A FEW GOOD
CARDINALS

Issaquah – PurposeDay – 2025

A FEW GOOD
CARDINALS

the rule, the key

&

human behavior

Carl Vincent

Description

Part history, psychology and esoterics, *A Few Good Cardinals* invites us to reflect on the question, "How many people cheat when they can?" Between 63 and 71% it seems. It appears to be the right time to find out why. The state of human behavior has propelled many to seek a way for improving the human condition. It appears that one character trait has most successfully escaped scrutiny despite being well known: narcissism. The impact of the narcissist on our world has been well documented. What is less well known, especially in the field of psychology, is where narcissism originates. In *A Few Good Cardinals* we explore how the narcissist may stifle meaningful progress, how they contribute to and even purposefully create trauma, and where the behavior appears to manifest most often. Complex trauma, war and economic devastation are the result of conscious choices by people who live in fear and deep rooted insecurity. The question we seek to answer once and for all is: Who are they?

Library Cataloging Data

A Few Good Cardinals – Exploring the Truth About Human Behavior
by Carl Vincent

ISBN: 978-0-9978166-7-9 (Paperback)

BISAC: BUS041000 BUSINESS & ECONOMICS / Management
BISAC: PSY017000 PSYCHOLOGY / Interpersonal Relations
BISAC: PSY021000 PSYCHOLOGY / Industrial & Organizational Psychology
BISAC: PSY023000 PSYCHOLOGY / Personality
BISAC: PSY045010 PSYCHOLOGY / Psychotherapy / Behaviorism

Publisher Information

PurposeDay, 1567 Highlands Dr. NE PMB 110-377, Issaquah, Washington 98029
— USA — https://www.purposeday.com
First Edition, Revised February 3, 2025 — 100% Human Intelligence

Follow us on X: @purposeday
Send feedback to 1159@purposeday.com

READ THE DISCLAIMER FOR IMPORTANT ADDITIONAL INFORMATION.

CAUTION: CONTENTS MAY TRIGGER STRONG TRAUMA FLASHBACKS. IF YOU ARE A TRAUMA VICTIM OR PERPETRATOR, CONSULT A LICENSED MENTAL HEALTH PRACTITIONER PRIOR TO READING THIS BOOK. The statements on this page and the disclaimer below form an integral part of the body of the book and shall not be considered separate at any point in time.

The paperback and hardcover editions provide expanded discussion and material on human behavior including an index. If you have previously purchased a Kindle version, note that the methodology of A Few Good Cardinals is identical to what is provided in this paperback edition.

To Renée

CONTENTS

It seems entirely possible
that everything is
exactly the way
it is supposed to be until
someone finds out that…

…not too long ago, washing your hands
with soap to avoid contamination and death
was considered unnecessary. The doctor who
discovered that it could prevent women from dying
after childbirth lost his license to practice, his job and
his sanity, dying in obscurity.

Despite extensive research,
his findings reportedly conflicted
with the scientific and medical
opinions
at the time.

Some people may always feel
they are

entitled

to deny and bury

truth

until it no longer suits them

DEFINITIONS

SLAVE:

- a person who is the (il)legal property of another and is forced to obey their owner

- a person who is forced to submit themselves to an influence by circumstance

- to work hard almost past one's capacity, or for extended time, under difficult conditions

TOXIC PERSON:[i]

- Someone who never genuinely apologizes for the harm they cause and does not meaningfully repair the damage

- Someone who frequently manipulates another person into something they don't want to do

- Someone who constantly creates confusion in the mind of another person with their behavior—and denies it

- Someone who *always* makes you feel bad about yourself in their presence

DENIAL:

- A "prison"

FAIR:

- *adjective:* respectful of everyone's rights; in accordance with the rules

- *adverb:* without cheating or trying to achieve an unjust advantage

FOREWORD

"And on the Eighth Day God Said, 'Let There Be Money.'"

How did we get this far without truly knowing who we are? Artificial intelligence is at our doorstep, yet we seem to barely comprehend the psychology of our own species. Time is going faster than ever before it seems. For thousands of years our ancestors made cave drawings, etched tools, built castles and churches, revered Gods, waged war, built hideouts, established cultures, circumvented the ocean in search of treasure, wiped out entire civilizations through disease and campaigns of terror, and disappeared.

Homo sapiens can be empathic and full of good will one moment, and overcome by an out-to-kill, regardless-of-the-consequences rage the next. When we are really honest with ourselves, we may have to admit that everything has consequences—bad and good deeds, now or later. After thousands of years of doing "just fine" without it, electricity emerged as a nifty tool for progress. Even though the first use of electricity was around 600 B.C. when the Greeks and Romans reportedly used it for electroplating,[2] it wasn't until the eighteenth century that Benjamin Franklin, among others, conducted extensive research on electricity and developed many of the basic concepts used today. About a hundred and twenty years later, we mastered the art of flight.

Not even forty years later, the jet engine was developed. Since then, we created nuclear power stations and spacecraft. It all seems so logical because our brain appears perfectly capable of keeping up with progress. At the same time, unfortunately, we keep waging war, abusing children, and running pedophile rings. Women keep saying men violate their rights, while men are slowly but surely coming forward with the abuse they have to endure at the hands of parents, school officials and other authority figures.

This is going to sound overly philosophical, but denial seems to be a powerful mechanism. It can deprive someone of something, or it can allow someone else to keep going when the odds appear to be stacked against them. Is the exploration of abuse and denial irrelevant when a growing population appears to ignore both—or when those in control use denial to make the case for their position of power? Checks and balances exist to make society livable, yet their relevance may be moot when people appear to thrive in their absence.

We are going to meet people for whom it can be argued that they charted a path to virtually immeasurable success while denying the extent to which they relied on the contributions of others or else, abused others to gain an advantage. Some encountered challenges along their way that forced them to reflect on the righteousness of their actions. Others didn't encounter such challenges or they successfully worked around them. The question why some people were successfully challenged and others were not may be critical for you and yet possibly utterly irrelevant for others.

What one person calls abuse may be denied as such by you or anyone else. What may be considered an appropriate remedy for abuse may be called unjustified by those in charge. There are possibly millions—humans and animals alike—suffering inhumane living conditions. Regardless of the fact that some have enshrined humane treatment and many other rules and regulations into a charter or law does not seem to prevent abuse because some deny it is happening—or they entertain a different definition of abuse—and they have remained in charge regardless.

Our exploration here aims to identify the factors of human existence that seem most closely connected to denial in its broadest interpretation. The goal is to facilitate reflection and discussion on the questions, "What on Earth are we doing? What are we trying to accomplish?" Nobody is expected to grasp the complexity of all of human existence. Even the author admits that many aspects of life have remained untouched here—that there may be a critical aspect of life left off the table, denied of its existence. The difference, hopefully, between this and genuine denial being that the author presumptively admits he denied the existence of one or more such aspects rather than proudly stating, "This is it, there is nothing else," while still being able to make a point that allows you to gain a better perspective.

What is bias and where does it originate? The *American Heritage Dictionary of the English Language*[3] appears to define bias as follows:

> (A) a preference or an inclination, especially one that inhibits impartial judgment; or
>
> (B) an unfair act or policy stemming from prejudice.[4]

In the behavior of practically every species, we can see something of ourselves. Consider cuckoos, for example, in how they have no problem with another bird raising its chicks[5]. Yet, from the moment a newborn emerges from egg or womb, there is something they all share: the challenge to survive. Bias toward their own may prevent them from seeing the bigger picture—just like a business that pollutes a river may ignore the fact that fish that feed a village swim in said river.

Besides a *will to survive* there seem to be two other conditions governing our existence: a *will to live*, in philosophical circles sometimes referred to as "conatus," and *meaning for life*.[6] The latter two are reserved for exploration outside of the context of this book. Rather, we are going to explore what it means to live in companionship with other humans in the context of the *need* to survive—men and women of every gender identity dependent on each other.

The United Nations Declaration of Human Rights[7] and the Committee on the Rights of the Child ("CRC") provide a right to survive to all. With regard to the latter, the principle of survival and development requires a conjunctive reading with all other rights and provisions of the CRC such as guiding principles and substantive rights—rights to health, adequate nutrition, security, an adequate standard of living, a healthy and safe environment, education and play.[8] Where does this moral compass originate? Nature seems to have quite a different idea. From the moment we are born, something tries to kill us: bacteria, viruses, natural disasters, animals higher on the food chain, and acts of God—which presumably includes the occasional meteorite and manmade objects falling from the sky.

Add to this list possibly our own mother in a severe state of post-partum depression, desperation or delusion, a person from within our community such as a random shooter on anti-depressants,[9] a drunk driver, or a malfunctioning airplane that crashes as a result of poor maintenance or a fake engine part, and we have quite a range of possibilities for our premature demise—while there may be many more. Our chances of survival thus seem determined by how supportive or adversarial the environment is at any given point in life.

The behavior of some people is occasionally considered, at a minimum, objectionable. People may be raised in the most loving of circumstances, by nurturing and responsible caregivers. Yet, what happens when the situation changes, when events outside one's control put undue stress on life: when someone competes for a job, or when the economy turns bad—for many years?

What effect does it have when a person's health fails? What happens when someone is exposed to long periods of offensive behavior or stressful circumstances?

Life may be governed by at least one fundamental rule: karma, commonly known as cause and effect. If we accept that for every cause there is indeed an effect, it may be helpful to know if there is a *key* for determining how a person is most likely going to respond in a given situation. Finally, *time* may have to be considered as a factor more critical in the outcome of said situation than ever before. In other words, we are going to explore what may be a realistic and useful root cause of most behavior.

The concept of slavery implies that one enjoys a superior status over another, suggesting the other person is subject to one's command. We are going to cover painful topics that may bring up horrific memories of trauma and abuse related to slavery. Nevertheless, we are going to stay clear of any direct association of a religious organization with slavery or with other practices like sexual exploitation. Likewise, this is not the place to discuss if a religious practice as the ultimate tool for enslavement—mentally or otherwise—goes against the basic principles of human rights. Finally, slavery may have far reaching consequences, yet it can be as close to home as addiction to a product or a habit.

You are going to say that it is not fair to single out certain individuals for the pain they have caused while ignoring the good that they may have done. *Behavior* appears to present itself in terms of the *context* in which it exists together with the *company* the primary agent keeps. In other words, it seems best that we explore how "good" people can be made to acquiesce to and even commit objectionable actions, while "bad" people can be made to look good before, while or after initiating them. This means that we are going to take an in-depth look at narcissism and what moment in time might be most closely correlated to its presentation.

Deception may be something God himself invented. Nature deceives when the occasion calls for it and so do we. How useful is deception, and is it fair? The Golden Rule[10] admonishes not to "do unto others what one does not want done to oneself," implying that if one deceives, one may be deceived at some point down the road. The effects of deception can be quite dramatic and damaging. Acts of hypnosis, poor nutrition, environmental factors, chemical exposure and other factors can make us gullible to deception if the experts are right.[11, 12]

At the root of deception, abuse, and goodwill is personality—which we share to a certain degree with others. How confident we feel, and how insecure we are, determines to a great extent how much we get accomplished. When we meet the kids we knew from kindergarten as adults, who turned into the driven, ruthless executive, the creative genius, or the skilled craftsperson? Each of them eating, sleeping and breathing on this planet, each of them with needs and desires. In terms of personality, how does one go from "focus, discipline, dedication, curiosity" to "manipulation, greed and violence"? The key seems to be that "focus" is a characteristic whose flipside is insecurity.

We are reportedly ever closer to a conscious encounter with one or more civilizations from outside our galaxy—or perhaps we have always had contact with extraterrestrials and we just don't know it. If we had an opportunity to get our house in order, what step should we take first?

Carl Vincent
Issaquah, 2023

ACKNOWLEDGMENT

This book would not have been possible without the generous contribution and unwavering commitment from many to my upbringing, education, emigration, relationships, health and development. Thank you and bless you!

DISCLAIMER

This is a book about human behavior from the perspective of a layperson. It is an attempt to explain certain fundamental principles of attitude, of relating between people, and that of people relating with their environment based on simple, day to day observations by someone not educated let alone licensed in the field of psychology.

I believe that everyone who is not considered a psychopath, sociopath or physically challenged in their mental performance, is inherently a good person, even though certain influences can make a person's behavior become corrupt, or at least deviate from morally and ethically just behavior, temporarily or permanently. Morally challenging subjects such as slavery and suicide are discussed here. If you know someone who is considering suicide, please seek help from a local mental health helpline or in the United States of America visit the National Alliance on Mental Illness website at https://www.nami.org/.

It is not my place to judge behavior, whether from a head of State, a religious leader, an executive at a corporation or from anyone else. The underlying premise of the research conducted for the purpose of this book was to observe rather than analyze behavior, and to distill it into statistically relevant form devoid of bias as much as possible. Said premise was based primarily on objectionable behavior and the context and company it had.

The author is not a licensed psychologist, behavioral specialist or medical practitioner. The inclusion of nutritional and dietary material herein does not constitute a claim to knowledge or license in this field by the author. The author is not a professional astrologer. There are many different interpretations of the stars and zodiac signs in the context of human behavior, just as there are many different systems that seek to interpret such behavior. The validity of said interpretations is not in question. While some aspects of Western astrology have been used as a foundation for discussion, the material referenced herein has been deemed to violate the inclusive premise of Western astrology and its system of ten planets and many interpretive points by professionals in the field.

You are encouraged to replicate the research presented in this book to form your own opinion on the state of human behavior in society. As our collective knowledge on human behavior is updated, the information presented herein may be considered inadequate in its representation of the human condition or become obsolete. Some or all of the material presented herein may conflict with local laws and regulations. The author assumes no legal responsibility for your enjoyment of this publication.

References to she, he, they and any other applicable pronouns may be used going forward in addition to their and them, implying any gender identity equally and without discrimination.

READING THIS BOOK MAY TRIGGER FEELINGS OF GUILT, SHAME AND INADEQUACY, PAST TRAUMA AND STRONG FLASHBACKS. BY PROCEEDING PAST THIS PAGE, YOU AGREE TO HOLD THE AUTHOR AND PUBLISHER HARMLESS AND TO PROTECT THE AUTHOR AND PUBLISHER AGAINST ANY LIABILITY AND HARM RESULTING FROM READING THIS BOOK.

"When I despair, I remember that throughout history the way of truth and love has always won. There have been tyrants and murderers and for a time they seem invincible, but in the end they always fall—think of it, always."
—Mahatma Ghandi

INTRODUCTION

"We may never know a person's motivation,
but it seems at least some people thrive
only when they have control over others."

Making soup conjures up an image of blending nutritious and delicious ingredients in a broth that forms the perfect introduction to the rest of the meal even if it's only bread. Whether your soup nurtures you, your family or friends, it brings the elements of nature and transformation right into the kitchen and your imagination. Starting with good stock, adding onions, protein and vegetables and flavor to our liking, soup is a dish virtually everyone can relate to. Writing *A Few Good Cardinals* has been very much like making soup. Starting with biology, adding will, purpose, gender identity, culture, psychology, and that critical ingredient that many take for granted: the moment one is born.

Every time we make soup, it tends to always taste a bit different from before. We also all have our own unique way of preparing it. Along the same lines, it is not too difficult to imagine that, while we may have much in common with others of our tribe, we each make our life unique. When we add inferior ingredients to soup, it may not taste very good but we will still eat it when we are really hungry. When we add bad ingredients, we may rather throw it out. So, how can we see the problems in our lives in a new light—maybe we need to change some of the ingredients or change our perspective: reduce the ones that taste unpleasant while increasing those that improve the flavor. The challenge is that everyone is always making soup somewhere, and it seems we don't always get to choose the flavor.

Do you swear to tell the truth and nothing but the truth, so help you God? The court room was silent and pregnant with expectation. Just minutes prior, the defendant had settled nervously into his seat. The plaintiff seemed confident. Magistrate Hansen listened to contradictory statements. She decided, after refusing to admit defendant's evidence, to find in favor of the plaintiff. This was a simple case. The plaintiff, a sheriff's deputy, claimed defendant had run a red light. Defendant claimed the light had been green. His testimony appeared to indicate that he had taken every precaution necessary—including coming to a full stop—before entering the intersection in order to make a left turn. The deputy's vehicle had been clearly visible.

The principle of considering someone innocent until proven guilty is considered sacred by some. When in doubt, courts may rule in favor of law enforcement. The clerk had warned defendant as such beforehand. When the stakes are low, we might argue the defendant should just pay the fine and move on. How then should we interpret a thirty-three year or more sentence for a crime someone did not commit? We may have to accept that unreliable evidence, a misinterpretation, available technology not being advanced enough, bias and thus a personality issue, or something else can interrupt an innocent life.

Motivation is something that has fascinated me for many years. Despite diving into sociology, psychology, and personality tests like the Myers-Briggs Type Indicator [13] and DiSC [14], it still felt as if I was missing a crucial point. From a layperson perspective, despite significant advances in technology, it still puzzles me how society can seemingly run around in a vicious, almost never-ending circle of inventing, creating and destroying without ever fundamentally solving the problems that keep plaguing us: injustice, economic inequality, chronic poverty, crime and environmental misdeeds. Of course, it could very well be that I am one of these people who will "never get it"—that a problem exists because *I* see it as such, and that it is not a problem for anyone else.

In about 1537, a certain European colonial power appears to have felt very confident. El Abra in Colombia, approximately 13,000 years old, is reported to be the site of one of the most ancient archaeological sites in the Western Hemisphere.[15] The Muisca negotiated with invaders from the Old World over the source of their gold. There appears to have been a misunderstanding. To the Muisca, gold could have been a symbol of accomplishment because they owned lots of jewelry made of this precious and highly desirable metal. The conquistadores insisted the Muisca show them the source. The Muisca pointed to their salt mines, from which they extracted the commodity so desired by other tribes it made for excellent trading value.

To the Muisca, the source of their gold was obvious: it was what they accepted as currency from other tribes in exchange for salt. Reportedly, the other tribes did not challenge the Muisca for their salt because the Muisca had developed expertise in mining it and were willing to put in the labor required for the job. Other tribes specialized in other activities and thus there was balance and harmony in the region. Frustrated, the invaders reportedly first killed their counterparts in the negotiation and subsequently, to show how serious they were, almost everyone else in the tribe for "good measure." In revenge, the surviving locals allegedly refused to assist the conquistadores in their search for El Dorado[16] for decades to come even if it meant a certain death.

If there is a cardinal one governing life, how can it not be karma—cause and effect? If I do something that is objectionable and that someone disagrees with, I can be sure that I will hear about it. Yet on occasion, I may have an opportunity to bend or even break this rule if nobody can see what I am doing— or so I may think. Another approach might be to deny that what I am doing will hurt anyone, or to blame a situation or another person. What would help me ease my mind most about the potential consequences? For one, I could decide to just do the right thing even if nobody is watching. We are going to explore the concept of rules in *A Rule is a Rule...Unless You Are One of Them.*

People who consider life akin to "war" may (un)consciously pursue their agenda at the cost of everything and everyone else around them. They might be Keith Ranieri of NXIVM or Elizabeth Holmes of Theranos. Holmes was the founder and Chief Executive Officer of a "revolutionary" biotech company whose promises were discovered to be a fraud.[17] Raneiri was the creator of a groundbreaking motivational system that inspired Hollywood elites and people like the Dalai Lama alike. He was convicted on fraud, sex trafficking and racketeering charges.[18]

The principles underlying human behavior appear to be more accessible than experts want us to believe when we keep it simple. The chapter *Behavior = Context*, gives an introduction of what theories have been developed to date. The intention here is to be able to more easily identify when someone does not have your best interests at heart. The chapter *Deeper, Bigger* introduces us to the concept of deception in order to manipulate and gain an (unfair) advantage.

People who seek control may acknowledge that rules are necessary for society to function, yet they may deny that the rules apply to them if said rules interfere with their mission.

In my experience, a healthy narcissist sets healthy boundaries. People who are born during certain times of the year, and who experience certain conditions growing up, appear to have a significantly increased risk of developing toxic narcissistic behavior instead. In *A Method to the Madness* we will explore how one or more of the following may contribute to toxic narcissism: (a) someone's date of birth, (b) location and time of birth, and (c) a combination of exposure to trauma, behavior from others and peer pressure. In *The Essentials* we go one step further by investigating the characteristics of astrological zodiac signs.

Birds of a Feather Stick Together discusses what makes people seek support and protection among others with similar beliefs. In 1911, Frederick Winslow Taylor published his book on the Principles of Scientific Management Theory.[19] His introduction of a theory for an optimized working environment for workers and management was considered revolutionary at the time. One of the first observations Taylor apparently made is that workers, especially when they underperform, may consider neutral or constructive attention as a sign that they are being recognized and perhaps even appreciated for their contribution. Improved productivity may be an immediate result even without a direct incentive. Sincerity, genuine concern and respect may be ingredients of the relationship between supervisor and staff that foster a constructive working environment and high productivity, blurring the line between "birds" who otherwise "stick together."

We may all have that moment in our lives when we had a first memorable encounter with someone who cheated or took advantage of us and it hurt. These and similar events may remain etched in our memory because they hurt our confidence. They traumatized our child brain, incapable of responding to a threat like an adult can with righteous anger or stoic self-regulation.[20] Worse still, people may suggest that we agreed to something when in fact we didn't, or that we remember something that didn't, in fact, occur. In *Truth Is Truth Until It Isn't* we explore the mechanism behind the illusion that memory occasionally tricks us into believing and how that affects our relationships.

A society may differentiate itself through the character of its judicial system and the recognition of property rights. People across the world have culturally and historically different concepts of morality, of what constitutes acceptable behavior, and of what are appropriate types of punishment for behavior that violates the law. In the chapter *Institutionalized Motivation* we dive into the effect of toxic narcissism on our efforts to produce things at scale, to reach people beyond our own backyard, and to affect climate policy, for example.

Bias is a concept that often gets paid lip service because it frequently gets in the way of on-the-spot decision making. In *Real Life is "Real"* we discuss how this often unconscious yet very important factor affects the quality of our decisions. Our self-confidence may depend on the need to survive. Confidence may be instilled by nurturing caregivers and a feeling of safety. One may be very confident yet highly insecure. *Live and Let Die* aims to guide us to a better understanding.

People are known to adapt their behavior to others in order to fit in or to set a new precedent. In *Tell* Your *Story* we reflect on how we learn by example because our brain directs us to, and what inspires us to be unique. Learning to use time to your advantage is an integral part of the journey of self-empowerment. A toxic narcissist uses time to gradually enslave, sidestepping the rules, while using fear and denial to intimidate. In *Who is Your Friend? A Fresh Look at Time* we explore different behavioral characteristics and how each use time to their advantage.

How familiar are you with the outcome of the Spanish quest for gold in the New World? As you may know, it didn't end well for the side that chose violence over logic. The Spanish did find gold eventually, except not where the Muisca lived. In fact, to this day nobody has reportedly been able to find the location, commonly referred to as El Dorado, where the Muisca's gold was originally extracted.[21] In any case, gold from other parts of the New World did make its way to Spain in large quantities, where it allegedly served to crash the economy with hyperinflation.

Empathy is an important step towards compassion. Once we have compassion for our mind and body, we can reimagine how society should function. Narcissistic people seem essential because they may be the final call for authentic and brave expression of ourselves. When narcissism turns toxic, that is the moment we need to pay attention. The chapter *How to Deal With a Narcissist* explores strategies and practical suggestions for thriving in a relationship with a toxic narcissist. While this first edition is heavily geared towards an American audience, you may resonate with the material no matter where you live. Future and translated versions of this book will focus on regional accounts of narcissism.

A RULE IS A RULE
UNLESS YOU ARE ONE OF
THEM

"Acknowledge that society is engineered to elicit frustration and suffering."

When nobody is watching, do the rules apply? What rules? When the stakes are high, the leverage is great and the future is uncertain, a rule may be easily bent or broken. If I were to force you to adopt my perspective, is that fair—ultimately? What is your definition of "fair," and does it even matter that we talk about it?

"That's not fair!" We have all said it at one point in time. We may all have been accused of not being fair. It is easy to say that "Everyone is born with a sense of fairness," but what difference does it make if we can't agree on what it means? The concept of fairness appears to have a built in bias that tends to favor my own perspective. Even the words that I write radiate bias and can elicit a sense of unfairness in you. This book was written by a Caucasian male who grew up in a privileged albeit small country that has dominated global trade since the fifteen hundreds. It is also a country that was invaded many times over, was once part of another monarch's empire or two, and wasn't even officially a unified country until well after the United States was founded. Better known for its famous painters like Vincent Van Gogh, cheese and wooden shoes,[22] The Netherlands reportedly controlled and enslaved people in their far flung colonies and trading posts for centuries. What is fair from my point of view may be very different for you.

People who migrate to a different country may do so because they feel they will have a better opportunity elsewhere. When opportunities are lacking, it may be that a certain group of people has a naturally unfair advantage because they live in a more resource rich part of the country, because they achieved an advantage by force or manipulation, or because they developed their skills and talents and contribute to society as best as they can. Every country has its own set of rules to which we may need to adapt in order to fit in. Countries may agree on rules that apply to all people around the world. Where rules originate may be a combination of what seems practical in the here and now plus what was already enshrined in law by our ancestors. How flexible we are in adjusting adopted law to our current circumstances may be a matter of personality and need. It may start with something as simple as a rule of the "house," my mother telling me to wash the dishes by hand because she thinks the dishwasher uses too much electricity, an appliance she didn't have growing up. It sounds like a bad analogy, but established practice can have a profound effect on our resistance to changing a rule when circumstances call for it.

If we feel we are better off under a certain set of rules, we may be more likely to consider the rules fair. It may take someone with great empathy to see fairness from another person's perspective. If we want to be really honest, we should consider that some of us are more rational and that "rational fairness" can often be perceived as "unfair" by almost everyone else. How we choose to perceive things can change what we think is fair.[23]

When you know who you are dealing with, you may feel respected. When I have an ulterior motive and try to deceive you, I might hide behind the mask of a fake identity. For an author, for example, this has long been a way to protect themselves from unwanted attention or to gain a foothold into a world dominated by men. In today's world of cybercrime and identity theft, it may be no surprise that the concept of identity has taken on a much different definition. Adopting an identity that is different from our birth name has long been considered a given online in order to protect our own interests. However, in cybercrime, the fake identity can present a bit of a shock when we find out somebody is not who they claim to be. The male, thirty-one year old FBI agent posing as a fourteen year old girl in order to catch a pedophile may be a good example.

Who else misrepresents who they are or what their position is in order to get what they want? Maybe the parent who comes up with an excuse so their child will show up for dinner, the teacher who offers to give a student a good grade if they have sex, or the politician who promises to end a war if elected. Perhaps it is the promise of making everyone pay their "fair share," disguising both the need for power to determine what "fair" means as well as the desire to destroy the middle (and upper) class as professed by the ideology of communism.[24,25] These and many other situations find us giving in to pretense for a position we covet—we do want dinner, but we want to finish a chat with a buddy first, we may not know what sex is but our hormones are raging and we sure want a good grade, and it would be great if we could finally pull out of that "needless" war.

The rule may be trust, while the conditions are set ad hoc and as arbitrary as those in power can make them. Yet, there is one tool in the arsenal of the narcissist that is probably the most powerful in getting us to do their bidding: to promise and failing to deliver, also known as "future faking." In 2022, Keir Starmer (born September 2), leader of the Labor Party of the United Kingdom, passionately announced that his plan to freeze energy bills was key to reducing inflation.[26] For two years, Labor campaigned on their assessment of the economy that the opposition Tories would leave them. After Starmer got elected Prime Minister by a minority, one of the first things on the agenda appears to have been to ignore that pledge and to scrap winter fuel payments for seniors[27]—rather than lowering the energy bill or keeping it stable, it is going up instead for this demographic of about ten million people or approximately 14.9 percent of the total population. Why does Starmer target older people? The answer seems clear: because they don't have the energy to protest. No pun intended. Starmer reportedly claimed, "things are worse than we ever imagined."

Politics has been fraught with promises and failures to deliver since the beginning of time. Indicating that one tends to take over the government after an election win with an "image" rather than a "clear understanding" does not seem to instill much confidence, especially when that image involves a budget shortfall of twenty-two billion Pound Sterling out of about twelve-hundred billion in government spending in the 2022-2023 budget, one point eight percent. Similar scenarios take place on a smaller or even micro scale everywhere yet often with like consequences. With one blow to your confidence in them, the narcissist accomplishes two goals: first, showing you who is in charge, and second, that your trauma is part of the conditioning for your future compliance—with every breach of your trust they weaken your resistance and self-esteem.

The Vietnam War seems to have left an extremely traumatic mark on American society. While the events leading up to the war, the various actors who alternately escalated or deescalated the fighting, the political maneuvering and the behind the scenes impact of military interests may be debated until the end of time, one thing happened that very few seem to have predicted beforehand. After the United States withdrew from the conflict and communism took hold of Vietnam, the bloodshed didn't end. As in Cambodia under Pol Pot (born May 19),[28] in China under Mao Zedong (born December 26),[29] and the Soviet Union under Josef Stalin (born December 18), the regime ensured that dissidents were ruthlessly reeducated or eliminated in large numbers even though communism consistently appears to fail to deliver on its promises.[30,31]

What does seem to work in turning the populace into a brainwashed mass of conformists may be a combination of propaganda, oppression, poverty and denial. The United States of America requires a pledge from nationalized citizens that they have no ties to the Communist Party. Yet, there appear to be many native born Americans—not to be confused with Native Americans—who would rather give up on the country's constitutional principles than fix what is wrong with capitalism and abandon their desire to introduce the most oppressive economic system the world has ever known.[32] Just like the rest of the developing world, every communist country that currently exists, or that has ever existed, relies on a market driven economy and on technology developed in the free West[33] to get where they are today. Their respective populations are allegedly kept craftfully in the dark thanks to a combination of an extensive effort to misrepresent history and limitations on free speech, press and internet access.

The general public expects to be able to trust the media based on the premise that journalism's first obligation reportedly is to tell the truth.[34] How disappointing it must have been at the time, when the radio show *War of the Worlds* appears to have led to the birth of modern fake news. Newspapers reported an alien invasion in October of 1938, an invasion that didn't happen. The reason behind this was that publishers apparently feared competition from a "new" medium: radio.[35] Did everyone suddenly lose trust in reporters? It seems a new generation of readers and listeners grew up instead and all was forgotten. Before we get too emotionally involved in the argument of what news channel may still be trustworthy, let us take a step back into the history of finance.

You may be no stranger to borrowing money to finance a purchase, or lending money to help someone. Either way, the incentive for the lender usually comes in the form of interest. However, this wasn't always the case. For example, Ancient Greece and Rome outlawed interest bearing loans while many

Christian denominations in medieval Europe considered the charging of interest at any rate sinful. There was a term for the demand of interest back then, which has since changed to mean "excessive interest" or "loan sharking:" usury. [36]

Over time, the definition of usury has changed just as much as the rules around money appear to have changed. In the Middle Ages, banking was governed by strict rules as to who could conduct financial business and what kind.[37,38] Perhaps in an attempt to wrest control from powerful Christian interests, at the end of the 19th century, a group of left-wing financiers and industrialists set their sights on taking over the British Empire and the world. They created distinct organizations: the Milner Group[39] and the Fabian Society.[40]

The origins of this initiative appear to go back to the Industrial Revolution of the 1700s. A new, powerful class consisting of international trade, finance and industrial interests had emerged from gold and diamond mining operations. They developed a monopoly on diamonds, through ownership by the Milner Group's De Beers of all South African diamond mines. Similarly, the Milner Group and their associates monopolized oil interests with the establishment of British Petroleum, Royal Dutch Shell, and Standard Oil, as well as certain other industries. These same interests extended their power through the control of a global network of financial firms like the Bank of England, the United States Federal Reserve System, and J.P. Morgan Chase.

As leaders of the Milner Group, figures such as Lord Milner, Lionel Curtis and Henry Hodson, initiated a competition for resources that would inevitably lead to international conflict. They focused on monopolizing material resources, whereas the Fabian Society concentrated on intellectual and humanitarian aspects. It aimed to capture the heart and mind of the Western masses with the promise of a just, socialist world and to control the people for the Fabian Society's profit.

Socialism and communism promote the centralization of control of all aspects of society. Rules are made and enforced by a select, privileged few. In a psychopathic drive for control, Milner-Fabian adherents reportedly sponsored revolutions in Russia and China, many military conflicts and two world wars. Mass cross-cultural immigration is one of their tools to subjugate the masses, while racial diversity has been imposed as a means to defuse conflict. Arab and Muslim leaders have eagerly become their partners, culminating in the systematic promotion of Islam in the West.[41,42]

Who first sets the rules tends to be the creator of a new business, a new religion, or a new country, for example. When you were born, your caregivers may have instructed you to listen to them because they set the rules at home. The Golden Rule is the principle of treating others as one would want to be treated by them. Adam was created last of all beings to teach him humility. If he acted in an overbearing manner, the Golden Rule[43] served to remind him that the fly preceded him in the order of creation. When a rule has outlived its purpose, it may be updated to reflect the current sentiment or necessity, or it may be discarded. Rules that have never changed may be, "Everyone who makes a practice of sinning also practices lawlessness; sin is lawlessness,"[44] and, "for every effect there is a cause, and for every cause there is an effect."[45]

To fully understand what a rule means, we may have to take the rule apart and study the meaning of the words themselves. What is sin? In the Bible, virtually every type of sin pertains to knowledge, pleasure, or a good name for oneself. Committing a sin may be as simple as not listening to my intuition, for which I am inevitably punished one way or another.

The principle of cause and effect may be considered the law of karma. When I do something only to feel better rather than help someone out of genuine concern, for example, it somehow always seems to come back to haunt me—an objectionable good deed.

Prior to engaging in war, anyone can claim they are going to win and that the cause is just. As an example, any soldier in Napoleon Bonaparte's Grande Armée prior to the French invasion of Russia[46] may have believed in the cause and supported their popular general wholeheartedly. For many, Bonaparte's accomplishments as ruler of the French Empire must have been sufficient evidence of his greatness. In hindsight, we may say that his record on domestic civil rights contrasts sharply with the alleged exploitation of conquered territories during his reign, adversely affecting his reputation.[47] Did he venture a "bridge too far," paraphrasing a failed stage from a theater of war in a different era?[48]

Some people know when breaking a rule seems to be the right thing to do, and when breaking a rule can make or break a future. There are those who admit (certain) rules exist, especially the one about cause and effect, but that they should be applied mostly to you and only sometimes to themselves—depending on who stands to benefit, obviously. Napoleon may have had a bruised ego after the failed campaign in the Peninsular War against Spain and Portugal.[49] Rather than laying low and solidifying his rule domestically, he sought to reestablish his military dominance with the Russia campaign of 1812, leading to a massive defeat in 1813. Napoleon Bonaparte was born on August 15, 1769 in Ajaccio, Corsica. If historic wars are not indicative enough of cause and effect, today's turf wars between drug cartels or those between drug companies in the pharmaceutical markets may provide a more contemporary clue.

People can be very protective of their territory if the invader does not provide a valid benefit in conjunction with respect. As an example of the latter, think perhaps of the invasion of the Netherlands by Nazi Germany in World War II. The Netherlands is a small country in a very strategic location when it comes to international trade. Germany historically relies on its neighbor's vital sea, river and rail infrastructure. While the Dutch set up an underground resistance movement the moment the Nazis invaded, there was allegedly also significant support for the German invasion. This resulted in an economic boom during especially the first year and a half of the Nazi occupation. As we discuss who decides when a rule applies, especially the rule of karma, it may be best to reflect on the observation that it took reportedly more than fifty years before the story of economic decline and exploitation of the Dutch by the Nazis in World War II, the traditional narrative, was questioned.[50]

During the Hunger Winter of 1944-'45 the Dutch had virtually nothing to eat because the Nazis took the harvest for themselves. This gave the impression that the Dutch did nothing but suffer under the Nazi regime. An effort to document the wartime experience of the Dutch shows that bias was considered an important factor to be prevented as much as possible in coming to terms with what really happened.[51] Meanwhile, Anne Frank's story and her death in a Nazi concentration camp hide the fact that a significant segment of the Dutch population appear to have aided the Nazis in their persecution of Jews and "undesirables": "The victim and his immediate social environment have a common interest in suppressing the threatening memories of the war and the more recent feelings of despair and confusion. In this way a 'conspiracy of silence' develops."[52] The truth eventually comes out, as it always does.

Rules exist pretty much anywhere there is a potential interaction between people. Rules exist for the behavior of people in a group of any size, from your local church to a nation state and between them such as international maritime rules and the Geneva Convention.[53] Rules exist for playing the card game bridge, for playing golf, riding a bicycle, and driving a car or truck. Rules exist for pilots navigating the airways, for captains of ocean going vessels and for astronauts venturing in space. Rules exist for a judge just as much as they do for the president of a country. Likewise, rules exist for the maintenance of a friendship—don't call me after 10 p.m., give a gift for a birthday, and congratulate someone for the birth of a child.

We introduce rules to make life more predictable, to establish a standard of fairness, and to express our desire to cultivate progress. Rules are meant to make it easier for you to purchase something from a foreign country, or to sell something to someone overseas. Rules exist to maintain order and to make sure you have a pretty good chance making it to your destination when you take a plane ride. There may be an ordinance stipulating how much noise you can make at which hours of the day. Customs and regulations dictate when your store may be open for business. The state or province where you live may have rules on which land may be used for agriculture and which for residential construction. The country where you live has rules governing who may get a passport for travel to a foreign country and what type of grain is acceptable for import. Rules may be burdensome and in need of review and cancellation from time to time.

Rules are everywhere—in sports, at work, in traffic, in commerce, for food safety and medical care, for financial transactions, for the transport of hazardous goods, and in space. Rules exist in the People's Republic of China and they appear to be quite different from those in America, but you wouldn't know it unless you studied them or visited both countries yourself. Rules need to be synchronized between countries to avoid gridlock in international trade. Yet, how can we judge the fairness of a society and the quality of life of its people if we don't know how the rules are interpreted?

The person charged with applying a rule may decide in your favor or not depending on their mood and how well they are paid. Imagine you are playing a game of football (or soccer, in America). How would you know if the referee is going to be impartial the entire game? Let's say that somebody scores a goal with their hand: a foul, and the point is invalidated. Most people would agree with this one, unless your name is perhaps Diego Maradona.[54] Players may apply certain tactics to agitate their opponent, enticing them to break a rule when they might not have an intention to do so at first. How would such gamesmanship[55] affect the attitude of the referee?

Historic moments in the sport of football may be interpreted differently depending on what country one rooted for. In the 1978 World Cup final between Argentina and the Netherlands, the host nation had a lot at stake—a first World Cup title. Argentina's squad is reported to have arrived five minutes late onto the field, which time the local fans used to get extra motivated or loud, depending on how you look at it.

The Argentinian team proceeded to complain about a Dutch player's medical condition for which he had been ruled fit to play several games earlier in the tournament. The referee sided with the host team.[56] Who was disappointed that the interpretation of the rules went against their team? The Dutch supporters, obviously. Was the referee's decision fair? Perhaps it wasn't. Maybe he chose to protect himself against a potentially dangerous situation after the game as suggested by a 2021 incident in Argentina's first division when a referee accused a Lanus player of threatening to kill him.[57]

In the case of the World Cup, if you are diehard fan of the game, you might rightfully argue that there are many better, more recent incidents with far more serious consequences. And if you are not a big football fan, you might say, "It's just a game." What these examples have in common is that I wasn't there to personally witness the event. And even if I had been there, you would be reading only one side of the story anyway. What if the Dutch players had been disrespectful towards a referee in a previous match?

The circumstances leading to somebody breaking a rule and somebody else allowing it may forever remain unknown. Conscience therefore appears to be the name of the game. Perhaps having a conscience matters when lives are at stake, money, or both. It is in "peace" time that we might become complacent to the fact that bullies and aggressors who charm with their grandiose plans for world power tend to start small. We might brush off how those with a utilitarian perspective—narcissists—deal with moral issues because "we are all human, after all." One could argue that everything involves risk and that one should be able to tolerate it. Risk may be governed by permanent, natural rules, or by manmade laws. It may also be affected by temporary factors such as a deadline, however arbitrary it may be.

There is logic and common sense, and then there is the rule of the deadline. On January 28, 1986, they competed to get seven people into space aboard the Space Shuttle Challenger.[58] The operator of the Space Shuttle, the National Aeronautics and Space Administration (NASA), had stipulated that there was a deadline for mission STS-51-L. The launch had been delayed before due to weather. Another delay was considered unacceptable. Unfortunately, a critical part of the Shuttle's propulsion system had been subjected to external temperatures lower than it had been designed for in the early hours of January 28. Some engineers recommended postponing the launch until the affected part had sufficiently warmed up.

Instead, management decided that the launch deadline took precedence. When the Challenger exploded shortly after liftoff because the part that the engineers had been so concerned about failed, it reportedly cost the US taxpayer about US$1.6 billion and the lives of all seven astronauts. Significant trauma on the loved ones of the astronauts who perished as well as on the many others involved with the Shuttle program ensued. Occasionally someone will say, "There is a reason for everything." Unfortunately, most of us don't have this kind of flexibility to "play" with the rules.

Two major industrial accidents that were also the result of cost cutting measures have affected the lives of many more: the Chernobyl[59] nuclear reactor incident in the former Soviet Union in 1986, and the Deepwater Horizon oil spill[60] in the Gulf of Mexico in 2010. When you picked up this book, it was probably not your intention to become proficient in nuclear engineering. Therefore, avoiding the boring details, let me just say that the cost-conscious design of the four nuclear powerplants at the Chernobyl site in Ukraine was not an accident—pun not intended. When something leaves little room for error, the impact of one person can be quite significant. On April 26, the attitude and behavior of deputy chief-engineer Anatoly Dyatlov—who was also the supervisor of a safety test taking place that same day—spelled doom for Chernobyl's reactor number 4: arrogance, over-confidence in his own skill, and denial of the severity of the situation. Shift personnel did not dare question his authority.

The situation in the Gulf of Mexico in April of 2010 was a bit different. The results were disastrous nonetheless—especially for the fishing industry—and on a scale not seen before. Authorities closed large portions of the Gulf of Mexico to commercial and recreational fishing following the Deepwater Horizon oil spill in an attempt to mitigate contamination. Many fishers sought alternative income solutions or chartered their vessels to help with the cleanup process.[61] The underlying cause of the failure of the Deepwater Horizon oil rig and the subsequent discharge of significant quantities of oil into the Gulf was reportedly a series of cost-cutting decisions not unlike those at Chernobyl as well as an inadequate safety system. The moral of the story is that regardless of the political system, corners will be cut with the wrong people in charge.

Towns and neighborhoods the country over appear terrorized by noise from loud muscle cars and motor bikes. A noise ordinance can give a community the reassurance that law enforcement has the tools to protect everyone's mental health and right to quiet enjoyment. After all, when there is noise, how is the quality of one's sleep and attentiveness during waking hours not affected?[62] As one might expect, law enforcement often has more important things to do leaving affected citizens angry and powerless in many cases. A brain troubled by noise cannot think well, rest well nor study for an exam preparing for a job that helps propel the community forward. Similarly, brain development in babies may be disrupted by noise of any kind when they try to sleep. The solution: headphones, they were invented for a reason. Buy a fast, quiet car and blast the imitated engine noise into your own ears, not in those of the neighborhood.

We may have a different interpretation of the rules depending on the situation and time of day—and depending on the chance of getting caught breaking a rule. In a group of a hundred people, one person breaking a rule resulting in harm to another may go unnoticed at first yet may eventually be remedied or punished. In a group of one hundred, eleven people breaking a rule may quickly garner pushback. At any point, we may ask ourselves when it is the right time to change a rule—unless it were proven the majority have somehow lost their mind or worse, they didn't have it in the first place. Our commitment to a rule may depend on how much impact it has on the welfare of the community, and how much we benefit from its implementation.

Some rules have been carried over from ancient times like Roman law which partially found its way into our modern legal framework, while others are newly crafted. Rules may be governed by social conventions adopted over hundreds if not thousands of years. They can be fundamental to one culture while awkward or non-existent in another. If there is one "rule" that stands out it may be the one that stipulates that we all learn from each other and our environment by observation. Consider it a biological principle because it operates thanks to something called mirror neurons[63] which were reportedly only recently discovered.

For people who deny that rules apply to them, ignoring the rule of karma seems to make life ever so slightly more convenient. When nature, God, or their fellow citizen, strikes back, they shift the blame to a third party. Psychologists apparently differentiate how people accept blame for an adversarial event: by accepting guilt or by feeling shame. Feeling shame is accompanied by transferring blame onto another person, group or event. On the other hand, people who feel guilt apologize, offer a resolution that is fair to all involved, and aim to prevent a recurrence. Try getting that kind of response from the person who feels shame: "I don't know what you are talking about" may be their preferred response instead.

You may live in a world where the rules apply to you but not to your neighbor. Imagine that you purchased some food for dinner for you and your family. Your neighbor walks by, sees the food sitting on the kitchen table and decides he wants to have some. He walks in, grabs half of it and walks out. How do you feel? The next day, you see that your neighbor has some clothes hanging on the wash line to dry. You see a nice dress and…do you take it or not?

Some people share from the goodness of their heart. Some cultures have this kind of sharing embedded into the principles of their society. But taking without asking, taking without a need? Let's see what happens when the situation is a bit different: it is war time and your neighbor is one meal away from dying after having escaped the enemy, while you need the dress as a disguise to stay safe.

Narcissistic behavior can inflict significant trauma and damage. Unfortunately, the narcissist may have a very different perspective. If changing our perspective on someone's behavior can change our perspective of the person, how would our perspective on narcissism as a condition change if we were to accept that the narcissist may be at war—at war with themselves, with the world, or both? War has rules and they are a bit different from those we maintain at peace time. War also knows more "life and death situations" than we tend to encounter when we are not at war—when life is an adventure or a puzzle instead.

Talking about war, the German soldier was apparently able to achieve remarkable successes early on in World War II. Known as the Blitz Krieg,[64] German divisions went around the French Maginot line,[65] quickly conquering France from the left flank. They managed to cover such a great distance in a short time thanks to putting every soldier on the drug Pervitin.[66] It may not have been the first instance when entire battalions were under the influence, but it sure made an impression even decades later. While this is not the right venue for a discussion about who started World War II and why, there does seem to be something worth mentioning about the prelude of the Blitz Krieg on France with regard to narcissism and the institutionalized variety: compartmentalized decision making.

Prior to Germany executing its strategy for the attack on France, French intelligence reportedly was well aware that Nazi Germany were planning some type of maneuver. As is quite common in national intelligence and counter-intelligence efforts, France had several services each trying their best at predicting hostile activities against the nation. The French in the days leading up to World War II were allegedly known to have been proud of their past achievements and eager to extend their long history of battlefield successes while trying to forget less memorable ones. It has been speculated that, through a mixture of intellectual laziness, bureaucratic complacency, and a conservative attitude, the French may have failed to modernize their military thinking.[67] Nazi Germany was keen to take advantage of this.

As we shall see further on in a very different and more recent theater of war, the French intelligence community pre-WWII was highly compartmentalized. In other words, none of the commanders of the various intelligence services shared their findings with others, while information passed up the chain of command that went counter to established doctrine tended to be ignored. The top decision makers who were the recipients of intelligence briefings were essentially in the dark about Nazi Germany's real intentions. We shall revisit this when we look at institutionalized narcissism.

Speaking of intelligence and war, how can we not take a moment to look at one of the most colorful characters in the history of espionage: Harold Adrian Russell "Kim" Philby, born January 1. In the dramatic series *Spy Web*[68] we learn how Philby managed to work his way up the ranks in the British secret service while serving his "real" masters, the Soviet Union. While he was revealed as a member of a spy ring known as the Cambridge Five in 1963, Philby escaped by first being reassigned to a less impressive posting in Washington, D.C. where his contact with the United States Central Intelligence Agency (CIA) was also a Soviet spy, and subsequently making his way to Russia where he died in 1988 in peaceful retirement. Of the Cambridge Five, Philby is believed to have done the most damage to the British and American intelligence establishment, providing classified information to the Soviet Union that caused the deaths of many MI6 and CIA agents. The damage was allegedly only lessened by Josef Stalin's notorious paranoia—himself a psychopath—that Philby may be a triple agent.

The reason of Philby's success as a spy lies perhaps most in his clever use of four distinct personality characteristics associated with his birth date, time and location in Ambala, India:[69] ambition, insecurity, determination and sensitivity to his environment. He reportedly had the personal policy of never confessing. Philby was known for his masterful use of charm in order to fool his superiors and escape those who tried to expose him. Considering that Soviet Russia in its final days considered him worthy of being honored by putting his face on a postage stamp, we can only imagine how valuable Philby has been for Soviet interests regardless of the fate of their version of communism.[70]

Where else do we see drugs take a significant role? In a dramatic documentary about famous jazz singer Amy Winehouse—*Amy*[71]—Amy's relationship with herself and the world around her stands out: an intense battle seemed to consume her to express herself, be herself and put herself out there. At times, Amy seemed to be at war with herself. In this "war" of sorts, she allegedly had help from, and was distracted at some point by, others. Her husband, for instance, reportedly introduced her to substances that might have made her feel as if they would give her more control, enjoyment or both, of the creative process: heroin and cocaine. Arguably, they must have greatly changed her perspective on music and life.

At some point though, it appears that Amy ran into a rule that governs life for all of us it seems: the limit to the capacity of the human body to handle stress, alcohol and other substances in the presence or lack of nutrition, sleep and other things that sustain us. This limit may be different for everybody and seems to depend on quite a few factors, but arguably it is still a limit.

Amy reportedly came clean off drugs, but the "rule" about alcohol and her body's capacity to deal with it had put a premature limit on her body's lifespan. If Amy was at "war" with herself, and if drugs can change our perspective—possibly making us feel more in control or capable—there may be another situation where drugs can and have been known to make a difference: actual war between full sized armies equipped with tanks, missiles, and fighter planes. In school, the Second World War had its rightful place in history class. The only thing missing from the perspective that I had on this global conflict was why it started in the first place, something more fundamental and basic than the "need to conquer Europe for our heritage": oil.[72]

What may be the difference between negotiating the price for a barrel of oil and invading the neighbors? Propaganda, deception, intimidation and…drugs.[73] Needless to say, the proverbial party didn't last because, well, drugs don't either. Eventually everything seems to come back down to earth and is subject to rules—karma being one of them—and conscience. For the narcissist life may be essentially war. Lose one battle, move on to the next. What makes the narcissist different from an empath? It seems to be an inability to entertain a different perspective.

Preventing a transgression of the rules can be accomplished by promoting the benefits of compliance and by "educating" people on the negative consequences of subversion through intimidation and coercion. Those who deny the rules exist for them may consider themselves at liberty to do as they please. It has taken philosophers and legal scholars centuries to ponder and discuss this issue at great lengths. Some hold the observation that karma follows the transgressor wherever he goes, to a next life even. Even if reincarnation were not only implausible but also nonexistent, what we do know is that even those who deny the rules apply to them at certain times appear to recognize that some kind of retribution is in store if their behavior is objectionable.

One pertinent rule in the intelligence community is that when a mission is compromised, it has to be reported. A few years into the Vietnam War, on January 23, 1968, the unthinkable happened. The *USS Pueblo* was a Banner-class environmental research ship that was converted to a spy ship in 1967 by the United States Navy. She had reportedly been gathering intelligence and oceanographic information while monitoring electronic and radio signals from North Korea. On that fateful day in January, she was attacked and captured by North Korea.[74]

According to James Bamford's book on the history of the National Security Agency (NSA), *Body of Secrets*,[75] the *USS Pueblo* incident[76] off the coast of North Korea resulted in a capture of codebooks by the North Koreans. Allegedly, the NSA duly reported the loss of these extremely critical assets. The North Koreans wasted no time and duly shared the books with China, who in turn passed them on to the North Vietnamese. Shortly afterwards, the Vietcong was allegedly able to translate every encrypted communication of the American military forces operating in Vietnam since. Despite the NSA's determination to inform everyone involved at the highest levels, reportedly not a single person in charge took their report seriously.

Domestic violence, emotional manipulation, car accidents, workplace harassment, and identity theft are but a few examples of situations where people fail to follow the rules—against human rights, property laws and many more. You may have suffered an injustice at some point or another because someone took advantage of the fact that you (have been conditioned to) obey the rules. The trauma that someone inflicts by violating the rules may stay with you for a long time if not the rest of your life. Meanwhile, the legal system in many countries appears to have extensive experience and liberties in applying the rules to their perspective.

Occasionally, a single individual claims to have a mandate to overrule anyone and anything. For example, one could consider the situation in Brazil around Alexandre de Moraes.[77] De Moraes virtually singlehandedly orchestrates an assault on free speech and constitutional freedom of Brazilians who disagree with the socialist leadership of the country by jailing the opposition no matter age, health or severity of critique. For Brazil, which seemed to be on a path to being recognized as a developed nation, this appears to be a serious setback in terms of human rights. Brazil's Congress thus far reportedly has been unable to stop de Moraes from denying that the country's constitution should protect the public from his excess use of power.

People who are set in their ways, and who interpret constitutional law in a certain manner that leaves very little room for discourse, may have certain personality attributes that the licensed psychological expert could educate us on. Unfortunately, it seems that those in Brazil's expert community would risk incarceration if they were to make an attempt. I will revisit the topic in the Epilogue.

Who is most likely to deny that something exists, that a rule has been broken or should apply? Statistics, when properly used, can tell us something about a condition. When we look for the answer to a problem, it seems best to start by measuring the validity of a criteria:

- exposure to a certain ideology that may influence someone's behavior

- a natural preference dictated by cultural conditioning

- profession, age, or social status

To understand people better, researchers often use a personality survey. The survey measures and evaluates a person's traits, characteristics and tendencies that make up their unique self. A personality assessment survey may yield results when properly structured, but the results of the ones that do are rarely available to the targets of abuse—before or after the abuse occurred. However, a survey has certain inherent limitations not least of which is the need to administer it. We need to find an alternative. The good news is that character traits associated with one's date of birth appears to offer a suitable one. The first group to be associated with rule-averse behavior appear to be born between two specific dates: September 23 and October 22.

Earlier, we addressed fear and insecurity as the flipside of focus. Some people born between these dates appear to have an uncanny ability to focus when they want to, such as: George Westinghouse, Margaret Thatcher, Serena Williams, Brigitte Bardot, President Dwight Eisenhower and John Lennon, all of whom have left their mark on society. Keep in mind that just because someone has a particular attitude on a personal level does not mean they fail to contribute to the greater scheme of things.

It seems prudent to ask whether it is fair that we establish someone's date of birth as a starting point. Finding that a certain number of people, large enough to make for a statistically valid observation, who appear to display a utilitarian or narcissistic view on life were all born between certain days of the year, is only a first step.

"How wonderful it is that nobody need wait a single moment before starting to improve the world."
—Anne Frank, German-Dutch diarist and Holocaust victim

BEHAVIOR = CONTEXT

"At the root of action…is a chemical reaction"

BEHAVIOR =

$$(\int DESIRE, PERSONALITY, CONDITIONING, TRAUMA, COMPANY)^{situation}$$

They introduced him as a mercenary from the former Socialist Federal Republic of Yugoslavia. Not just any mercenary, but a former member of that country's intelligence service. He mentioned that he had been offered good money to kill the prime minister of a Scandinavian country and that he had politely declined. His name was Ivan Von Birchan.

It was the fall of 1985. A few months later, on February 28, 1986, Olof Palme would be walking to his home in Stockholm with his wife after attending a movie late at night. About ten minutes after leaving the movie theater, they would cross paths with two bullets ejected from a Smith & Wesson .357 revolver. To this date, the killer technically remains unknown.

Sweden today seems more known for its high crime rate and as an example of a failed immigration policy rather than Ikea furniture, ABBA and Volvo cars. Olof Palme had been elected Prime Minister of this once mighty seafaring nation for a third time in 1985. Palme was a pivotal and polarizing figure domestically as well as in international politics. He was steadfast in his non-alignment policy towards the superpowers, accompanied by support for numerous liberation movements following decolonization including, most controversially, economic and vocal support for a number of Third World governments. He was the first Western head of government to visit Cuba after its revolution, giving a speech in Santiago praising contemporary Cuban revolutionaries.[78]

If any successful assassination offers multiple yet not necessarily competing perspectives it would be this case. Von Birchan's rejection would, unbeknownst to him at the time, lead to a very different outcome. Famous crime novelist Stieg Larsson would spend ten years researching Palme's death before he passed away of presumably natural causes without a resolution. An architect looking for building blueprints, Jan Stocklassa, would get "Palme fever"—as he refers to the passionate speculation and search for the killer by his fellow Swedes—after discovering Larsson's abandoned material in a storage facility. He allegedly spent another ten years untangling the knots. Eventually, the Swedish investigators would blame a witness who had already passed away of natural causes by the time the investigation was officially closed. But for us there is yet another side to it all: how did Palme get to the point of being a target in the first place?

While the mystery surrounding his death may never be solved, there were plenty of clues that his behavior rubbed some the wrong way. Though Sweden's historical role in European and Scandinavian affairs may be up for debate, Palme enjoyed the fruits of his compatriots' labors, inventive spirit, and commitment to freedom. Still, partially as a result of his personal convictions, he seemed ready to change course and embrace communism. Political rivals and foreign governments alike took note of his visits to and connections with Cuba and the Soviet Union. Did he consider the countless victims of this ideology that seeks equality for all except for the ruling elite? Between fourteen and sixty million, mostly Christians, are suggested to have died in Russia during the Bolshevik revolution and Stalin's reign alone—reportedly largely financed by secular Jews.[79,80,81] Brutal gulags were established, the state police could pick anyone up from the streets of Moscow at random and send them away for life, the state controlled every aspect of a Soviet citizen's existence.

Sweden is a country known for its environmental stewardship. Palme seems to have ignored or perhaps not known about the environmental disasters as a direct result of the Soviet regime's mismanagement of resources.[82] Likewise, Palme was apparently willing to ignore that technological advances in the Soviet Union were mostly the result of Western technology having been copied and stolen, even from Sweden perhaps.[83,84] What stopped him from having a broader, more nuanced perspective?

There are potentially many contributing factors to Palme's death, some politically more sensitive than the one described above. It may be necessary to

A Few Good Cardinals

consider that the convictions and subsequent actions of one could have jeopardized the existence and freedom of many. *The Man Who Played with Fire*,[85] a miniseries about Palme's murder investigation, appears to suggest that "freedom of many" is relative. As a leader of a country with a historically and geographically significant position in the northern hemisphere, Palme must have been excited to contribute to the political changes taking place in a country far away—South Africa. The Black South Africans Palme embraced and supported had long lost their native ways as a result of Western influence and slavery at the hands of the Dutch, French, English and Portuguese.[86]

Agricultural expansion by the Boers and other settlers and the discovery of gold in the region transformed the area dramatically. Prior, the Bantu had abandoned the thousands year old hunting and gathering practices they inherited from the San who occupied the land between about 130,000 and 1,800 years prior.[87] After a period of slavery, the Bantu had been forced into a system of poorly paid jobs and a Western style economy instead. In other words, the playing field had been significantly changed since Jan Van Riebeeck[88] first claimed the area for the Dutch East India Company (V.O.C.) in order to supply ships on their way to and from the Far East. Born April 21, 1619, Van Riebeeck reportedly set up the "Council of Policy". The council's meeting minutes dated December 1651 are considered the moment written public records were first introduced in South Africa as the indigenous people allegedly had no written culture. In 1658, he banished a local translator named Autshumato to Robben Island—known ever since for housing political prisoners—for committing crimes against the V.O.C.

The discovery of a diamond on a farm in the British controlled Cape Colony in 1867 and of gold in the Afrikaner "Boer" controlled Transvaal Republic transformed South Africa's agricultural-based economy into a segregated, White-controlled capitalist industrial society. Over the next two decades, the country became the economic powerhouse of Africa. The British colonial administration scrambled to expand their political control over all of southern Africa through the use of war and conquest over Boer-controlled colonies and over what was left of the traditionally ruled African (Black) territories.[89,90] Into this complex dynamic, Palme thought to valiantly introduce change for oppressed Black South Africans, which reportedly irked at least some in the intelligence community.

Our behavior in a particular situation, like Palme's in the case of his interaction with black South African leaders, takes place in the context of what is called a contextual framework. This framework includes such factors as the environment we grew up in and the social and political identity we developed for ourselves. It includes our educational background, our interactions with others during our formative years, any trauma we may have suffered, advice we may have received from elders, and many other things that I at least am mostly unaware of in day to day interactions.

Being inclusive—as such term is fondly used by many today—may be an almost insurmountable task when it comes to highly complex political situations. Yet, Palme in his position as a representative of a Scandinavian nation whose citizens may not have been able to understand what life in South Africa was like, perhaps did not care as much about the consequences of his initiative for his fellow Swedes as he was enthusiastic about a cause which ultimately wasn't his to resolve. That is, it would have required him to admit that there were many on the Anglo and Boers side of the equation who may simply have gone along with the regime because they, like their black compatriots, had little choice in the matter.

What are we missing from the picture then? Almost everything it seems. In order for Palme to appreciate the dire situation for black South Africans in the Apartheid era, his contextual framework was limited (1) to what information he received from his attachés on the ground, the media, the Swedish Ambassador to South Africa, domestic and international intelligence briefings and reports from locals, (2) to what he had learned about South Africa and its history—such as chronicled in James A. Michener's *The Covenant*[91]—prior to becoming prime minister, (3) his own background, (4) the political circumstances at the time of his government and the will of the Swedish people, and (5) his aspirations, mood and other circumstantial factors. Most of these contributing factors the general public would not have known at the time let alone would be available now. We, as outsiders, would basically be in the dark trying to make sense of Palme's motivation.

The trauma bond is possibly the most significant psychological factor in narcissistic dominance.[92] Once a narcissist has committed an act of abuse, they are considered capable of doing it again. In order to preclude further abuse, people pleasing may ensue as a survival strategy. From the need to survive through impatience, a superiority complex, deep rooted insecurity, or a combination of these and other factors, violence may be the ultimate trauma inducing tool in the toxic narcissist's arsenal.

Olof Palme could have gone into history as an empath had he chosen to be one. He instead opted to ignore important aspects of his own country's history, position in the world, and of the economic and political situation in the regimes he so admired. Whether his murder was the right course of action to avert Sweden becoming a communist country is not part of our discussion. Decisions were made by those involved, and action was taken. Hindsight is always twenty-twenty. What personality characteristics contributed to triggering someone to kill him is something we are going to come back to later.

Aside from the need to get things done, behavior seems to originate from a desire to feel like one accomplishes something, to receive a reward for one's contribution, however little, and perhaps even to be recognized. A reward from an action can come in many forms: self-validation—when I look in the mirror and am pleased; a feeling of content after I iron my shirt; a feeling of accomplishment after I cook a meal or assemble something; a feeling of control when I am in charge of a project; a feeling of achievement when I own a piece of property; a feeling of acknowledgment when people listen to me; a sense of power when people do what I tell them to do.

Kurt Lewin[93] in 1936 first proposed that behavior presents as the function of the person and their environment.[94] Here we are expanding on it since we have developed a much better understanding of how unresolved trauma can affect behavior. We will revisit this later on when we discuss the case of Robert Durst.

Validation can come from an external source such as praise, from spirit or God, material objects, and social status, or from inside— humbly acknowledging that one is worthy without expressly sharing such a statement with the world. Some people seem to need lots of validation by the nature of their behavior and their material possessions. People who live in fear, who are insecure and have a utilitarian perspective on life seem most liable to seek (near constant) validation.

Receiving validation for some appears to function like a drug whose supply is ever useful. Control of a relationship is a mechanism through which validation may be achieved provided that the target remains more or less in place: sending multiple follow up texts to a friend asking if they are still going to the party on Saturday; repeatedly requesting that somebody submit a survey; sending frequent email marketing messages that alert the sender when the recipient reads the message. This type of behavior on the part of the sender can result in stress on the part of the recipient—stress which can affect their decision making, relationships and productivity. Someone with a utilitarian perspective who denies that maintaining control this way results in harm or suffering may be unresponsive to an attempt to change their behavior.

A good example may be the struggle for affordable health care in America. Consumers—also known as patients—have reportedly faced significantly increased costs for health insurance and care since the introduction of the Affordable Care Act, also known as Obamacare.[95] Providers "ping" their patients with vaccine recommendations and annual checkups. They control the target by mandating which parties may talk to patients about health and what information they may provide. If I were to be at risk for cancer, for example, my doctor may not talk to me about vitamin D. In an effort to validate their position and address the issue, lawmakers in the State of Minnesota—representing the consumer—recently attempted to introduce legislation aimed at reducing health care costs. One of the main providers of said care, also seeking to validate their respective role in society, responded quickly, allegedly successfully curbing the assault on their control over the marketplace.[96]

Self-validation may come in the form of parenting. How precious isn't the newborn to their parents and caregivers. Yet, raising a child is subject to many variables the most significant of which may be the personality of its parents. The overly protective parent may not allow their child to pursue a particular interest. This type of parent may seek validation for their role as a caregiver: from the child through obedience, from the community by expecting recognition for being a "responsible" parent. One could argue that setting a limit on outside playtime is a healthy signal of a caring parent toward their offspring especially if the neighborhood is unsafe. Is the mandate accompanied by constructive dialogue with the child explaining the reasoning behind it? Does the parent become more relaxed as the child grows older, or if the neighborhood becomes safer? Does the restriction on outside activity include verbal abuse when the child disobeys and comes home eleven minutes late? Is there another adult who supports the child in breaking the rule, undermining the authority of the controlling parent?

A Few Good Cardinals

Negotiating with a controlling party may be a long-term affair. In the case of the tug of war between law makers and health care providers, the proverbial battle may consist of decades long give and takes whereby the most skilled, the best leveraged, and the most empathic or shrewd party may (temporarily) gain an edge. Nevertheless, a goal is at stake in either situation: quality health care at a cost consumers can afford in our first example, a child growing up to be a responsible adult who can take care of themselves in the second.[97]

Frustration with others often expresses itself through rudeness. The checkout line at the grocery store that does not move fast enough may find that you exercise patience and compassion while the person ahead of you tries to find their money or the cashier is looking up the code of an infrequently sold vegetable. There are plenty of moments where people seem to be "asking for it," or where another is acting out their frustration by being rude. Studies on the net effect of intolerant behavior may rarely be on the radar, but it seems a study on neonatal intensive care unit (NICU) performance may illustrate a point that negative behavior can have an effect, while simultaneously alerting us to bias exhibited in study design.

The NICU in a hospital looks after babies and infants that need intensive support. Neonatal means any baby under 28 days old. An NICU team looks after very ill and/or premature babies. Iatrogenesis is a technical term used to describe harm caused by deficient medical care. Often, it appears this type of harm results from performance deficiencies among medical team members. In a medical setting, performance may be judged by a diagnostic and a procedural component separately. A randomized trial investigating the impact of rudeness on performance identified team-targeted rudeness as the underlying cause of deficiencies—that is, rudeness that did not target a specific individual of a team as harassment or bullying might. Individuals exposed to rude behavior were considered being less helpful and cooperative. Now, this is where bias entered the discussion: there appears to have been no effort to identify the performance characteristics of the staff who exhibited the rude behavior.

It was discovered that rudeness appeared to have adverse consequences on the diagnostic and procedural performance of NICU team members. To resolve the performance issue, the researchers identified information-sharing as a solution to mitigate the adverse effect of rudeness on diagnostic performance, while seeking help allegedly mediated the effect of rudeness on procedural performance.[98] What can be the effect of iatrogenesis, or harm caused by deficient medical care? In the case of a neonatal care unit where the patient is extremely fragile and has a whole life ahead of them, it could be a lifelong medical condition or a life-threatening event. As Frederick Taylor observed in his work in the early nineteen hundreds, when workers receive attention that they ordinarily don't get—which lack of attention has led to negative performance issues—performance may improve even without direct intervention.

A 2001 performance study[99] on iatrogenesis by itself, without considering team member behavior per se, looked at the incidence of medical harm for two 3-month periods before (A) and after (B) alerting team members that they were subject to observation and possible intervention. The study reportedly found that although the prevalence rates (over a specific period of time) of iatrogenic events were comparable in both period A and B, the incidence rate (newly identified cases) decreased significantly during period B.[100] Does this mean that NICU teams perform better when the threat of enforcement of the rules is looking over their shoulder, were they subject to a dictatorial leader who urged them to speed up tasks (and cut corners) in order to improve the "numbers," or were some team members themselves at fault?

When control is exercised beyond a reasonable degree trauma may result. Taxpayers may be left footing the bill for skyrocketing medical costs. As a result, they may be financially strapped if wages and health insurance fail to compensate. They may be forced to forego care needed to ensure they can remain a productive participant in society. In our second example, the child may develop something we came across in the previous chapter: cPTSD.[101] The stress from living with a controlling caregiver for many years may result in the personality adopting a survival strategy that they carry with them into their adult years. In other words, the validation sought by one party can have a noticeable effect on another party. The need for validation may be observed in someone's behavior.

This is going to sound overly complex, but how is the *behavior* of a person not subject to the *context* of the situation at hand *plus* the *company* they keep (and how many), and:

1. predictable conditions, such as:

   a. cultural norms;

b. the person's physical condition (*i.e.*, if they are in pain they may act differently);

c. ambient noise (*i.e.*, loud noise testing their patience may trigger the demand for a quicker resolution and excessive demands);

d. personality (*i.e.*, a stubborn individual will negotiate differently compared to an altruistic person);

e. if the subject is acting alone and feels backed by a cause; and

f. if the subject is acting alone and feels backed by a group of people;

PLUS

2. unpredictable factors, such as:

a. how much experience and training the subject has with the situation at hand;

b. emotional state and mood,

c. noise (how sensitive is someone actually to noise, especially when we need to consider her current stress level),

d. if the subject experiences a flashback to a past event or trauma due to a specific similarity in the current situation,

e. what recall the subject has of a similar past event or emotion;

f. how the subject scores on the scale of autism spectrum disorder,

g. if the subject is an in- or extrovert and how it applies in this situation,

h. if the subject has epilepsy,

i.   what alcohol and/or drugs, if any, the subject uses,

j.   if the subject is being intimidated or bullied,

k.   what long term stress the subject has recently been exposed to,

l.   her general sensitivity to distractions and ability to focus,

m.   what distractions are present in the current situation and how they affect our subject—something I call the *hypnosis factor*,

n.   her conditioning/addiction level to dopamine as a reward motivator;

PLUS

3.   conditions that immediately preceded the situation.

Behavior can involve action even if it means withdrawal or doing nothing at all. Action may be based on a gut feeling and may be impacted to some degree by one or more of the above factors. As scientists gain knowledge of other factors influencing behavior, I am thinking specifically in terms of advances in neuroscience, we may be able to expand the above list. As I understand it, a caveat to any behavior that is considered the result of one or more of the above contributing conditions might be amygdala-induced behavior as we saw earlier, and the effect of oxytocin.[102]

In a personality assessment, the question is what happens when we extract one individual out of a particular situation and insert a different person. How different will their response be? For our second subject, the circumstances of the situation remain virtually the same: the distractions, the noise, and the time of day. The remaining variables are their unique personality, their past trauma, and what preceded their participation.

When we subject a person to a singular event, we have only limited observable behavior at our disposal. It gets much more interesting when we can observe a person over an extended period of time, and when we can study the history of their behavior. Due to possible self-embellishment and bias, asking someone to describe how they would behave in a certain situation will never give us the full picture. It is important to acknowledge that our own bias as an observer may diminish the value of our observations in a similar fashion. Nevertheless, observations over an extended period of time have the distinct advantage that the effect of factors such as mood, the effect of drug and alcohol use, emotions and stress on the personality may be greatly neutralized. Such observations are generally possible for people in our family, social life, and the workplace.

The foundation of personality may be established at the earliest moment of life, at first breath. We may, when we pay close attention, be able distinguish certain personality characteristics in an infant from a very early age. These characteristics may present practically from the moment a child is born even though some experts consider them simply a response to external stimuli in combination with a need for survival—such as attracting attention, primarily from the mother.

The personality for our purposes appears to consist, roughly, of three elements: wants, needs and presentation or mask. The first, wants, is reportedly closely linked to the day a person is born. It is the primary indicator of behavior and whether a person is in- or extroverted. For example, people who have a wider and deeper perspective on life than most people, resulting in a highly sensitive, inspired and sometimes absentminded personality.

The second, needs, indicates, among other things, what satisfies us when "all else fails" in extreme circumstances. For example, order, correctness and being of service. When nobody has a need for his person, they may feel depressed and at a loss until they realize what mood they are in and encourage themselves to "get it together."

The third, presentation, shows how the world sees us as well as how we present ourselves—our mask. For example, a "helpful, critical, and analytical" person. Aspects of behavior such as our physical condition—whether a person is disabled in any way or was exposed to environmental chemicals possibly resulting in diminished brain function—and mental health—whether the person has been diagnosed with a personality disorder, suffers from (complex) PTSD[103] or any other kind of mental condition—fall outside of the realm of our exploration. Many books on the subject appear to be available for further research.

From an early age, a child learns to fit into her environment or to resist it. Caregivers correct the child's behavior with phrases such as, "No!", "Behave yourself," and "Control yourself." Rules are intended to level the playing field, for maintaining social order, protecting against injustice, and, most importantly, preserving and improving one's chances of survival. Most of the rules of society are intended to govern behavior you may never see yourself engaging in thanks to your moral compass.

Her mother was stern yet fair as long as she obeyed the house rule: inside by 9pm. Charlotte loved playing outside with her friends, or just to chill and hang out. It was early summer and the sky was clear. Mother had reminded her that it was almost time to come inside. Charlotte hid and stayed out. The stars were bright and the weather was just so…perfect. Now it was passed the cutoff time and Charlotte knew punishment was coming. She heard her mother calling, "Where are you? Come inside at once!" as any mother who is concerned about the safety of her child would and who cares about the image of her authority as a parent at the same time. Rules are rules. Charlotte stayed out of sight. It was getting dark. All of a sudden, Charlotte saw something very bright pass overhead, far away, yet awe inspiring. She stood mesmerized. Then she heard her mother close by and realized it might be best to give herself up. "Right here mum," she yelled out. "I lost track of time," she instantly made up an excuse. "Did you see that? What was it? I want to find out!" Charlotte was so excited, it later turned out this evening inspired her to pursue a career in astrophysics. She broke her mother's cardinal "9pm rule," but it was worth it. Sometimes we need to break a rule.

Every time we have an interaction with the world around us, something happens in the brain. Neurons are created, links between them are established, etcetera. The theory and practical implications of this is left to the expert literature on neuroscience. When we are repeatedly exposed to a certain stimuli, neurons start forming permanent connections. In order to learn and retain language skills, for example, it helps to trigger neurons formed in class again and again. But what about neurons and their connections that are established as a result of repetitive negative stimuli from our caregivers? What if a parent repeatedly denies a child an opportunity to play with friends? What if a child is exposed to certain chemicals that affect brain development? The child may be repeatedly, and over a long period of time, witness to arguments between her caregivers, confronting the child with a sense of helplessness—and perhaps worse, responsibility for the plight of the victim. Breaking a rule once may not leave much of an impact except if it is a special occasion. Doing it repeatedly may have a similar "training" effect on the brain as being witness to drama between adults: habituation—a form of non-associative learning by which a non-reinforced response to a stimulus decreases after repeated or prolonged presentations of said stimulus.[104]

Many books have been written, both in academia and in the area of self-help, to deal with the effects of exposure to trauma at an age at which the brain has not yet developed its adult capacity to process emotions that the adults in the situation are displaying and inflicting as it were on the child. Reportedly, lack of confidence, a sense of guilt or shame, and potentially also a desire to take revenge for the victim are possible outcomes for the child. How does the resulting neuronal development in the brain affect its development into adulthood? A useful book that discusses the effect of abandonment, the influence of trauma and that of drug/alcohol use by parents is *Ghosts from the Nursery*.[105]

How the child deals with the consequences and the degree to which she heals herself are of course a matter of significant interest. For the purpose of our discussion here, though, what interests us most is not just the personality of the child, but that of caregivers as well. Gender (identity) appears to have very little to do with how the child is treated. A parent may take it out on a son or daughter regardless. The characteristics of personality do not appear to discriminate, nor does social status, wealth, genetics, physical attributes, or race appear to affect the foundation of personality. What does appear to affect the expression of personality is the amount of control an individual has, how supported she is, how well liked, how many like-minded individuals she finds in her community.

DEEPER, BIGGER

"How does it not start with entitlement?"

Deception can be a game for some, an annoyance for others, and life threatening for the unfortunate. Is deception fair? When the chance of dying at the end of the day is pretty high, we might change our perspective. In World War II, deception was a life or death situation for those engaged in battle. Operation Fortitude was one of many initiatives where deception played a critical role for the Allies in gaining a strategic advantage over the enemy.[106] And that is what deception boils down to: gaining an advantage over another, fair or not.

Politics and power dynamics can make us wonder why politicians say the things they do, but even people closer to "home" may have a reason to deceive on occasion. People who are supposed to be there at the most critical moment of life—childhood—in some families ignore their offspring instead, or worse. People who command another person to do things that go against their very nature can make their followers obey. The threat of punishment and the promise of reward may be used to gain compliance. Contrast this with the approach the empath prefers who would rather rely on access to resources, experience and expertise as motivational tools.

The self-absorbed person with a utilitarian perspective manipulates others any way they can. Maintaining the status quo may be the preferred response despite oppression because the need to survive may trump the wish to escape. There appear to be a number of mechanisms that can thwart an attempt to change the dynamic. One is called Stockholm Syndrome[107]—a coping mechanism for an abusive situation in which one aims to please the perpetrator—the other self-justification, a similar coping mechanism that justifies why one should postpone an escape: "I was here yesterday. It wasn't so bad. What are my chances of getting out alive anyway"[108]

Life may very well be an exercise in learning from each other and growing as individuals without ever being able to explain it to anyone. Intelligence, emotional maturity and cultural norms seem to vary quite dramatically from one civilization to another. If we want to thrive, we are going to need tools. Who could have predicted that curiosity and passion would eventually lead to the invention of an electrical apparatus in England[109] and not in, for example, Africa or the Middle East? One need only look at the technological progress of Western civilization since the Industrial Revolution to admit that the gap with other cultures has widened quite a bit. Yet, how sure are we to assume that the next breakthrough technology would come from, let's say, China?

Even in Western civilization itself there are enormous differences. For example, the kind of technology that defense specialists and intelligence agencies reportedly have access to seems far beyond anything the average citizen can dream of let alone would need to lead a fulfilling life. Still, everything we do is marked by one constant: the presence of the human mind. If one mind can manipulate another while the former denies their own contribution to the situation, how is that not toxic? Some people act alone while others form a group to "institutionalize" their behavior.

We could argue that the perpetrator of manipulative tactics simply lacks intelligence to judge the potential impact of their actions. This argument appears not only contracted by reality, but also by a body of research such as what Nayef Al-Rodhan argues in *The wrongs, harms, and ineffectiveness of torture: A moral evaluation from empirical neuroscience*. His findings imply that manipulative and coercive behavior, in the long run at least, can have an effect opposite of that which was intended.[110]

Historically, self-centered behavior is referred to as narcissism. In a Greek myth about Narcissus, we learn that he allegedly saw his reflection in a pool and fell in love.[111] Narcissism can morph into a toxic form and eventually present as psychopathy and sociopathy even though the latter are not officially recognized by the psychiatric profession. As far as I understand it, under certain conditions narcissism may be helpful. It appears to give the subject a much needed focus and ability to concentrate effort. The trouble starts when this focus on one own's endeavor turns into toxic behavior. Toxic behavior rewards one person over another, distributes resources unfairly and denies that others contributed to the success of the team. It can cause real emotional, mental or physical harm. It is in this toxic state that narcissism seems to put a severe strain on human relations.

At its most basic, life seems to come down to survival. You, me and everyone else and everything around us survive an onslaught of natural forces like solar radiation, hurricanes, hungry bears and viruses, together with human made factors like red-light running cars, household chemicals and microplastics on a daily basis. For you, survival may be a given. What makes life uncertain is *how* we survive and the conditions under which we live. Yet, we can't change if we are unable or unwilling to accept that another option exists. For some of us it is much harder to accept the need for change.

For some, skim milk is the natural choice. Since its introduction, the American Heart Association appears to have been at the forefront of its suggested health benefits: clear arteries and a lean body[112] while a source for information on organic living claims it contains many nutrients, can help build lean muscle and boosts weight loss.[113] Unfortunately, the opposite has happened when it comes to body weight. A veritable obesity epidemic seems to have engulfed Western societies. Arguably, sugar consumption appears to blame to some degree.[114] But wait, there is more.

A 1994 study only went as far as suggesting that skim milk *may* reduce the risk of coronary heart disease.[115] Yet, the debate over the health benefits of skim versus whole milk got a twist in 2013 with the publication of an *Archives of Disease in Childhood* study that claimed skim milk consumption by children can lead to obesity.[116] What about adults? It seems producers of dairy have noticed a change if a 2024 report on the global industry[117] is an indication. Still, the last time I checked the dairy aisle in my local supermarket, skim milk is not just sold by itself but also as an ingredient of many yogurt, ice cream and other products. What is the truth then? It appears that as early as 1930, it was known that "skim milk 'is not only the very best supplement for growing pigs, but is of almost equal value for fattening purposes.'"[118]

> "Before World War II, skim milk—a byproduct of butter processing—was not sold in stores, but either discarded or fed to chickens, hogs, and calves as a protein-rich replacement for costlier animal feed. The development of skim milk […] came about because dairy producers […] seized on postwar marketing opportunities to sell what once had been hog slop to housewives and families."[119]

The history of skim milk, therefore, seems to be one of deception and misappropriation of a survival mechanism. In other words: toxic narcissism.

Narcissism reportedly presents on the scale of Narcissism Spectrum Disorder (NSD),[120] from a very personal form that may not be detectable by others to extreme sociopathy, the violent criminal who knows no bounds. Brain structure may explain why people present the condition to varying degrees. Although narcissistic traits have been linked to structural and functional brain networks, including the insular cortex, the findings appear to have been inconsistent.[121] Furthermore, people may be classified as learned or natural narcissists if I understand it correctly. According to the experts, what makes a natural narcissist is apparently still up in the air. Fortunately, and this is why we are here, it seems we have a solution.

A learned narcissist gets their behavior exactly as the term implies, by learning from others—from the natural narcissist or other learned narcissists. A learned narcissist appears to relinquish his acquired behavior traits when his chances of survival have improved, the situation no longer calls for a "fit in at all costs" mentality, and when he is surrounded by empaths and exposed to fair and just behavior. Going forward, I will refer to learned and natural narcissists together as narcissists because until they reveal themselves, how are we supposed to know the difference?

Imagine that you meet a Tinder date. How would you know if you are dealing with a narcissist? Their response to your questions could give you a clue if this person is a somatic empath, a well-off altruistic narcissist—a good person—or a toxic individual pretending to be rich—provided you are not so overcome with emotions and your brain isn't overwhelmed with visual and other stimuli that you have no time to absorb their data dump. Their body language could be another clue: do they look you in the eye just long enough to establish trust? Do they make implausible excuses for their behavior in the past? There may be many more clues. Yet what specifically could be the most important tool in the narcissist's kit may be the tendency to cover their tracks and intentions by confusing you—by hypnotizing you with small hand gestures and verbal timing cues into ignoring what they may be dropping right in front of you.

How pervasive is hypnosis in the language and behavior of the narcissist? Reflect on how much experience you have dealing with others. Now imagine that people in general, narcissists and empaths alike, want to make a good impression on you while hiding their less attractive qualities. Do you think you have what it takes to identify who is who? Then consider my conundrum in the following, very simple exercise on memory.[122] On a large table in a room is a model train on a circular track. The train consists of a number of freight cars, each with one word written on them in big letters. Four test subjects join me for this exercise which is conducted by a psychologist. He indicates that soon he will set the train in motion. At some point, he will stop the train and ask if we remember seeing a specific word from one of the train cars.

I did this exercise a few years ago and pride myself on being highly aware in these kinds of situations in real life. If anyone can remember a word, it will be me. Knowing that there are four other people participating in the exercise may put some pressure on me to get it right. Except, I was not in the room. I was sitting at home in my living room watching the exercise on television. In other words, no pressure but my own. The psychologist flips the switch and the train starts running. It makes a few rounds while I try to remember as best as I could each of the words on the cars. After a few minutes, the train comes to a halt. Then comes the question: was "chicken" one of the words on the cars? Nobody got it right, not even yours truly.

Deception is as old as nature itself. Animals do it, plants do it, humans do it.[123] However, of these three, we seem far less willing to admit to the reality of death that often accompanies being at the receiving end of deception. Narcissists seem to be more aware of the fragility of life than others, and of the need to preserve resources. In their self-absorption, a narcissist seeks to ensure their own survival not only above others, but often also at a cost to themselves—which cost they blame on the situation or a third party. The survival tools they have at their disposal seem well developed from an early age, possibly as early as birth.

Like with the moving train exercise, narcissists may deceive with circular language, intonation, hand gestures, by walking in a certain way—literally by using anything they have found useful in creating an impression that diverges from and hides their true self. Deception may be coupled with a very mild form of bullying such as by repeating the target's name every other sentence in conversation. Hearing one's name can have a hypnotic effect, emphasizing that the other person is fully aware of our presence. In a nefarious context, it might be considered as a kind of "reeling in" of the target's attention. Doing it repeatedly can have the effect of hammering in that the perpetrator is fully focused on the target—a tremendously valuable validation tool. Individuals manipulate with deception to get the attention we might not otherwise grant, groups do it to gain members, and organizations do it to sell a product or promote a cause that may otherwise not be worth it.

What happens after the initiation phase, once you commit to a follow up to your first Tinder date? Assuming that you are dealing with a toxic narcissist, a number of tools are at their disposal:

- trauma bonding—e.g., "I forgot my wallet, can you pay?"

- controlling behavior—e.g., "stop talking to your friends, they are so annoying"

- denial that something was said or happened (creating cognitive dissonance),

- changing the rules of engagement, and more.

Once the toxic narcissist has a hold on someone, it may be a while before an escape becomes a possibility. The bad news is, that sometimes I am not acutely aware that I am being deceived. The perpetrator may have created not only a scenario of extreme cognitive dissonance, they may have introduced a number of distractions as well. In addition, I may be too gullible and complacent. I have to admit that sometimes dealing with deception may be more effort than I want to spend.

Consider what happened to Sue Hughes, a psychiatric nurse in England. Being used to dealing with patients and their mental illness on a hospital ward, she may have been conceited about her ability to sniff out problems in real life. A woman who became her closest friend manipulated Sue into spending an alleged £117,000 on an imaginary boyfriend.[124] At the time of this writing, it seems no birth date is available for the convicted perpetrator, Anna Bonner. The deception took place over more than twenty years. Hughes was warned, but, at first, ridiculed the person who tried to help.

Wealthy investors, well known politicians and power brokers alike were taken in by Elizabeth Holmes's vision. She was so intent on "saving the world" that she did anything to make it happen: adopting a male voice, wearing the outfit of her idol—Steve Jobs—and hiding the truth in the proverbial basement, away from the prying eyes of federal investigators and regulatory agencies. Hiring bodyguards and bullying by her and a strong male partner completed the picture. It took two employees in seemingly insignificant positions to pull away the veil of deception, but not before a senior engineer committed suicide as a result of intimidation and lies.

How does Theranos compare to what Dr. Anthony Fauci appears to have contributed during the Covid-19 mRNA vaccine scandal: more than one million dead in the United States?[125] Will he face similar, or more severe consequences as Holmes did for having orchestrated the deception of the century while investing in the lab from which the Wuhan virus reportedly originated,[126] or will he slip away into obscurity? The stakes may be so high that we as outsiders will never know the whole truth.[127]

Misty Griffin is the author of *Tears of the Silenced*.[128] In her Amish community, abused children had no one to turn to for help. The Child Rights Act petition[129] that she started aims to bring awareness of the deception that allows religious communities to perpetrate unspeakable acts of sexual abuse and violence against children. The question inevitably arises as to how far society today is aware of the pervasiveness of narcissism and its cousins psychopathy and sociopathy. Tinder dates, the above acts of deception and the occasional cult are one thing, but what about religion as a whole, the culture of multi-national corporations, financial institutions and the field of medicine? In how far are organizations that impact us all infiltrated by and representative of toxic narcissistic behavior? Meanwhile, my local supermarket allegedly uses a clever tactic to convince me to donate to charity or buy the oranges that are on sale.[130] How bad can narcissistic and deceptive behavior be, my subconscious may be asking itself.

It is suggested that all problems can be solved if we want to. If money prevents us, let us reexamine how we value time and labor, and the products and services they produce. Is it pollution, let's tackle the problem at the source, improving product design, production systems and distribution. Is it human welfare, let's evaluate if should have a basic income in conjunction with labor participation in accordance to one's capacity. With technology, many things are already possible and even more in the years to come if our current progress is any indication. What is keeping us from moving forward faster besides a natural resistance to change seem to be established, vested interests.

A balanced approach to innovation may be the best course of action, but how do we define "balanced?" If a less polluting energy source is available than "fossil fuels," how fast should we be developing it? If a large international department store gobbled up all the local stores in your town, how can the local retail scene be replaced with a meaningful alternative? We are not alone in experiencing dramatic change. Nature is right there with us and is often worse off. What is keeping us from going with the flow?

How people define fairness seems to vary quite a bit. What is fair to the narcissist appears to pivot towards their own self-interest. The next time you are in a negotiation, try saying, "I want to do what is fair," to see what reaction you get although it is a term perhaps best used with discretion. When an injustice is perceived to have been committed, one may feel like screaming at the top of their lungs, ready to move mountains to rectify the situation. Violence may be used to "teach someone a lesson."[131]

Talking about violence, it goes without saying that women the world over suffer under the threat and perpetration of abuse by men—and to an extent also other women, and that they have done so for millennia if not longer. What seems to go largely unnoticed, is that it takes at least a man and a woman to put a violent man on the planet. A baby, in its mother's arms, is apparently not violent. It does not make a threatening face at the human who cherishes it, it does not hit her nor does it try to get away. Research seems to point to emotional and physical factors influencing that moment, what came before, and what happens next until the first time someone threatens to or actually assaults a woman. Robin Karr-Morse describes some important findings in *Ghosts from the Nursery*.[132]

What stops us from educating parents-to-be accordingly? I would hate to suggest it, yet is there some kind of toxic-narcissistic scheme in place to purposely omit such knowledge from mainstream education, and to somehow cultivate violence in society? Call me naïve, ignorant and anything else, but what would it take for women, collectively, to undertake a concerted effort to improve their lot if men are indeed as missing in action as they seem to be made out to be? At least in Sweden, where a music festival was recently made "female-only" as a result of misbehaving men,[133] or in the Netherlands, where British men have been barred from visiting as tourists,[134] it seems some kind of after-the-fact initiative seems to be in place to prevent violence. Narcissism as a condition does not discriminate. Men and women are known to be afflicted to the exact same degree. The presentation may vary because of biological differences, but the result is the same: trauma and a victim, while the perpetrator often walks away scot-free.

Just like there are different kinds of empaths, there may be a reason why someone may be an altruistic rather than a toxic narcissist. An altruistic narcissist may deny a personal issue while being responsive and respectful of others. The natural narcissist raised in a loving, nurturing environment devoid of displays of narcissistic behavior may develop a similar stoic, logical personality as the empath. The second rule of life, learning by example, virtually ensures this. If a natural narcissist who grew up in adversarial conditions, experiencing trauma, being exposed to altruistic behavior can mitigate the negative consequences of his upbringing may be possible. Someone may grow spiritually because of the challenges life throws at him and become more respectful of others. But does altruistic narcissism guarantee open mindedness in human relations?

Those who admit to having caused harm in the past seem reluctant to identify what steps they would be willing to take to stop themselves from engaging in harmful behavior again when faced with a similar situation. One in particular had committed financial crimes for which he was punished with jail time and restitution. While in prison, he allegedly found Jesus. After having his sentence reduced for good behavior, the individual joined a local church and taught its board members how to become savvier with church finances. Despite being surrounded by a supportive church community, he was subsequently found to have defrauded the church in a similar way as the crime for which he was initially convicted. The toxic narcissist may not be able to rise above the need for self-validation.

As mentioned earlier, the cause of narcissistic personality disorder appears unknown.[135] The individual with narcissistic personality disorder is known to display a pattern of behavior characterized by exaggerated feelings of self-importance, an excessive need for admiration, and a lack of empathy. People who are affected by it often appear motivated in life solely by the achievement of success and power. Their primary motivation is colored by two distinct characteristics: fear and lack (of abundance). In the pursuit of their goals, they often take advantage of others without fair compensation because they fear there is not enough for everyone. Lest someone beats them to success, time is of the essence. The American Psychiatric Association speculates that the behavior typically begins by early adulthood, yet a study by the University of Washington appeared to indicate that babies show a sense of fairness at fifteen months.[136]

Measuring narcissism in a person may be accomplished with the Narcissistic Personality Inventory (NPI) developed by Robert Raskin and Calvin S. Hall.[137] The NPI makes an individual choose between pairs of statements that assess levels of modesty, assertiveness, and willingness to manipulate others. The scale recognizes that a person might still exhibit a fundamentally healthy personality. The most distinctive characteristic of such an assessment is that it does not rely on outside observation. In other words, if you experience someone acting as a narcissist towards you, you have no recourse if the person rates themselves outside of the range considered to be that of a narcissist.

While some experts argue that the cause of narcissistic personality disorder may be unknown to them, to me the cause seems increasingly clear. This realization comes partially from a field of study that many experts deny exists. As it so happens, denial is one of several narcissistic traits. Denial appears to be a very potent force and quite prevalent. It is one of the primary reasons I decided to write this book because I couldn't keep denying that so many of my fellow human beings are in denial not just about things they do or don't do, but about things they have said, committed themselves to, and subscribe to. In fact, it seems denial is possibly the most important enemy we have in human relations.

Numerous philosophers and psychoanalysts have attempted to answer basic questions such as, "Why do we think" and "Why do we do the things we do." Their travels through the territory of the mind have yielded terminology to distinguish individuals who display personality traits that seem to be less desirable for the proper functioning of the modern social unit—the individual and their online friends (if any), the family as we have come to see it, or the community, whoever may be its members. Anti-social behavior as a whole can be harmful, but for the purpose of our exploration here we limit ourselves to the trait that serves one's own interests to an unhealthy degree: selfishness. In common discourse, there are considered to be three variations of this personality trait in ascending degree of severity: narcissism, psychopathy and sociopathy. Only the first is officially recognized by the psychology profession. The result of the behavior—trauma—is universal. When the behavior of a narcissist harms primarily others the person may be considered toxic. Finally, narcissism could be considered to present on a scale and be referred to as narcissism spectrum disorder.

Experts spend a significant amount of effort trying to determine what lies at the root of aberrant behavioral traits in order to better understand what leads to events such as school shootings, the collapse of a large international corporation like Enron[138] and the Ponzi scheme operated by a former Chairman of the Nasdaq stock exchange, Bernard Madoff[139]—and war. The Enron Corporation was an American energy company based in Houston, Texas. In October 2001, news of widespread fraud within the company became public. The company subsequently filed for bankruptcy. Its accounting firm, Arthur Andersen—at the time one of the five largest audit and accountancy partnerships in the world—was dissolved. In addition to being the largest bankruptcy reorganization in U.S. history at that time, Enron was cited as the biggest audit failure. Kenneth Lay and Jeffrey Skilling were key players in Enron's unscrupulous activities.

There is a tremendous amount of data to sift through in order to understand, for example, the desire of one individual to kill not just one other person but multiple, or for one person to be able to convince thousands of others that it is perfectly fine to make up non-existent investment returns and promote that as a legitimate business. When it comes to a mass event like war, people who represent us in government often portray it as necessary. Considerable, often heated, deliberation precedes it. The group whose position does not often make the news is usually referred to as the silent majority. Similarly, for every victim of a serial killer, there are many who were in the path of the perpetrator yet did not get killed.

When I met renowned documentary filmmaker Liz Garbus, she was in the process of shooting her documentary *The Farm, Angola, USA*[140] in which a death row inmate describes that he killed someone because that person had an "evil eye." It seemed to imply that even people society considers outlaws appear to be able to separate the "good" guys from the "bad." Striving for fairness and justice could mean that one gives up healthy competition and striving to be better than one's neighbor. The alternative may be acknowledging abundance: there is enough opportunity for success for everyone within the context of their own, unique life.

It may be an illusion that society has meaningfully progressed over thousands of years. Instead:

1.   strong, charismatic rulers frequently manage to convince enough serfs to pick up arms and kill the neighbors;

2. one group, fearing for their tribe's survival, may infiltrate the neighbors, conning the host into giving up the essentials while thinking nobody will ever complain;

3. another group may decide they are "superior" because "God" has "chosen them," invades a territory and sells the locals into slavery to a third group under the guise of "good business practice."

Fast forward to today, and slavery appears still very acceptable in certain parts of the world. The "neighbors" are now pretty much just the field or body of water next door where one can dump anything no longer needs. If someone needs to sell something fake fast, there is an Internet auction for that.

If there is one good example of an environment that resembles a Western version of the tight-knit survival-based tribal structure of the islanders in the Pacific Ocean, it might be the astronaut corps of the United States National Aeronautical and Space Administration (NASA). One small mishap in space can mean the failure of a mission or worse, the death of an astronaut. Got an ego? Leave that on Earth. A slightly bigger mishap could have consequences far worse: big money is involved, multiple, highly trained lives are at stake. That is, for the astronauts at least. But does the same go for the people at mission control, the managers and the decision makers? Can they get away with a lie like an astronaut might be tempted to tell but is trained not to when he forgets to take a crucial tool on a spacewalk?

As a species, we live in a social structure of one kind or another simply because we can't do everything ourselves. We are accustomed to relying on the support and expertise of others: Janet takes care of everyone's dental care, Peter grows food, Wendy teaches young children in math, Pat helps people recover from illness, John protects the village, and so forth. When a community is small, resides in a remote location and relies on nature for its sustenance, people help and support each other from an early age. When one person defies the norm or challenges common practice by disrupting the status quo, he is expected to be challenged directly. If that person takes something that isn't theirs and deprives the community of that resource, it is noticed and addressed. Anonymity is not an option. Everyone looks out for one another. Purposely disrupting the community spirit for self-gain is not only frowned upon, it is not generally practiced. In other words, exposure to disruptive behavior is minimal.

An important discovery to come out of recent neuroscience research is the principle of mirror neurons. In more worldly terms, we learn by example.[141] If we were to find ourselves surrounded by parents, grandparents, aunts and uncles, and other community members on a twenty-four hour, seven days a week basis with near constant supervision and feedback, learning by example could be an intense experience of selection, integration, and trying to be liked by the right people.

The motivation for comparing my fortune to that of another, for considering anyone a threat to my existence, and for scheming to eliminate said threat may reside in insecurity, a deep rooted kind of insecurity. For the narcissist, overcoming said insecurity may be an endless road to deeper experiences and bigger toys. Should I consider myself fortunate or not that I don't seem to harbor such a need to feel bigger, better and stronger?

A METHOD TO THE MADNESS

Power, status, prestige

Insecurity, how is it not a burden? Maybe we are all naturally insecure. Earlier we found that people born between September 23 and October 22 seem to be naturally averse to rules they do not like. If a study among seven hundred and seventy-six people is any indication, there is a second group worthy of attention: those born between December 21 and January 20. If insecurity has a match, people born in this timeframe seem to fit the bill even better. What right do I have to link insecurity to an observation among fewer than eight hundred cohorts? Just because my father was born in late December, for starters, and he was definitely insecure to an extent? He also accomplished much, seemed passionate about his career and was known as ambitious and determined. What else was he allegedly known for? Womanizing…and acting as if certain rules did not apply to him. Doesn't anyone not act like the rules don't apply every now and then? When they otherwise do no harm, the most honorable solution may be to let them live.

"Harm," now there is a loaded word. Does it mean the same to the person with the utilitarian world view as it does to an empath? Take Prince Yasuhiko Asaka of Japan, born on October 20, 1887, for example—within the September 23 to October 22 timeframe mentioned above. Reportedly, he was responsible for coordinating the Japanese atrocities committed in China between 1937 and 1945.[142, 143] Perhaps he followed orders and merely executed a policy that reflected the attitude of Japan towards its neighbor across the East China Sea. Or maybe there was a personality component contributing to his behavior. Harm can have a financial component like in the reported US$233 to $521 billion annual loss to fraud that the United States Government Accountability Office reported for the 2018-2022 accounting period. How many veterans would not like to get better medical care, how many infrastructure projects could be tackled, and how many other worthwhile initiatives lack funding because of this kind of mismanagement?[144]

An antidote to insecurity may manifest as a drive to succeed at any cost. Rules may have to be bent or broken. The ego must not suffer. Who else might be working hard to uphold an image of success? People born between March 21 and April 19, and those born between June 21 and July 22, also appear to have an increased level of insecurity compared to those born during other times of the year. It seems a higher level of insecurity is correlated with an increased risk of developing narcissistic behavior traits. Reportedly, childhood development, trauma, and exposure to narcissistic behavior from others is a factor as to how strongly said narcissistic traits present. In addition, peer pressure can apparently legitimize denial and abuse. Psychology identifies two kinds of narcissism: learned and natural. The former presents in a situation where the person adopts narcissistic behavior as a survival mechanism. The latter appears to be present from birth.

In 2003, a Midland, Michigan, woman who had received international acclaim using a cadaver-sniffing dog to resolve murder cases was charged in federal court with planting evidence at crime scenes.[145, 146, 147, 148, 149] Sandra Anderson, the "world's most famous" dog handler, had fooled many. There appear to be quite a few other instances of dog handlers misrepresenting their canine's capabilities in court or failing to follow proper procedures to ensure credibility of the evidence. Even police officers occasionally appear to fall foul of such practices. That these kinds of practices occur isn't really the most important issue. What is important is the reaction, or should we use the term "vendetta," that cops inflict on one of their own when the latter suspects fraud.

In a documentary on the Anderson case, the junior officer in the department—who was the first to suspect foul play—was portrayed as having been shunned for betraying the group consensus that nothing appeared to be wrong. Even after Anderson was found guilty and sentenced, she and her dog Eagle still had their staunch supporters. Captain Bill Murphy apparently considered Anderson the "best in the business" even after the trial was over and the evidence of her wrongdoing had come to light. Asked if the charges Sandra faced made him doubt Anderson and Eagle, Murphy's response on camera was apparently a resounding, "No."

If psychology as a science lacks the tools to anticipate or at least interpret the behavior of the parties involved in a situation like the Anderson case, perhaps we need to look elsewhere for a key to human behavior that could help us rectifying an "anomaly" such as a dog handler dismissing the rules for professional conduct and the consequences for those accused of crime. A historic figure whose travails we discussed earlier, was not born in any of the above four time frames. Was Napoleon Bonaparte not insecure? If so, what led him to seek revenge for his first ever loss in battle against a combination of Spanish, Portuguese and British forces? Lost pride or a false sense of duty to his wife Marie Louise of Austria and his country may have made him overestimate his chances of victory against Russia. In 1811, Napoleon reportedly exclaimed: "In five years, I shall be the master of the world, Russia alone remains; but I shall crush her..." His underlying disposition toward combative mastery and control was allegedly laid down in a Corsican family; his abilities and his dedication to hard work were strengthened by a French education, and in his reading of the philosophes and history; his Corsican style of craftiness was practiced in factional island quarrels.

The French Revolution opened up opportunities to his great military and administrative gifts and revealed his superiority to himself and to a large public. Great rewards may have reinforced the disposition to seek mastery of everything in view and to push events to the utmost. Yet, great success and the exercise of command from the self-isolation of his office blinded him to the reality of what was possible. Restless, illimitable striving eventually entrapped him into a double war against two relatively invulnerable powers, England and Russia. Like Louis XIV and Louis XV before him, he lost on both fronts.[150] Napoleon's invasion of Russia may have been his biggest and deadliest campaign, but it sure put an end to both his army and reign.[151] It seems we may need to look beyond dates alone if we want to solve this puzzle.

Astrology is considered one of the oldest sciences known to man. For many it has been a tool to predict events although often with less than satisfactory results. Fortunately, astrology is a much more useful instrument for understanding human relations better. It seems ironic how many books have been written about personality attributes, yet practitioners often still give their own interpretation. The good news is that astrology does seem strikingly accurate at describing basic personality attributes and human behavior as long as we keep it simple.

I have been studying the astrology of personal relationships for more than twenty years. In that time, I obtained some insight into human behavior from a psychological perspective as well. In fact, I now wish the social sciences would have long understood a bit more about astrology if only because it would seem to make sense to use psychology and astrology side by side. The reason why is something we are going to look into a bit later.

The avenue through which an astrologer attempts to describe someone's personality characteristics and position in the world is called a horoscope. For the calculation of such a horoscope many different systems are available, each with their own unique method of calculation and interpretation. Despite thousands of years of research, it seems astrology is often found lacking in describing the entire person and their aspirations. Instead, it appears much more suited to predicting behavior. In many cases, even just a birth date alone is not enough to gauge if insecurity, for example, adversely impacts someone's attitude. Besides a correlation between birth date and behavior, there may be one or more contributing factors. The system that I used for my research is called Western astrology. Western astrology recognizes the twelve zodiac signs of Pisces, Aries, Taurus, Gemini, Cancer, Leo, Virgo, Libra, Scorpio, Sagittarius, Capricorn and Aquarius. It projects these signs, each correlated with certain fundamental characteristics, on a wheel. Each sign takes up thirty degrees of the circle, adding up to three hundred and sixty degrees together. While the zodiac signs are positioned on the outside of the wheel, the wheel is then divided a second time into twelve segments called "Houses" in an inner wheel.[152]

Each of the houses refers to an area of life. For example, the second house represents values and property, the eighth house birth, sex and death, the tenth career and social status and the twelfth hidden enemies and our connection with imaginary worlds. The houses in Western astrology are generally not equal in size. In each of the houses, astrology then places the planets—the Sun and Moon are considered planets, alongside Mercury, Venus, Mars, Jupiter, Saturn, Uranus, Neptune and Pluto—and "points," the latter being of a more esoteric nature and not relevant to our exploration here.

The most important parts of the horoscope are the Sun, the Moon and the position (also called a cusp) of the first house—the house that describes the relationship of the person with their environment and how other people see them. The cusp of the first house is commonly referred to as the Ascendant or Rising Sign—indicating the zodiac sign that is about to surface at the horizon at the moment and location that someone is born.[153] These three "points" are together called the Big Three.

To obtain a horoscope, a calculation needs to be made based on the date of birth, time and location. For the location, a city or town is often sufficient. Astro.com is a Web site that many use for this calculation because it offers a wide variety of options for interpretation and guidance. In order to determine a horoscope or natal chart as astrologers call it, I use the services of Astrodienst, which owns Astro.com.[154] For the interpretation of the meanings of the planets, houses and other aspects of the astrological chart I was inspired by the writings of, among others, Stephen Arroyo, Reinhold Ebertin, Robert Hand, Dane Rudhyar and Noel Tyl. My personal observations of people in real life and work situations, and my research of celebrities and political figures, form the basis of this exploration. An example of a chart wheel used for the interpretation of the horoscope is provided in Figure 1 below.

Figure 1. Sample Chart Wheel.

Researching the nature of narcissism, it appeared that not only do those born in the above mentioned time periods have an increased chance of developing the condition, so do people whose horoscope has the signs of Cancer, Capricorn, Libra and Aries on the Moon or Rising Sign. Astrology refers to these signs as "Cardinal" signs. Taurus, Leo, Scorpio and Aquarius are traditionally called "Fixed" signs, while Gemini, Virgo, Sagittarius and Pisces are considered "Mutable" signs. Even though astrology stresses that one of the life lessons for the cardinal signs—besides applying their natural gift of focus and ambition—may be learning to establish healthy boundaries, this aspect of these four signs is often ignored in practice.

What about people who have none of these signs on the Big Three? There appears to be one additional criterion for narcissistic behavior that can lead to extremes. Astrology identifies four elements: Air, Water, Earth and Fire. An abundance of Fire can trigger a sense of permission to exceed natural boundaries when it is not balanced by the modality or another, technical component of the horoscope. Going forward, it seems best to distance ourselves from established terminology that fails to capture the essence of narcissism in astrology. Instead, we will refer to the Mutable signs as "Visionaries", to the Cardinal signs as "Designers," and to the four Fixed signs as "Builders"—recognizing the contribution each makes: the visionary dreams up the future; the designer distills it, and the builder gives it concrete form. One or more of these three functions may be present in the Big Three of a single individual.

THE ESSENTIALS

"Existing in a state of continuous panic turns one into a self-centered,
obnoxious glutton. It ruins relationships, the body, one's life. The billionaire
magnate obsessed with a fear of lack cheats on a stock trade, lies about it, and
does not *fear going to jail—they deny it."*

—Anonymous

f I care to pay attention, a relationship is where I may get to know a whole other part of myself. How others see us, how we feel in their company, whether we are introvert or extrovert, and how each is appreciated by the people we associate with, these are things that get attention from experts and are discussed in professional and popular journals at great length. In addition to the psychology of relating, something more basic needs our focus: the quality of our personality. In astrology, this is initially represented by the zodiac sign that was on the horizon at the moment of birth, the Ascendant or Rising sign.

When we meet someone new, the sequence through which we reveal ourselves tends to go like this: Ascendant, Moon sign, followed by Sun sign— once we feel safe. The Ascendant represents how other people see us and what we show of ourselves to others. When we meet someone who has the same Sun sign as us, the Ascendant takes a back seat at first and the sequence is reversed—unless I perceive them as a potential adversary.

It is my impression that people tend to see me as somebody who tries to fit in, helping someone out without being asked (and without asking anything in return), reserved and self-effacing. These are some of the attributes associated with the zodiac sign of Virgo when it presents on the Ascendant. The Ascendant can be the trickiest part of the whole personality equation because we don't get to see that part of ourselves unless it is mirrored back to us. The other two members of my personality team are a Pisces Sun and a Virgo Moon.

One day, I met another Pisces with whom I hit it off really well at first, professionally speaking—a woman who joined our team. In the beginning there was that all too familiar vibe of "Hey, what have you done with your life so far?" like two good friends who haven't seen each other in twenty-one years. After the "catching up" phase, there is the "I need to take care of something, catch you later" phase. That is the role of the Moon, which represents "needs". For my Virgo Moon that would be like, "I need to get my thoughts in order." In contrast, my new Pisces acquaintance has a horoscope with the Moon in Sagittarius. Sagittarius is a sign that loves traveling, learning from other cultures, and pondering the philosophical questions of life.

Sagittarius as a Moon sign needs to be respected for their opinion. My colleague's life story was full of wild experiences in places my cautious Virgo Moon could only dream of. She loves sharing her adventures in rural Russia just after the fall of Communism, for example. When she listened to my story, she said she was so impressed with the kinds of places I had been to. I tried to tell her that her experiences sounded way more exciting—my Virgo Moon isn't as adventurous as my Pisces Sun wants to be—but she insisted that I had a much more exciting life.

After the "I need to get my thoughts in order" phase, there is the "showing one's other colors" phase. This is when the Ascendant kicks in.

You are going to say that the Ascendant would be the first thing two strangers see of each other when they first meet, but recognizing oneself in another person who has the same Sun sign can make us turn the meet and greet upside down. When it comes to romance and dating, sometimes we feel so comfortable in the presence of another person that we want to be vulnerable right away. We might call it "falling in love." I can only talk about my own Sun sign, but I have seen it happen with two Aries who told everyone around them how they had fallen head over heels in love, only to discover later that the other had some very annoying personality quirks that changed the relationship from the most romantic to an all-out war like only Aries could wage.

In the case of my Pisces colleague, she has Libra rising in her chart. In my experience, Libra can have a pleasant, sensitive demeanor at first, yet may have a need to rock the proverbial boat from time to time. Symbolized by a pair of scales, it seems to never fail that Libra seeks peace where there is discord and war where there is peace. The moment "war" has broken out, the cause of which Libra thinks they are very clever at hiding—or at least denying lest anyone thinks the Libra is the "bad" person—Libra will be jumping in to say how they alone can solve the problem.

We worked together for about three years after which something peculiar happened. I almost got fired over something my colleague had withheld from our boss. I don't know about you, but my Virgo Ascendant doesn't have a need to mess up a perfectly good working relationship. What is critical in understanding the personality is that the three parts of Ascendant, Moon and Sun sign are all important in their own right. How often do we not hear people talking about the Sun sign exclusively? Astrology seems to emphasize it even because it is "easy."

The Ascendant is a critical part of our personality, yet it is intricately connected to the Sun and Moon. The nature of the Ascendant can hide if Saturn, a planet associated with control, insecurity and discipline, is present close to the cusp of the first house. A close friend of mine, whose chart has Aries rising, may be a classic example. Saturn is in the first House of her horoscope and thus hides (*i.e.*, controls) the otherwise fiery expression of the Aries Ascendant. She comes across as very shy to any stranger except perhaps another Sagittarius— her Sun sign. After pleasantries have been exchanged, my friend will bring out her proverbial lightsaber and start "whacking" the other person just so they know her opinion about things—opinions are a very Sagittarius thing.

How is the Designer zodiac sign in its primitive, unevolved form not a (toxic) narcissist unless they had healthy role models growing up? The person with too much fire in their horoscope may give us all a sense of exuberance and limitless possibility. When we add a Designer touch through Aries, toxic narcissism may introduce itself to the equation—ignorant as they may be to the potential pitfalls of their grandiose plans. The answer of how to guard ourselves against the impact of narcissistic behavior may very well lie in the brain and our capacity for what is often referred to as executive function.[155]

Executive function, according to the experts, is our capacity to manage our time and energy, prioritize tasks, respond to requests for help, and deal with people in authority. Inevitably, we are going to have to deal with someone who seeks to manipulate us into helping them against our wishes. Such an individual may have an ingenious tool at their disposal that is reportedly, for maximum effect, best applied as early in life as possible. It goes by a one word term: "no."

How does "no" sound when it is said repeatedly and specifically for the purpose of limiting our excitement and desire to explore the world? It may be hard to identify the impact of "no" when our brain is still in its growing stages, at least it was for me. As we get older, it may become increasingly easier to counter a denial of a request, but we may have to do something in order to obtain the desired result. For example, let's say that I want ice cream. My mother tells me "no" without an explanation. Subsequently, I need to decide if my desire is strong enough to warrant a second, equally polite request or if I need to take it a step further. If I do nothing, two things may happen. I may lodge the denial of ice cream as a singular event. At a later stage, I will remember that I had no success before, and I may adjust my tactics for obtaining ice cream. Alternately, I may simply conclude that now is not the right time for ice cream and my mother is correct in declining my request. I will ask again in the future in the exact same way.

If I decide to ignore my mother's rejection, though, again I have two choices. One is to ask again, the other is to emphasize the need for ice cream in some way. Imagine that the request is denied every time you try no matter what you say and how loud you say it. Next week, another request is similarly denied. The following month, I want to buy a video game that all my friends are playing. Again, my request is denied. Over time, these rejections may result in low self-esteem, low confidence, and depression—and a failure to learn negotiation skills.

Everything in life happens as a result of a negotiation, whether internally or with others. Caregivers have a duty to instill healthy negotiation skills in their children so that they can establish their authority and earn respect among their peers. Repeatedly denying a child the opportunity to exercise these skills and build confidence may result in setbacks, lower income, poor job performance and other challenges. As we will see, it is not just the mere fact of being denied something that hinders the child, it is also the way in which the caregiver communicates that can make a difference. The method of communication and the attitude of the person with whom we negotiate determines to a great extent our appreciation of the relationship. We can identify three distinctive communication styles, four unique temperaments and a level of control that is unique to each, ranging from very strict to extremely relaxed.

Restricting the natural inclination of a child can reportedly impede healthy development of critical thinking, management and organizational skills which are part of the executive function. The controlling parent seems to blame. A negative outcome of executive function issues can reportedly present for infants and young children as tantrums and difficulty in self-regulating emotions, while adolescents may have difficulty achieving independence and making plans for the future.[156]

You may be familiar with the time of year that you were born and what your zodiac Sun sign is: Aries, Gemini, or Virgo, for instance. The daily horoscope that you may be familiar with from your favorite news site is based on this. When somebody asks you what sign you are, that sign is directly related to the day that you were born. For me the Sun was in Pisces. However, what you read about the signs is more or less a caricature. Nobody is a pure Aries, for instance. Astrology considers many other factors when it talks about you as a person. Each of us has an influence of several signs and that influence varies depending on a number of factors that are beyond the scope of our observations. If you see a reflection of yourself in one of the examples, know that the example does not represent you per se. Furthermore, you may have the ability to transcend the negative manifestations of your zodiac sign by controlling your exposure to harmful experiences. However, when you feel trapped, or when you have been under prolonged or repetitive stress, do you see yourself adopting some of the negative aspects associated with your sign?

Generally speaking, the Sun as an object in the horoscope represents our inner essence, who we are and what we want. The Moon represents our needs, emotions and, curiously, also the public. The sign of the Moon represents, in our simplified approach, what we need to feel comfortable at work and how we function optimally. The signs each have various qualities associated with them. Some signs are more dominant than others. Even though we generally say "He is a Leo," or "She is an Aries", the person with the Leo Sun may have a Moon in Capricorn and because Capricorn energy is more dominant, it may take over the characteristics of their Leo essence. The workplace can bring out the worst in someone, or the best. This should not come as a surprise. In terms of our focus on zodiac signs, the way a sign expresses itself is influenced by the culture of the organization.

In other words, put an Aquarius in a formal environment and (s)he will behave one way. Put that same Aquarius in a company that prides itself on innovation—giving autonomy and accountability to come up with the best ideas—and you may see a completely different work ethic. Don't people deserve to be treated with respect when they do what you hired them for? An Aquarius may brush off poor leadership because it is a socially oriented sign that tends to do everything for the cause. In contrast, a Leo—if it weren't for their natural loyalty—might expect to be treated better and not stick around for long.

What does each sign want, need and project:

the *"Visionary"* – Primary Motivators: Progress and Creativity

    Gemini – quick witted; WANTS: information;
        NEEDS: communication, data, variety
        PROJECTS: intellect, wit, charm, adaptability

    Virgo – ambition, service;
        WANTS: to analyze and be of service;
        NEEDS: to analyze, to be correct, to be needed;
        PROJECTS: service, logic, taste, judgement

    Sagittarius – opportunity;
        WANTS: a venue, a theory, something new;
        NEEDS: to be respected for their opinion;
        PROJECTS: an opinion, optimism

    Pisces – inspiration;
        WANTS: to know everything;
        NEEDS: to understand;
        PROJECTS: an ideal, infinite possibilities, compassion, trust

  the "Designer" – Primary Motivators: Fear, insecurity and Lack. Has an elevated risk of becoming a (toxic) natural narcissist.

    Aries – initiating;
        WANTS: action;
        NEEDS: to be number one;
        PROJECTS: initiative, impulsivity, excitement, fearlessness

    Cancer – caring;
        WANTS: a sense of belonging; to give protection and security;
        NEEDS: emotional stability; someone to nurture, and someone to blame;
        PROJECTS: sensitivity, compassion, caution

    Libra – intellect;
        WANTS: harmony; a hammock;

NEEDS: social or intellectual pursuits;
PROJECTS: politeness, comfort, sophistication

Capricorn – ambitious;
WANTS: a venture, and a team to manage;
NEEDS: control, to manage something;
PROJECTS: determination, ruthlessness,
success

the "*Builder*" – Primary Motivators: Continuity and Stability

Taurus – steadfast, determined
WANTS: results, value, practical solutions;
NEEDS: stability, consistency, anything tangible
PROJECTS: confidence, loyalty, affection, an
easygoing nature

Leo – demonstrative, loyal;
WANTS: attention, validation, a stage;
NEEDS: attention, validation;
PROJECTS: confidence, optimism, generosity,
warmth

Scorpio – transformational; (self-) destructive and
regenerating;
WANTS: authority, control;
NEEDS: information—in order to control their
work or that of someone else;
PROJECTS: persuasion, loyalty, determination,
shyness

Aquarius – conscientious; social;
WANTS: a social endeavor;
NEEDS: a secretary, communication;
PROJECTS: curiosity, quirkiness, individuality

Astrology can make people look like monsters or heroes, but in reality we are still products of our environment as well. Do you know who created air conditioning? There are several people in the history books, but let us look at somebody who was successful. He has a November 26 birthday. Someone who lived a few decades later had the same birthday. She allegedly raised twenty-seven foster children while hundreds more at some point in time were under her and her husband's care. Who should we consider a hero?

Margaret (Margie) Cantrell[157,158, 159,160] pushed law enforcement to investigate allegations of abuse by a group of adults in Mineola. Seven people were convicted of child sexual abuse, and the scandal rocked East Texas. Several of Margie's adopted children testified against adults in multiple lawsuits that sent four people to jail for life. It was later determined that the testimony of the children was coerced and should have been considered inadmissible. No physical evidence had ever been found to establish guilt. While one of the adults died from Covid-19 complications in jail, the other three adults should have had their names cleared. Sadly, their sentences were not entirely removed from the record. Instead, in order to save face, the local district attorney's office offered a plea deal which the defendants accepted.

How did Cantrell establish her authority over the children in her care to the extent that they obeyed her and assisted her in the legal proceedings that their foster mother orchestrated? Let us take a look at her horoscope for November 26, 1949 at approximately 10:15am: Sun in Sagittarius, Moon in Aquarius and Capricorn rising. The Aquarius Moon indicates a need to be involved in the community and to make a socially relevant contribution. One of her Capricorn Ascendant's characteristics is considered to be "ruthlessness." In contrast, Willis Carrier's horoscope for approximately 5:00am on November 26, 1876 shows a Pisces Moon and Scorpio rising—the deciding factors that make his personality very different from Cantrell's.

How people relate to their environment comes out via the sign of the Ascendant in the horoscope. The element of the sign can be indicative of the nature of a person's expression. Fire, for instance, is easily recognized: this person radiates enthusiasm and drive. Leo rising people are known to "light up a room." Earth as a rising sign translates into somebody who is practical in their approach, who shows ambition and organizational skills. Virgo rising is not only a practical person, but also someone who is eager to help analyze the problem at hand. Air as the element of the rising sign can make the person seem aloof or distant, while water can make the person more emotional than their Sun and Moon sign may imply.

The other aspect of the rising sign that we need to consider is the mode of behavior. Is it a Designer type sign, a Builder or a Visionary—insecurity compensated for by one of the sign's distinctive characteristics as noted above, determination, or creativity? In terms of human relations, there may be one more critical aspect that hinders open communication and progress: denial. I can tell myself that I never deny it when I am wrong. Ordinarily, I may not deny

A Few Good Cardinals

responsibility, but when someone has been pushing my boundaries for too long, would I adopt a different response?

There are so many reasons why relationships falter. When people don't hang around, who do I have to blame? When it comes to our children, though, do we have a different attitude? If we lie to a child in such a way that they lose respect for us—the adult who is expected to display responsible behavior—what happens to our feelings towards that child? How much do we care that the child does not want to see us anymore?

In recorded footage of the aftermath of Margie Cantrell's legal battles, we hear that at least some of her foster children simply don't want any more contact with the adult who provided a home for them. Margie reportedly states that she denies she did anything wrong. To date, no judge or law enforcement officer appears to have been held accountable for accepting Cantrell's doctored testimony that led to the convictions. In this case, denial is most impactful here. It seems best we keep an eye on the rising signs most liable: Aries, Cancer, Libra and Capricorn. Deep engagement and time[161] may be our best tools to mitigate the potentially disastrous effect of denial. That and our own wits. At some point, we need to move on and do what seems best under the circumstances. Record the decision, stay motivated.

BIRDS OF A FEATHER...STICK TOGETHER

"A few bad strangers messed it up for the rest of us"
—Jerry Seinfeld in *Curb Your Enthusiasm*[162]

A toxic narcissist who manages to gain a foothold so strong that they establish a foundation that may last years, decades or longer may be considered very successful or a thorn in the side of morality. Arguably, few can do the job alone. Toxic narcissists seem to have a penchant of seeking each other out and growing "the business" together. Unperturbed by a sense of duty to the community as a whole, the organizational narcissist seeks to propagate their cause in much the same way as the individual except at a larger scale.

In business, there are pros and cons to narcissism. A small business may weather competition better because of the stronger focus on self that narcissism affords. The more is at stake, the bigger the advantage of the nimble empath gets. They run the enterprise for the long term and with the benefit of all stakeholders in mind. A narcissistic emphasis in the executive suite can result in some significant gains early on. In the long term, a denial of strengths and weaknesses, overreliance on outdated processes, and being reluctant to foster talent may jeopardize long term success.

An excellent, albeit dated, example in my opinion seems to be that of Salomon Brothers, the infamous trading firm at the roots of the 2008 financial crisis, as told by Michael Lewis.[163] The firm's executive leadership, pretty much in the hands of one person, appears to have run Salomon's chances of survival after the 1987 Wall Street crash—and subsequently the entire firm—into the ground by failing to adapt to changing market conditions.

Assessing a single individual as a narcissist must always be done with caution. Just because I see it, doesn't mean it is true. It is about looking at a person from every angle and in every context, as a private individual and someone with a public persona: "She is a great woman because she built a school for disadvantaged children." Perhaps, but it seems Oprah Winfrey (born January 29, 1954) could be a narcissist because she denied that her administrators would be capable of abusing the children, failed to put in safeguards against abuse, and gave administrators the benefit of the doubt despite complaints from the children's parents.[164]

Noel Tyl is a well-known astrological pioneer who made the dissection of behavior transparent for everyone interested in the field in his book *Synthesis & Counseling in Astrology*.[165] If there is anything astrology can do, it appears to be showing how scattered or focused we are likely to be in career or love, what our needs are, and how others see us. If we dig a little further, it also appears to show us what challenges we face pursuing our goals. One of those challenges may be our own attitude—fear and insecurity, over-confidence and hubris, or faith that everything we need is at our disposal at all times as long as we keep an open mind. One way to overcome insecurity is by getting others to support our goals.

I hinted at it in the introductory chapter on narcissism, "*Deeper, Bigger*," but if there is anything in life that stands out about Western civilization, it may be the pursuit of technological superiority over nature. Some of the basic building blocks may not have arrived on the scene until just before Michael Faraday's breakthrough invention of the electric motor,[166] but I can't imagine that the question on the mind of many historians and anthropologists would not have been why then, in the early eighteen hundreds, and not sooner—and why there, in the damp climate of England. Surely, others who had also been experimenting with electricity on the mainland of Europe and in Scandinavia may have been close. Faraday reportedly found inspiration in the works of others such as Hans Christian Ørsted and André-Marie Ampère. Birds of a feather stick and grow together.

The foundation for Faraday's breakthrough may have been laid about two hundred years earlier: the end of a tumultuous time in the history of England, the English Civil War.[167] An invention usually requires peace and quiet for sustained and prolonged effort. Not having to worry too much about food, medicine and other life necessities can create an ideal climate for inventors to thrive.

We are known to draw inspiration not just from each other, but from nature as well. At the dawn of the industrial revolution architects and civil engineers strived to one up not just anyone who had gone before but of course their contemporaries. To err is human is a saying attributed to Alexander Pope,[168] a famous poet who lived in England in the same period as Michael Faraday, the early eighteen hundreds 'To forgive is divine' makes his famous saying complete. If making a mistake is natural, who pays for the consequences?

When a bridge functions as intended, everyone is happy and not many people notice its function. Riding a train, driving my car, or walking up to it intending to cross whatever it spans: a river, a highway or the entrance of a port, for example. Building and maintaining a bridge so that it may be used safely for many decades if not hundreds of years seems quite a bit more complicated. Many people are involved from a variety of disciplines. Not wanting to bore you with complex engineering details, let me just say that when a bridge fails, the origin of such a failure may be due to a fault in the very smallest part of the structure.

What does structural engineering have to do with a book on human behavior? Everything we create starts with intent and desire, and a bridge is not different. Collaboration from an army of experts is required in design, manufacture and assembly. We want to make sure that our creation meets certain standards and that it will be properly maintained. Some of these steps may need to be revisited from time to time. Building a bridge is thus first and foremost an exercise in human relations.

The Tay Bridge in Scotland was the proud work of Sir Thomas Bouch. Bouch had been knighted after Queen Victoria had crossed the bridge six months prior to its collapse in December of 1879.[169] In episode three of *Epic Engineering Failures*,[170] Stephen Ressler takes us through the basics of the design and construction of the Tay Bridge and why it failed. When we consider how much effort goes into the construction of a bridge capable of supporting the safe transit of trains, how many people contribute and how many resources are used, how can we not be in awe of our collective accomplishment of such a feat? And yet, the success of a bridge often comes down to the opinion and preferences of just a few people. Consider today's frequent mass shootings in America, something arguably a bit more dramatic that happens, sadly, far more frequently. What do mass shootings appear to have in common with the Tay Bridge disaster in 1879? It might be this: warning signs.[171]

Going back to Scotland in 1879, who alerted higher ups that something was not right with the Tay Bridge in the months leading up to its December 28 collapse? Maintenance workers had reported an issue with the bolt holes for the lugs used in connecting various elements of the bridge. The holes had been cast with a taper; as a result, the contact between the bolt and the lug was essentially against what could be best compared to a knife's edge at the outer end of the hole, causing the lug to move whenever wind or a passing train put pressure on the bridge. This design weakness led to a gradual weakening of the entire structure. There are many other contributing factors in this story which we shall ignore for simplicity's sake because the one thing we are interested here is that this, and other warning signs, were essentially ignored if we can believe the results of the investigation conducted after the bridge's collapse.

The Skagit Bridge incident in Washington State[172] did not result in the loss of life. The lessons here were of an engineering nature and of applying common sense while operating a motor vehicle. While the bridge had been designed as a two lane span, one lane in each direction, demand quickly increased requiring additional capacity. Rather than going through the expense of replacing the bridge or building a second one alongside it, in order to save money, it had been decided to add two lanes and remove the shoulders on the existing structure. As a consequence of this decision and the arched support span across the bridge, there was a height limit difference between the inside and outside lanes for either direction. On May 23, 2013, an oversized transport approached the Skagit Bridge. The vehicle had been cleared for its route with a permit and was accompanied by a pilot vehicle driving ahead.

Just prior to striking the arched support span and causing the collapse of the bridge, two things went horribly wrong for the driver of the oversized transport. The driver of the pilot vehicle was on their cellphone, reportedly not paying attention to feedback from the height monitor—essentially a stick longer than the height of the load being transported just behind. In addition, the driver of the truck was being passed by a semi at the very moment they reached the bridge. If you have ever passed an oversized load truck on a highway, you may have given it plenty of space while you passed in your passenger car. In this case, the driver of a semi-trailer truck approaching the narrow, height restricted Skagit Bridge did not allow the driver of the oversized load vehicle to move into the left, inner lane with a higher maximum height clearance.

To err is human, and of course everyone has been forgiven while lessons were learned. For the purpose of our exercise here, the lesson is that some may ignore the warning signs and play down the potential consequences. In real life, up until now at least, after a disaster a renewed commitment is generally announced with the promise that those in charge will listen to the people who sound the alarm. While fatigue, stress, hubris and self-justification may affect decision making at any time, when we deal with a complex system the consequences may not surface until far into the future. I am thinking of a building in Surfside, Florida that partially collapsed a few years ago. There had been insufficient funds for proper maintenance after thirty or so years of uneventful existence. A major refurbishment had been postponed. Decision makers had "stuck together" rather than raising alarm.[173]

Success and failure of a complex system may affect those who were not even born at the time of its introduction. Money is oftentimes a valid argument to make design, engineering and maintenance decisions that shortchange real needs and safety considerations. Yet, financial decisions are like engineering decisions made by people just as well. What ultimately prevents adherence to proper procedures, due care and maintenance, is the impact of personality in each stage of conception, design, construction and maintenance.

The Larsen-Nielsen system was conceived in Denmark as a cost effective construction method for medium height residential buildings up to about seven stories. In England, the Ronan Point apartment building had been constructed according to this system. The main difference between Ronan Point and how Larsen-Nielsen had been conceived was that Ronan Point was twenty-two stories high. On May 16, 1968, Ronan Point partially collapsed as the result of an incident seemingly unrelated to the building's construction.[174] Four people died and seventeen were injured. What emerged from the ensuing investigation was that of the construction safety mechanisms inherent to the Larsen-Nielsen system, none had been properly implemented. In effect, the system should not have been used for the type of high rise building that was Ronan Point in the first place, and on top of that all of the safety elements had been botched.

Investigations often run into an issue common to a situation where multiple parties share blame: sealing of the evidence. In other words, engineers are not allowed to share what they knew before and during construction, the fire department is not allowed to publicize its findings, and the building's owner is similarly not talking. What this means is that the human element, the psychology of blame, gains the upper hand. How can people learn a lesson from a disaster if the most critical information is being withheld from the public? What use is an investigation for future construction projects if nobody is allowed insight into which mistakes mattered the most and how they were handled?

Fear seems to be at the root of the desire to withhold critical information. Naturally, people want to protect their interests and limit their liability to the maximum extent possible. Still, the approach that some take after the guilty have apologized and the blame has been fully accepted is one of forgiveness and a desire to move on. Those who live in fear seem to have a hard time doing just that. Moreover, they are insecure enough that they have a hard time accepting that another person would ever forgive them for their mistakes without pushing for large scale compensation through legal means.

England found itself staring another disaster in the face fifty years after Ronan Point: the Grenfell Tower fire.[175] BBC News called it "one of the UK's worst modern disasters."[176] Seventy-two people died. Declared as a major incident, reportedly more than two hundred and fifty London Fire Brigade firefighters and seventy fire engines from stations across Greater London were involved. Residents and critics of the building's managers had been sounding the alarm on Grenfell Tower fire safety deficiencies for years:

> "The Grenfell Action Group has a long history of raising concerns about the almost criminally lax manner in which the KCTMO treats fire safety issues," wrote the Grenfell Action Group, a tenants' interest organization, on their blog as far back as 2013.[177]

Grenfell Tower is a now abandoned residential building in North Kensington in London, England. The building was finished in 1974 as part of the first phase of the Lancaster West Estate. The property lends its name after Grenfell Road, which ran to the south of the building, while Grenfell road itself was named after Field Marshal Lord Grenfell, a senior British Army officer. The Grenfell fire is the subject of multiple ongoing investigations by the police, the coroner and a public inquiry. Among the many issues investigated are the management of the building by the Kensington and Chelsea London Borough Council and Kensington and Chelsea TMO—which was responsible for the borough's council housing—building inspections, fire safety systems, the materials used, companies installing, selling and manufacturing the cladding, and failures in communications. The local council's leader, deputy leader and chief executive all resigned.

The fire was allegedly started by an electrical fault in a refrigerator on the fourth floor. Grenfell was originally built in concrete. Gaps around window openings were irregular and had been filled with combustible foam insulation to maintain air-tightness. This foam insulation acted as a conduit. A ventilated cavity between the insulation board and rear of the cladding panel existed; however, at least some were found to have been improperly installed or not suitable which exacerbated the uncontrolled spread of the fire.[178]

What concerns us the most here is not the tragedy itself nor the inevitable trauma for the survivors, their families and of course those who were injured. Something that stands out amidst the complexity of the incidents that are Ronan Point and Grenfell is a culture of denial. A culture of people who cover for each other, who may have grown up together, who went to the same schools, who share friends, sports interests and the like.

For an organization in order to survive the weather of time, a healthy amount of foresight and self-reflection appear to be considered critical cultural elements. Without a willingness to face hard facts and brainstorm ways to overcome challenges with a mind as open as possible, the end may inevitably come soon. Dissent in such an organization may be considered the equivalent of an unnecessary evil. People who live in fear share one particular perspective that stands in stark contrast to how somatic and affective empaths approach life: they cannot comprehend that an alternative solution may save them from a certain calamity. If they did not think of it, it doesn't exist. Some disasters may happen because, well, nature.

Other disasters may happen because of the narcissist. If there is not enough money to cross and dot the proverbial Ts and Is, what does the narcissist do? They cry foul, they create drama: their world is falling apart, they do not get what they deserve, a great injustice is being done. They may have an audience eager to please them—other narcissists, and an unlucky empath swayed by the charm, perceived urgency for the cause, or both. Often, the result is that additional funds are committed far in excess of what was originally estimated to prevent the problem—investors pour in money or new bonds are issued. As to the question of who will eventually pay when investors want a return on their investment or the bonds are due, we may hear "We will cross that bridge when we get there."

We may not always have a birth date at our disposal when we want to analyze a situation from the human perspective in order to determine the utilitarian or narcissistic effect, but when we do it may yield an interesting insight like it does in the next example. A project that is often cited as an infamous example of construction shortcomings is the Tacoma-Narrows Bridge in Washington State.[179] Its designer, Leon Moisseiff, had been selected primarily because of his experience on several prominent projects while working under the guidance of another engineer. Now it was his turn to shine. Born on November 10, 1886, Moisseiff's horoscope had a Scorpio Sun and Moon in Aries. Toxic narcissism may present as an inflated ego. An Aries Moon out of its comfort zone may manifest as an inner need for prominence.

For Moisseiff,[180] this was his first project as the lead designer. Money was reportedly an issue from the outset, but so was Moisseiff's desire to make this bridge the "most beautiful and flexible." Engineers, meanwhile, underestimated the effect of wind on the bridge, a perspective similar to that which affected the fate of the Tay Bridge in Scotland almost a hundred years earlier. Even so, if anyone voiced a concern, Moisseiff—with his horoscope's Aries Moon dictating his need to be the most important person in the room—was eager to preserve his vision of grandeur and not as open minded as one would want someone in his position to be. He may not have heeded a warning if there was one. The result is history—the "most beautiful and flexible bridge" collapsed on November 7, 1940, just six months and six days after opening to traffic.[181]

How does our principle of "birds of a feather" apply to the case of the Tacoma Narrows Bridge, when it may be obvious that the charisma of one seems to have had major implications on the design and engineering of the project? The answer lies in the fact that many other engineers were involved in the selection of materials and components who, in the absence of a crisis, may have been reluctant to raise an alarm. We will never know because you probably weren't there, I certainly wasn't there and all we have is video, hearsay and an after-the-fact report or two from people whose bias may also be never known.

What I do know is that the father of my best friend in childhood was a bridge designer. He spent most of his spare time drunk, trying to forget the anxiety that the responsibility over a new span across a major waterway in our city brought. The bridge used a new design not dissimilar to that of the Sunshine Skyway Bridge except that the central part of the bridge was less than half the size. His bridge is still standing after forty years without any incidents so it seems he did a pretty good job.

In other words, it may be easy to "stick together" when no immediate danger is in sight. As we saw earlier in the case of the convicted dog handler, Sandra Anderson, all of the police officers stuck together except one.[182] At the conclusion of this case, the officers would still have to work together provided that nobody got suspended or worse. The pressure to conform to group consensus may be very strong. Birds of a feather may be a principle that rests on just one commonality like "passengers on an airplane."

In the case of sudden depressurization or turbulence, this is demonstrated by the effect of injuries inflicted on people after having been violently ejected out of their seats. The "Fasten Seat Belt" sign may be off giving people a false sense of security. The idea is that they are a "passenger" on a plane and have a right to enjoy the flight, which enjoyment from their perspective does not involve being tied to a seat. When they are supported in this by others of the same attitude, they quickly form a group even though they may not be seated together: the group of "people without their seat belt on." The other side of the coin is that a passenger is also a parent, an employee in a business on the ground, a sister, or a caregiver, for instance. Yet, in the absence of immediate danger, "What is the problem? Lighten up!"

When a political cause is the impetus to form a movement, its members may come together to effect change, a powerful catalyst. Perhaps a good example of this is the case of Bassam Youssef and his Egyptian version of the "Daily Show with Jon Stewart."[183] Assembling a devout team of supporters, Youssef was a prominent feature on the government's radar during the Arab Spring. Youssef became immensely popular for giving a voice to the public on television. Eventually he fled the country for the United States to secure his own safety, leaving his followers and staff to fend for themselves as the government cracked down. Almost immediately, the argument could be made what if he had not done anything, would he have been considered weak? Would the outcome of the citizen uprising have been different? We may never know except that many years on, the effects of their participation in his movement may have cost his supporters dearly.[184] The question here is not one of heroism, validity of the cause, or if Youssef and his supporters not each followed their own, true purpose in life. The issue is whether narcissism contributed to the way Youssef handled the situation. He was reportedly born March 22, 1974.

What a medical doctor is allowed to tell a patient about their condition, the types of treatment available for a diagnosis, and the manufacturer of the medication the doctor may prescribe are all highly regulated. The "birds of a feather" are not just the physician but all clinical staff. Control over treatment options is further exercised on the financial side when venture capital (VC) firms buy hospitals for investment purposes, strictly monitoring their financial performance. We are encouraged to appreciate the value proposition that VC provides as if with their financial resources and industry knowledge, VC firms "empower healthcare entrepreneurs to transform their visions into tangible solutions that improve patient care, enhance medical outcomes, and reshape the healthcare landscape." What seems lost in translation is that simultaneously, VC firms:

> "help drive innovation [...] and bridge the gap between groundbreaking ideas and *commercial success*."[185] (emphasis mine)

An allopathic doctor is not just judged by their financial performance, they are also bound by a professional code such as a the American Osteopathic Association (AOA) Code of Ethics.[186]

How important is it that one professional sticks to his proverbial guns and another backs them up? For the construction worker, the mother, the manager, the bridge engineer, or the baker turned patient, it may be more important than one realizes though not necessarily in a good way. Allopathic medicine is well established and supported in many countries around the world. A nephrologist and medical scientist whose name I purposely withhold to protect his interests, purportedly conducted a one thousand cohort, peer reviewed clinical study on the prevention of kidney dialysis. Reportedly, the study results were considered highly positive and his method was subsequently awarded a patent. Unfortunately, implementing his treatment protocol that promised to significantly improve the quality of life for dialysis candidates would seriously reduce the "commercial success" of dialysis.

Dialysis appears to be a highly lucrative industry if the market statistics of renal dialysis equipment makers are any indication.[187, 188] Being associated with the Veterans Administration hospital system in the United States, it seemed he could make a significant impact for the many war veterans suffering from kidney disease or for those close to a diagnosis. Almost immediately, he admitted, he had been considered an outsider for going against protocol and subsequently lost his position. Having studied at Harvard and Oxford, his connections with fellow students—who are now in government positions around the world—are allegedly many. None appear to have had an interest in his findings on dialysis prevention. Fortunately for his own patients, this has not stopped him from using the method in his private practice.

When it comes to doctors accepting payments from the pharmaceutical industry in order to promote certain prescription medications or treatment plans, the principle of "birds of a feather stick together" may be no more appropriately used than here. In the case of pharmaceuticals, would I feel any different about my doctor's care for my condition if I knew that they receive a financial incentive from the company that makes the drug my doctor suggests I should take?[189] The debate around the effectiveness of Covid-19 vaccines is ongoing as of this writing, but at least we know that physicians received a bonus for every vaccination.[190]

The implications of the principle may be far and wide. If a connection between two people may invoke the "birds of a feather" concept so easily, where else could we see it in action? If you travel anywhere on your own, you may have been in a situation where you must have looked out of place and momentarily confused. When that happens to me, someone inevitably approaches quite readily. The individual with nefarious intentions may fire off a first question inevitably along the lines of, "Where are you from?" How crucial is our reaction in such a situation? It could be the difference between life and death if the announcements at many an airport against accepting a ride from a random stranger are any indication.

TRUTH IS TRUTH…UNTIL IT ISN'T

"A human being is a part of the whole, called by us 'Universe,' a part limited in time and space. He experiences himself, his thoughts and feelings as something separated from the rest, a kind of optical delusion of his consciousness.

This delusion is a kind of prison for us, restricting us to our personal desires and to affection for a few persons nearest to us. Our task must be to free ourselves from this prison by widening our circle of compassion to embrace all living creatures and the whole of nature in its beauty. Nobody is able to achieve this completely, but the striving for such achievement is in itself a part of the liberation and a foundation for inner security."

—Albert Einstein

"Conformity to fact or actuality." "The reality of a situation." Truth or "the" truth, what is the difference? What is "actuality?" Truth has been the subject of philosophical discourse for millennia.[191] In a legal context, one may be asked to, "Tell the truth and nothing but the truth, so help you God." One is expected to respond in the affirmative. But what is truth, really, and when could we say that "truth is truth until it isn't, then it's *their* truth?"

The truth is that "truth" seems to be quite flexible. When I am being asked to tell the truth, what they don't ask me is to "tell the truth as I observed it, and as I recall it now." That would be too much to ask because, as instruments such as the video camera—invented long since the foundation of the United States of America and the establishment of its legal doctrine—appear to demonstrate beyond a reasonable doubt, memory seems to be quite fallible.

Can you remember the first time that you traveled from a new home to your workplace? Did the route seem particularly long compared to the following day or the next week? That is not a coincidence. Do you make the same breakfast every morning like I do, but sometimes one or two things are different? Then you may have been stymied just like I was when someone asked what you had for breakfast exactly and you didn't remember, exactly. The brain doesn't record routine, even when there is a slight variation.

I don't usually get frustrated with jury duty, but when I do, it tends to be because of a logical error by the judge or prosecution. One day, I was selected for a jury pool, or so I thought. Seated among a representative group of our local community, including two elderly people who were uncomfortable sitting the entire afternoon on the hard benches in the court room, I listened intently to the prosecution's case. Someone was on trial for the fourth time for the same incident: alleged murder of his spouse.

In America, technically one cannot be tried more than once for the same crime, but in this State they had found a loophole it seemed. The defendant was from another State. They had moved him from one county to another. The alleged crime: he had been hiking on his honeymoon with his new wife; she had allegedly slipped into a ravine, had hit her head in just the wrong place and had died on the spot—he must have pushed her. The prosecution had alleged that it was intentional. There appear to have been no witnesses. Three juries before ours found him not guilty. He had a solid defense and an even more solid witness team which included members from his wife's family who backed up his version of events and his love for his now dead wife. During *voir dire*— which in the United States is the process by which prospective jurors are questioned about their backgrounds and potential biases before being chosen to sit on a jury—the judge fell asleep.[192]

The prosecution, a zealous District Attorney (DA) intent on improving his career prospects with what he claimed—in the media—to be a slam dunk case, insisted that memory is "infallible." The defense tore apart every single argument the DA had made five minutes earlier with solid scientific studies on memory. The DA ignored all of it, obviously. The case proceeded to trial. A few weeks later it ended with a hung jury on the least significant count, and a "not guilty" on the remaining three counts. The defendant was finally free. In my case, it turned out they had included my group, about half of the pool—seated in the back—just for show.

A Few Good Cardinals

What is "truth" and what is "the truth" then? Truth is the general version, "the truth" may be more specific. It is true that the Sun revolves around the Earth—until someone determines it is the other way around. My interpretation of an event is going to be different from yours, but according to the law that may not be so. At least, they are not going to tell you it is. That is why a defendant tends to be a bit nervous. At least I assume so because while I have been a defendant, I wasn't nervous because I knew the truth—and so did the plaintiff, presumably. Unfortunately for me, the plaintiff's version of events was not the same truth. Also, the plaintiff was an officer of the court in the community, a Sheriff's deputy. The judge didn't even seem interested in my version of the truth, but out of politeness listened to my truth anyway. The plaintiff's version of the truth prevailed and they won. That is how I interpreted it. To the plaintiff, their truth was not a "version" of the truth, it was "the truth." And now comes the weird part. When under stress or adversely impacted in another way, it seems possible to miss certain details and have the mind fill in the blanks.

When I suggested that the day after your first commute to work the route may have seemed shorter, I was referring to a tendency of the mind to blank out objects it has seen before in order to "save space" in the memory banks. There may be another version—I may be so preoccupied with "stuff," so busy with a sick child, a big project and a leaky dishwasher that I may plan certain activities in my mind ahead of time. Next thing I know, something interrupts this well thought out plan. I handle the emergency and "think" I am getting right back on track until someone calls me out on something I didn't do. Yet in my mind, I "see" that I did it. How do I respond? What are the consequences? In some situations, the consequences may be quite dire. I may tell myself that I am great at remembering things but then the unthinkable happens—someone tells me my version is not true.

Imagine that on your way to work, you stop to get coffee. One day, I did just that. Unfortunately, I had told someone I was on my way to the office. They estimated how long it would take me and called me at the time they expected me to be there. Being "on my way to the office" doesn't preclude me from getting coffee, dropping off dry cleaning, talking to the security guard in my building, or checking the mail downstairs and taking a bit longer because I received an important bill and decided to verify if it was correct—I am still on my way to work. Imagine my surprise when the person who expected me to be at work in twenty two minutes accused me of lying. Lying about what? I politely inquired. I never regained the trust this person had in me just because of three minutes and a cup of coffee.

Some people can be real sticklers it seems. Now imagine someone finds themselves in the middle of a stickup at a gas station. The perpetrators escape. The police apprehend the only person left who happens to be an innocent bystander. Whose version of the truth will prevail? There are organizations that help people caught up in situations like that and much worse: the Innocence Project,[193] for example. Sometimes it takes decades or longer for truth to reveal itself; sometimes all it takes is for someone to realize the folly of their imagination.[194]

In the Senate hearings following the 2008 global financial crisis, representatives of Moody's[195] and Standard & Poor's[196]—among the most well-known rating agencies of financial instruments—were asked a question. Members of Congress wanted to know what had convinced the agencies that the collateral debt obligations at the heart of the economic meltdown had been worthy of their respective top rating.[197] The response seemed to indicate that, while their rating of said instruments was ordinarily considered a testament to the quality of the underlying obligations—in other words, investors could count on the fact that the issuers of said obligations were solvent and would make all payments on the loans—the rating was nevertheless just an "opinion."

Another interpretation of "opinion" may be, "not entirely the truth." For the representatives of the credit rating agencies, though, the truth was always "truth." The individual with a utilitarian perspective may adapt a different interpretation of the truth depending on the circumstances and the time an inquiry is made: what is your truth today, and what was it yesterday? How would one ever really know the difference?

Truth matters because, at the end of the proverbial day, what do we need? We need to accomplish something. Life may be considered a series of steps so small yet so significant. Life may go on forever and ever, never changing in its intention. When you stop reading this book, you may go on with your routine as if you are not affected in any way by the words your mind consumed. When you decide what you are going to do next, it may be easy to ignore and forget all the steps that led to this very moment. And yet, how are these steps not all connected to who you are today, right now?

The woman who gave birth to you, the people who raised the animals whose milk you drank in school, the maker of the toy you played with, the publishers of the book you had to memorize in order to pass an exam, the driver of the bus you took to go to work, the people who built the plane you fly to go on vacation, everyone depends on something being true and someone being truthful. In order to fit in and contribute, everyone sells something every single day: themselves. How can I help? When it comes to survival, relationships and social structures may be complex or simple yet the concept of truth is what they have in common. We want the other person to see and hear our truth, to feel it, to understand it, and maybe also adopt it.

"These tests have been in retail employment for over 20 years. To get into upper management, you have to be a diagnosable level of narcissist, or psychopath. They literally screen those people into the store managers slots—that's why it is so awful to work there, it's deliberate. They have preferences for different levels of manager.

That is how some people race up to assistant or co-manager, inside a few years, and others don't get even a department manager slot, over a decade. You can be too mentally 'well' to be placed in any level of management there. The only competency based management role there for most stores is sporting goods department manager. They're legally required in most places to have that person be somewhat sane." — *Anonymous*

At the same time, you may want to hear the other person's truth and find out what you have in common in order to learn and grow. Naturally, none of us can share everything all at once. Neither can we share every little detail that contributes to an opinion we hold dear. Intelligence experts and psychologists alike have made it their mission to find out when a person is not willing to meet you halfway, to be honest and truthful. Studies on facial expressions, body language, and much more have resulted in highly advanced personality assessment techniques used in day to day situations as well as scanning equipment used in law enforcement and the military to detect potential criminals. What we read in the media may be far behind what is actually available to those in power.

Another person may or may not hear you, understand you, or be willing to adopt your truth. Somebody may purposely withhold information because they consider it not to be in your best interest. Somebody may purposely withhold an intention to do something, arguing that doing so is not a violation of their relationship with you because, to them, an intention does not equal an act. "That is life" is a common reason to accept such situations. "Deception" is the term most commonly used to describe them.

Giving or taking is a social construct and can be taught to everyone regardless of their personality. We learn from each other in order to fit in, and most importantly, we learn from our caregivers what is acceptable in order to survive. What happens when we attain status, when our leverage exceeds that of others? How does our motivation, and our behavior towards others, change?

For takers, the world around them is their instrument. People, material objects and power are tools for survival and self-gratification. For them, results are more important than the process of obtaining said results, and certainly more important than the tools themselves. For takers, a sense of lack is a primary motivation together with the fear that there will never be enough. They see the cup as half empty. No, not your cup. Theirs. And you had better fill it, now— and at your own expense, if they can help it.

For givers, life may be a privilege—and a God given duty and obligation. Life for them is not devoid of pleasure and enjoyment yet it may look different. For them, enjoyment may be watching you recover from a busy day eating a meal they prepared. Givers are aware of the consequences of their actions and the impact they have on the world around them. Givers clean up the mess they make at a party. Givers don't have fun at your expense.

"Ridiculed -> violently opposed -> accepted as self-evident"
– Arthur Schopenhauer

TO LIE OR NOT TO LIE,
THAT IS THE QUESTION

"They would offer huge amounts of money; we could have been rich! But if you
ever got caught, that was it, you would be banished....
I was a prefect so I had to lead by example...
You did not disrespect, you did not steal."—Sam Hill[198]

Life can be full of challenges and afflictions. Before the age of the
Internet, many challenges may have made the headlines, but on a personal level
it may have been much easier to tune them out. A disaster in a nearby town
mentioned in the local paper that people read once a day made a different
psychological impact than a similar event instantly broadcast on social media—
while labels such as "BREAKING" can give a completely different sense of
urgency.

We are now more than ever aware of events that happen in parts of the
world you might not even know existed unless you paid really good attention in
geography class. Some events appear to happen in the spur of the moment.
Others appear to require your immediate attention and compassion until you
find out the news flash refers to something from six years ago. The operative
word being "appear." Watch a video clip on YouTube, turn on ESPN, watch
your local station's prime time news coverage and you may interpret any event
you see as spontaneous: The athlete who wins a medal; the politician who gets
elected; the bank that goes under; the new miracle drug that is being introduced;
the dog who rescues his boss from a frozen lake.

In graduate school, a professor instilled in me a duty to always ask *why*:
Why am I doing this, Why this way and not another way? A few years ago, I

found myself asking why it is that some people torture others to get some information out of them. It may have had something to do with the waterboarding scandal that was plaguing the Central Intelligence Agency. Whereas people have been fighting wars for millennia, and the reasons for war are often pretty clear—territory and resource scarcity come to mind—the rationale for torture appears more evasive given its seemingly limited effectiveness.[199]

When I need information, I appreciate it when someone gives an answer that is useful. If you are a bit like me, you probably don't like it when you receive a response that appears inconclusive or that makes the provider look competent, but that is based on insufficient or faulty data. Nevertheless, as Carol Tavris and Elliot Aronson point out in *Mistakes Were Made (but not by me)*,[200] we appear to have a variety of reasons at our disposal for justifying the choices we make. The person providing misleading information may have a motive and a justification.

For some people the distinction between a lie and the truth may be very rigid. This may or may not be the result of a traumatic experience. When my wife asks me if the bakery is open until six and I tell her I am "pretty sure" it is, she considers it a lie on my part when it turns out they close at five. For me, there is a grey area between truth and lie and sometimes that area is pretty big. I have to admit that this has not always worked out in my favor.

There may be another reason why people lie: to gain an unfair advantage. Some may do it unintentionally and apologize, correcting themselves after the fact. This is referred to as "source confusion." Source confusion is considered, generally speaking,

> "misattribution of memory involv[ing] source details retained in memory but erroneously attributing an...idea to the wrong source."[201]

For example, I went to the grocery store two weeks ago and noticed their opening hours. When my wife asked me about the opening hours of the bakery on the other side of town, my memory recalled the opening hours of the grocery store instead. It happens—to err is human. Psychologists spend a great deal of their time analyzing human behavior. Many studies have been done apparently linking behavior to context—logic, position of authority, time and place to name but a few examples. It doesn't take an expert to notice that people don't go about physically torturing other people, but they may be emotionally hard at work to show who is in charge. In order to avoid the next grilling, telling a (white) lie may be considered a necessary "evil."

While context is important, it would arguably be quite difficult to anticipate if someone we don't know is going to tell the truth in a particular situation. Asking questions like, How comfortable are you dealing with this? How have you resolved this in the past? can be time consuming and may not yield a useful answer. Many people are inherently uncomfortable saying "I don't know" because they might lose face, or they may fear for their career. The question is, then, given these obvious limitations, what tool might we have to estimate someone's potential truthfulness either before or after the fact—but preferably before it is too late. In other words, what are the chances that someone, regardless of context or potential bias, is telling the truth?

Just like torture can leave scars on the human psyche, lying also appears to have some negative side effects. There are psychologists, for example, who specialize in the treatment of people who were victims of parents who lied to them about their rights, duties and responsibilities. Between the life and death of a child are a range of experiences varying from a completely nurturing, richly explorative and responsible childhood to sheer neglect and abuse, physically, emotionally, mentally and spiritually. Some experts argue that children at a young age don't really know the difference between a lie and the truth. And yet, when I see a three year old punching another boy hard because the victim refuses to let him play with one of his toys, and hear the perpetrator explain the crying victim lying on the floor to the babysitter that "there has been an accident," how can I not help but think, aren't the answers right in front of us?

In order to survive—whether we are living in solitude or in a community—as a species, we tend justify our behavior. Yet, what is justification when it involves twisting the truth about a condition to such an extent that it becomes an outright lie, and when this lie has potentially serious and costly adverse consequences? For example, after World War II, it became common practice to feed cattle grain instead of grass because grain appeared to speed up their growth rate significantly hence a shorter time to slaughter.[202] Farmers and the food processing industry to which they supply conveniently ignored the side effects: health conditions in cattle such as acidosis, necessitating medications and antibiotics which create prime conditions for the *Escherichia coli* bacteria, commonly referred to as *E. Coli.*[203]

Western society is known for its ingenuity and thrust for invention. One of the consequences of the industrial revolution was observable decline in overall human health. Around 1915, America's first flying doctor and avid inventor, Dr. Forrest Shaklee, set out to create one of the world's first whole-food multi-vitamins.[204] For the next forty years he continued on his quest to discover the truth about nature and how it can aid humans in staying healthy. Doctor Shaklee, and others like him, allegedly considered the human body not healthy unless it is free of disease and has the capacity to overcome disease. It has been said that he cured himself of cancer—as a result of radiation exposure from laboratory equipment—with his own preparations.

There are some who argue that human ingenuity can bypass the need for natural intervention in health using synthetically derived alternatives. Hence the rise of allopathic medicine and its use of pharmaceuticals, sponsored by John D. Rockefeller.[205] Some may argue that allopathic medicine is the result of a compromise we make with life itself and a matter of economies of scale. Yet every compromise may eventually reach its limits. My late father was an internist and medical researcher who did not believe in the efficacy of the medications he prescribed his patients. Still, if you were his patient, he would have prescribed you a drug for your condition. If he got sick himself—which apparently happened rarely—he only took a holistic, natural approach.

Who else did so? John D. Rockefeller himself. Prior to 1908, every clinic and hospital allegedly used primarily ancient traditional natural medicinal treatments. Rockefeller realized that synthetic versions of natural curative vitamins and medications could be developed from petroleum he owned. He successfully sought to control and monopolize multiple industries at once: petroleum, chemical and medical.[206] Rockefeller reportedly continued to use chiropractic and homeopathy for his family while using his influence to prosecute homeopathic physicians.

Two things have brought us as humans closer together than ever before in human history. The first is the population explosion from around two and a half billion people in 1950 to around eight billion today. The second is the globalization of manufacturing and trade. The result is that we are not just dealing with our immediate neighbor's version of truth, we are also dealing with the truth as told by the tomato grower in Canada, the coffee plantation in Kenya, the manufacturer in China, the hotel in New Zealand, and the cheese maker in France represented by the French trade association. Negotiations impact many as well as their interests, today, tomorrow and far into the future. Everyone wants to have their truth be heard, nobody wants to lie if they don't have to. Where does the narcissist stand in all of this? As an institutionalized version of the individual, narcissism may be a formidable foe. And yet, at its root, the narcissist organization has a narcissistic individual.

INSTITUTIONALIZED MOTIVATION

Psychopaths appear so prevalent in upper management that psychologists coined a term for it: "corporate psychopaths."[207]

What appears to distinguish the narcissist and his more extreme cousin, the psychopath, from the empath and altruist may be just one crucial trait: insecurity. The reason narcissists often work together to further their cause, while belittling and shutting out empaths, appears to be because they find strength in numbers. This may sound obvious, but in twenty one plus years of research it seems I have yet to find empaths who will stick together for a cause long enough to make a meaningful impact. Once a narcissist smells something good going on, they inevitably beg to join then sow discord or create a crisis just to convince everyone only they can rescue the operation—preferably as the new leader.

This is going to sound convoluted and hard to grasp, but people who feel ultimately secure in themselves—even though they may still suffer from low confidence, worry and anxiety—don't seem to have an intrinsic need to team up. This appears to be the greatest weakness for the cause of the empath. Psychopaths know how to take advantage of it almost from the moment they are born. As we saw earlier, it seems they, the psychopath, are born as a narcissist, but that the extent to which they develop their respective traits may depend on early childhood environment, exposure to narcissistic behavior (earlier we saw how we appear to learn and copy from each other thanks to mirror neurons in the brain), trauma and peer pressure. The result is narcissism spectrum disorder. When narcissists team up, we are witness of the effect of their behavior on an organizational or institutional scale that may cross every border in the world.

How many empaths have successfully and meaningfully shut out psychopaths and managed to sustain the result? Over the years, I have been involved with a number of constructive causes aimed at alleviating suffering, promoting mental health or providing, for example, women entrepreneurs access to resources. In none of the organizations involved did I have an executive decision making role. Some of these organizations were founded by a utilitarian, others by an empath or altruist. Over time, they were eventually all reduced to a skeleton of their original selves. In the case of the utilitarian founders, often because they failed to anticipate or adjust to change, or because the focus was on the image of the top people rather than the health of the organization.

There are simply too many examples of organizations that stumble and fall. So many, that it would be incredibly easy to dismiss any notion of personality being at the root of their demise. Luck, timing, likeability, access to vital supplies and financing, competitive positioning, the economy, natural events like storms and earthquakes, and stock market conditions, these are some of the many factors that can prematurely make a founder go back to the drawing board.

Behind all of the things that could impact the potential success of any endeavor is something very simple: a human being, a mind and a personality who together initiate an activity. From the moment I wake up, I want to do something—my brain demands it: I want to feel good, I need the feeling of accomplishment. The small business owner wants to run his car repair shop, the chief executive officer wants to run the mega corporation, the general wants to run his army. Meanwhile, the farmers and fishermen want to provide food for them all.

What is the difference between these examples and anyone working strictly for themselves in terms of how dependent they are on the "system"? Not much it seems—they all need other people to succeed before they can. The owner of the car repair shop needs people to make cars, buy cars and bring them in for maintenance. In a small community, people who deliver each other products and services can be fairly easily held accountable for the quality and integrity of their contribution. If I take my car to your shop and you don't do a good job or overcharge me, we can discuss it. You know that if you don't fix the problem, I will tell everyone else and you may have to skip town.

When a large corporation buys your repair shop, the customer service relationship may become very one sided. If you have ever been the recipient of an uncaring, indifferent customer service department located in another country, you know what I mean. The utilitarian individual takes advantage of the separation between the person who makes the product and who delivers it. But it is not just the relationship between customer and supplier that is adversely affected by corporate narcissism. In an effort to minimize cost, for example, managers are often tempted to push their own workers to the very limit as well.

Imagine that you are a sailor in England in the eighteen hundreds. Your boss has two options when it comes to your welfare during a months-long journey to the Far East and back: take enough food onboard or take on a new crew at the ship's destination. A common disease whose origins was not well understood reportedly affected about fifty percent of all who sailed the mighty seas: scurvy.[208] A solution was found in lemon juice by surgeon James Lind. This was dismissed at the time by not only the United States Navy, but also allegedly many a fleet commander and ship captain.[209]

Before lemon juice was introduced as a remedy against scurvy, the death toll among seafarers due to poor nutrition is estimated to have been two million in the period between Christopher Columbus's first voyage to the Americas and the mid 19th Century. In what perspective should we judge this number? Perhaps a good benchmark might be the death toll of African slaves en route to the Caribbean and beyond: a reported one million eight hundred thousand.[210] That's right, more sailors who got paid to work died than the precious cargo of the slave traders even though the numbers are not too far off. It goes without saying that there seems to be no way to actually verify if the data is anywhere close to being correct.

What does this say about narcissism or corporate psychopathy? It might have helped if a ship captain in the eighteen hundreds had access to the Internet. Even then, they would have to look up potential cures for scurvy and find them acceptable. Having no access to the multitude of data sources we find at our disposal today, for the purported benefits of lemon juice they relied on word of mouth, the charisma of lemon juice salesmen and the bias of the ship's doctor, for starters. They would also weigh the cost of taking lemon juice, adding to that the cost of hiring a fresh crew for the return journey at the ship's destination, while discounting increased morale of the original crew and the chance of a mutiny by sailors who were healthy enough to protest conditions onboard.

Can you imagine not providing the best for your crew? You may be an empath. Yet, for the corporate psychopath, there seems to be no "best" for the team: everything is a calculation; people appear to exist solely as an expendable utility. The ultimate "corporate" psychopath of days gone by may have been the Roman military commander, the Spanish conquistador or the Khmer Rouge guerilla leader.

When a human is considered a utility, their death is a number. How badly may progress have been thwarted in the past due to the premature death of an unlucky yet otherwise intelligent individual who stood in the proverbial and perhaps also literal line of fire of a psychopathic ruler—a ruler whose primary intent may have been to expand their "empire" solely because they had a personal feud with the neighbors? It may be difficult to admit that people in the most deprived social conditions are capable of rising to the occasion despite hardship and oppression. A good example may be the quest for affordable inventions in lower income countries termed "reverse innovation."[211] In all, it seems there is a desperate need to identify the psychopath before damage is done.

One way in which a society may differentiate itself from that of another is through the character of its judicial system and the recognition of property rights. Because people across the world have culturally and historically different concepts of morality, of what constitutes acceptable behavior, and of what are appropriate types of punishment for behavior that violates the law, laws and regulations vary from one country to another.

Culturally, there appear obvious differences in how unwritten moral laws are interpreted, applied or ignored. Moral and cultural rules exist and persevere because they were once made up or developed out of necessity, a power play or combination thereof. Subsequently, legal systems emerged as a result of the necessity to create and maintain social order, as a power grab by those considering themselves more entitled or educated, or a combination thereof.

Individuals or a group may consider themselves above the law, flouting the moral code, the legal system or both. Likewise, there are those who consider it sacrilegious to break said moral code of conduct or to challenge the rule of law and authority. We have a choice whether:

1. to respect the sacred moral right of another person to exist and survive, as an individual or as a group;

2. to take advantage of the situation with the sole motivation to ultimately benefit oneself, the organization or both; and

3.   whether to resolve conflict through mutual understanding or through deception.

This choice inevitably leads to the question of whether the legal system exists so that those who naturally respect the rule of law are kept in social and economic confinement, or if the legal system provides genuinely neutral and objective protection to all regardless of one's inclination to respect the rights of others.

Perhaps it is necessary at this point to expand our scope of reference and add to our perspective of the legal system that of political and military structure and attitudes. If, for instance, your country's raison d'être is to recognize certain inalienable rights for all because all are considered equal, how could one's access to financial and political resources provide a certain level of protection against the rule of law? This question doesn't just affect matters of state, it affects equally the most mundane of behavior and action.

Everything anybody does happens in context. It relates to what has gone before, to one's belief system, and certainly to one's motivation. When people surround themselves with others who share their beliefs and motivation, we could call it institutionalized behavior and it may gain an air of legitimacy. Actions undertaken as a result may be considered justified because of precedent. But does that make them morally just? Do wrongs become rights because those in power regard them so? Those who fight against institutional abuse may already know that it does not quite work this way.

Today we know that, at its most fundamental, institutional abuse has at its roots an individual with Designer influence in the horoscope. This influence, as we have seen, appears to indicate an individual's life perspective of lack and fear and that this alone is the foundation of the individual's decision making. The actions of a head of state with Designer influence in the natal chart who orders a lethal attack on innocent civilians should not be considered any different from those of your neighbor with a similar astrological influence who chooses to blast his stereo at three o'clock in the morning disturbing your sleep.

At this point, I should stress that this exercise of uncovering the fundamentals of human motivation is not meant to judge past behavior. Rather, it is intended to find out why people may have acted the way they were *observed* to have done. Subsequently, we can work to not only prevent similar behavior in the future but also avoid condoning it because of misinformation, willful ignorance or apathy.

Consequently, does it appear that our beliefs and the resulting political, legal and economic systems are the children of a perspective of fear and lack? If that is the case, it would certainly tie in perfectly with the astrological observation that there appear to be three fundamental classes of people, regardless of gender, race, ethnicity, political status, heritage or any other classification.

In early 1986, one of the most visible, dramatic disasters in US space history ever took place in the skies over Florida. At the time, the Space Shuttle was the crowning achievement of the National Aeronautics and Space Administration's (NASA) human space flight effort. The orbiter itself was a highly sophisticated vehicle the size of a small jetliner with space for up to eight astronauts in its cockpit. For launch, two reusable solid fuel rocket boosters and a large fuel tank were attached to the orbiter.[212] For each mission, the Space Transportation System, as all the components of the Shuttle Program together were called, was assembled on site at the Kennedy Space Center in Titusville, Florida.

Some parts, like the solid rocket boosters, had to be shipped via rail over long distances. The boosters were manufactured by Morton Thiokol in Utah. As a result of the need to ship the boosters to Florida, certain design modifications were made which affected the conditions under which the Space Shuttle could operate. For instance, the solid rocket boosters consisted of several sections that were only connected to each other after they arrived in Florida. The connection between two sections was described as a "field joint" because it was assembled away from the manufacturing facility in Utah, "in the field" in Florida. This field joint of the two segments consisted, among other things, what were called a Primary and Secondary O-Ring.

The O-Rings were made of a flexible material. In effect, they were designed to seal off the narrow space between the segments and thus prevent the ignited propellant inside from escaping the joint at lift-off. These O-Rings were sensitive to the weather in that their performance deteriorated as the outside temperature dropped. It was reportedly not known what the exact temperature limit was for a successful launch. Even so, a year earlier, on another chilly and otherwise successful launch day, an anomaly had been observed when the outside temperature had reached a low of around fifty-three degrees Fahrenheit.

As a result, some engineers felt comfortable that they had sufficient data to call off a launch in the event of similar adverse weather conditions. NASA had a fleet of four Space Shuttles at the time.[213]

On January 28, 1986, NASA's Space Shuttle Challenger broke apart seventy-three seconds into its flight.[214] Each shuttle flight cost approximately US$1.6 billion, making the incident a one point six billion dollar piece of fireworks resulting in the death of seven highly trained crew members. The incident did not happen because somebody wasn't paying attention. In fact, everybody with any kind of responsibility had been paying attention in the days leading up to it: to the weather, to the conditions under which the orbiter could fly, to the state of the crew, to everything as they normally would for a Space Shuttle mission. The reason for the incident could initially not be ascribed to a single individual or factor, they say, though there is one line in a report on the calamity that appears to hint at something: "The mission had already been canceled due to weather before, and, as far as NASA was concerned, another cancellation due to weather was unthinkable."

The night before launch on that fateful morning of January 28, the air temperature had dropped below freezing at Kennedy Space Center. In fact, the recorded low was eighteen degrees Fahrenheit (minus eight degrees Celsius). After thirty minutes of heated discussions between management and engineers of Morton Thiokol and NASA, the go ahead for launch had been given despite the misgivings of some of Thiokol's engineers: there was no prior experience with the effect of temperatures this low on the functioning of the O-Rings. How did management then reach a decision to launch, knowing that Challenger had been sitting exposed to the elements on the launch pad?

Purportedly, the decision making process whether or not to launch Challenger that morning went like this: "Thiokol management requested the chief engineer to 'take off his engineering hat and put on his management cap,' suggesting that organizational goals—a "self-imposed" deadline because "the President would be watching"—be placed ahead of safety considerations."[215] It seems that the purpose and timing of the mission was given higher priority than the management of risk to the mission. Furthermore, dissent from some of the engineers was ultimately ignored and sidelined altogether—by one person at Morton Thiokol in particular, who did not pass the reservations of these engineers on to NASA's decision maker, who was ultimately responsible for the launch decision. What makes risk management so important, and what personality would be best suited for the decision making role in each stage of the decision hierarchy?

There are obviously many details that I am leaving out for simplicity sake. Yet, imagine that you had decided to call of the launch. Some people might have called you names for addressing a potentially fatal event by postponing and reassessing it. You might have lost your job. How would you have felt about your decision? The one or two people who gave the go ahead on that fateful morning of January 28, presuming they had been properly briefed on the dissenting opinion of the engineers, do not seem to have cared all that much about the $1.6 billion launch expenditures wasted nor about the lives of the crew members because (a) it is not their money, and (b) they would still be alive to talk about it at the cocktail party next week. It was the mid-eighties, I can imagine they had cocktail parties back then. How an organization manages a dissenting opinion, fact or stronger appears to be a critical determinant as to how deeply engrained narcissism is.

Hindsight is twenty–twenty. Important revelations came to light about NASA's management structure and culture as a result of the investigation following the Challenger disaster. The "only" problem on the engineering side was that the technical issue that led to the failed Challenger launch had allegedly already been identified and flagged for management to address before the first Space Shuttle was built. I understand that after the first anomaly in the performance of the field joint was observed, engineers had initiated work on a solution. NASA reportedly considered the proposed solution, introducing a third O-Ring, "too expensive." The good news is that people usually have a tremendous capacity to overcome setbacks. Time heals all wounds so they say. Except the wounds of trauma perhaps. Peter Levine couldn't have done a better job providing a diagnosis as to how traumatic events affect us and a path to healing from trauma in his book *Waking the Tiger*.[216] This means that there might be a way out for the many victims who are emotionally "stuck" after having experienced trauma, whatever the nature of the event.

One thing that is often overlooked in traumatic situations appears to be awareness. In the case of a potential rape victim, they might not be acutely aware what is about to happen, apart from feeling very strange about being with a person they know and have come to trust. The rape victim might thus be excused for lacking awareness. Yet, much was known about NASA's management structure and deficient organizational culture prior to the failed

Challenger launch. While the Senate hearing and ensuing investigations into the Challenger disaster revealed that organizational weaknesses had apparently not been sufficiently acknowledged prior to the fateful day, rape victims do not ordinarily seem to have the "luxury" of compassionate attention and trauma care. On the contrary, many may freeze or fawn instead, the latter being a coping mechanism in advance of a threat[217] perhaps just as much as in its aftermath that many therapists appear to underestimate.

Something similar may have happened in the lead-up to the September 11, 2001 terrorist attacks on the World Trade Center in New York City and the Pentagon, the BP Deepwater Horizon Spill in 2010 and the handling of the Great Pacific Garbage Patch:[218]: some saw it "coming," but their voice was not heard. Even so, large scale, impactful events are so rare compared to everyday calamities that we might be tempted to consider them interesting case studies that don't apply to "us" because "we have the situation under control." Under such circumstances, it seems not uncommon for the voice of dissent and warning to go unheeded for a long time. What mechanism needs to be in place to facilitate the ignorance and denial needed to allow a threat to develop sufficiently into an actual crisis and catastrophe? Is one person in control, or are a critical number of narcissists working in concert required to do the "trick"?

There is a field of study whose aim it is to understand the dynamics between people in groups and between groups of people: organizational psychology.[219] Considering how little we still seem to know about the individual human mind/body/emotion dynamic, it is commendable that we have already devoted so much energy to understanding how people function in teams and organizations.

One of the core principles of human functioning is survival. It may not be on your mind on a daily basis, but survival is what matters most. From the moment we are born, something or someone is actively engaged in trying to kill us: viruses, bacteria, nature, our fellow human beings and perhaps even yourself when you lose control of your car because you were texting and driving, slamming it into a tree or shop window at high speed. Staying alive may require substantial effort, let alone leading a meaningful and successful life. But can you do it alone? Can you lead a successful life without any support or intervention? It may depend, among other things, on how you define success. There are plenty of examples of people living as a hermit for most of their life. I guess they never need a dentist. What is their secret?

One of the characteristics of narcissistic behavior is an inability to adapt to changing circumstances in the absence of an attractive enough incentive. Anyone challenging the status quo is often considered inherently suspect and it was apparently no different at NASA in early 1986. When we consider who is in charge, we are tempted to consider this person as the key decision maker. In order to assess how negatively impacted an organization is by narcissists, it is therefore tempting to look at this key decision maker and say, well, if this person is *not* a narcissist we should be okay.

Reality may be quite different. Something that was left out in much of the discussion of the Challenger disaster, though it was featured in the documentary about the investigation,[220] is that there appears to have been just one person who ultimately decided to approve the launch. This key decision maker apparently had no knowledge of the reservations the engineers had about the launch, nor of the underlying data for a positive launch recommendation, because those reservations had been filtered out of the launch directive long before it reached his desk. In other words, management considered it unnecessary for the person who took the final launch decision to have access to the most crucial piece of information: that the engineers considered it a no-go that morning, and that management had overruled them.

Naturally, many accomplishments have been celebrated in our history without much fanfare or challenge. It goes without saying that we rarely accomplish anything without at least a small setback. Yet, for the same token, other significant incidents have happened before the Challenger disaster and since as a result of intentional neglect the world over. What sets them apart from unintentional incidents is not that they happened despite neglect. What sets them apart from incidents that appeared unforeseeable is that they happened because individuals who were ethically incapable of good faith, fair judgment, were in a position of decision making authority from which position they ruled over the (mostly innocent) lives of others. Let me clarify that.

If an incident is foreseeable and it has a dramatic impact, you would expect someone to be held accountable. If an incident is unforeseeable, the organization is expected to respond along the lines of "we will do our best to anticipate future occurrences and be more prepared for similar events." When we dig into the nature of both kinds of events, though, it is often found that at least some people were well aware of the potential risk for either kind of event to occur – both an unforeseeable and a predictable event. What we need to know then is what the effect would be on the organization to allow this awareness to rise to the surface prior to an incident that negatively impacts people's lives the success of the organization. What sets these types of incidents apart from uneventful successes is that risks are being taken that people could have known were irresponsible but didn't act on because of their personality and that nobody had the authority, willingness or both to stop them. How do we deal with that?

There are two ways that we can deal with lack of awareness. One is to further study the nature of human behavior and adapt training and ethics standards accordingly. Another is to introduce technology—for example, artificial intelligence (AI)—that may help identify weaknesses and potential failure well ahead of time. There appear to be pros and cons to each. The pros fall mostly along the lines of improved human relationships, increased organizational efficiency, better understanding of potential risks, and thus, hopefully, increased performance. The cons for studying the nature of human behavior are that we might become aware of associations between biochemistry and human behavior that disrupt mainstream opinion, for instance. What if we had to collectively admit that:

A. a core biological principle for the male psyche is that it is biologically (I can't stress the word "biological" strongly enough) programmed to respond to a threat that is perceived as existential[221] with violence?

B. that women are *biologically* programmed to judge a potential mate for their ability to fend off a(n) (potential) existential threat rather than to *prevent* it?

C. that those with a utilitarian perspective pick and choose their preferred method to fend off an existential threat not based on what is best for everybody, but only what is (ultimately) best for them or their image—now, and/or in the future?

One way to gauge human behavior is by creating data models that avoid having to query the subject in question. Data gathering on social media and online purchasing habits has become one of the main tools at the disposal of the behavioral analyst. If you ever wondered how Amazon determines what product you might like to purchase next, data modeling is at the core of its recommendations. One step further still and we find ourselves in the realm of artificial intelligence or AI. No longer do we need your purchasing habits.

Instead, we pull all your data from every site you have ever visited, every location you have ever been and checked in on Yelp, every bank transaction you have ever made, and much more if it is available, and lo and behold, somebody thinks they can predict who you are going to vote for in the next election.

What is not commonly understood or acknowledged is that the design of data analysis models is affected, inherently, by the needs, preferences and bias of their creators. In other words, human behavior and personality traits effectively translate into how AI is designed and programmed: bad programming in, bad behavioral predictions out. Let us take a look at how an organization dealing with life and death such as NASA deals with personality traits if only because of the high-risk nature their work tends to involve.

The documentary *I am in Space*[222] describes what personality traits NASA looks for in its future astronauts and the psychological nature of the training they are subjected to: "Achievers evolve from personalities with strong narcissistic traits by overcoming the threats and dangers of a suffering self." The narrator shares that NASA selects its future crew members for criteria such as "dexterity, concentration, memory, vigilance, and the ability to make decisions." Apparently, astronauts are also expected to be "balanced, patient, receptive, focused, creative, and able to forgive." What seems to be an astronaut's biggest fear? According to the documentary, their biggest fear is being shamed because of a mistake.

Considering that to err is human, how is shame constructive feedback? Doesn't NASA know that making mistakes is part of being human, and that we can mitigate it by instilling a healthy sense of responsibility and a systems approach to critical thinking? Unless we consider the type of environment astronauts work in and that a mistake can be literally deadly. Perhaps shame is what one personality needs to stay focused, while it would be trauma inducing for another. Arguably, despite its focus on recruiting narcissists, NASA's astronauts have accomplished much in what have been described as some of the most challenging and dangerous conditions besides perhaps mining, the military, and the nuclear industry.

Let us retrace our steps for a moment. We noted that "vigilance" is among the criteria for admission into NASA's illustrious astronaut corps. Vigilance is commonly found most prevalent among victims of narcissists, not the other way around. How about "being able to forgive"? I have yet to come across a narcissist who genuinely forgave a normal person for a "mistake." There is usually some type of retribution associated with it: "I'll forgive you, but you have to [fill in the condition]." Narcissists are known to have selective memory when it comes to things they promise to do. On the other hand, the narcissists I know sure remember what I promised to do.

What if NASA's recruitment efforts are run by narcissists, would that explain the training regimen? One of the core observations of the behavior of the narcissist is that, for leadership positions, like attracts like, while opposites "attract" for subordinate positions. In other words, narcissistic managers tend to hire mostly empaths for staff positions because empathic people tend to be more subservient. Suppose that NASA is right and that narcissists make for great astronauts, would the same be true for management?

When we take things to a higher level, the global economy might come to mind as a good example of where narcissists may come to jeopardize the status quo. No better example perhaps of an organization aiming to understand the role of the global economy in the progress of civilization comes to mind than the Mises Institute[223]. Founded by Ludwig Von Mises, born September 29, 1881, Mises philosophy aims to educate about fundamental economics, yet appears to ignore the reason the economy gets messed up from time to time: personality.

How is it not that people create and sustain the economy, while it is also people who crater the economy? The difference is that they tend not to be the same people. A characteristic of the zodiac sign of Libra is that it likes to make peace where there is chaos and chaos where there is peace. They just do not seem to want to admit it. The Mises Institute may eventually acknowledge that a certain personality type causes financial disaster rather than certain people per se. This might lead us to finally develop a way of fixing the problems people love to argue about—and a new mindset devoid of denial, fear and insecurity.

As we saw earlier, behavior appears closely linked to context. When we consider the many energetic and successful people born between March 21 and April 19, it goes without saying that Aries, for instance, in particular makes for an excellent entrepreneur, artist and inventor. Think Charlie Chaplin, Eric Clapton, Thomas Jefferson, Diana Ross, Jair Bolsonaro, Mariah Carey, Lady Gaga, Christopher Walken, and Ewan McGregor.[224] Working alone or in a small team, they often display enviable drive, focus and passion.

What happens when they go outside of their comfort zone and bear responsibility for managing large teams or even entire organizations may be another story. The inherent fear and insecurity associated with their birth dates may, in a more public role, drive them to hide these character traits with the display of behavior associated with an overbearing and dominant personality. Examples may include King Leopold II of Belgium,[225] responsible for the abuse and death of millions in the Congo Free State during his reign; Kim Il-Sung of North Korea;[226] and Philip IV, King of Spain[227] during the Spanish Empire's participation in the Thirty Years War, which period saw millions perish as a result of the conflict.

If history is a guide, on occasion it does not take a crowd to affect change. What follows may sting or even arouse strong emotion, but the good news is that there is a good chance you will make it through that moment alive. Something which cannot be said for the many millions who have reportedly perished at the hands of the followers of a passionate instigator of a cause. There are good causes and there are causes that may be good for some—while it lasts—and not so good for others. Mao Zedong was born on December 26.

Without expressing judgment, it goes without saying that his charisma and drive to do good for the People's Republic of China (PRC, or China) bear fruit to this day. Without saying whether the fruit is rotten or ripe, toxic or nutritious, the world is witness to the institution that is the Communist Party of China. The personality characteristics associated with the period December 21 to January 20 include discipline, desire for control and structure, dedication, ambition, focus and the display of hard work in order to achieve great things. In addition, for people born during this time the ability to focus appears to be associated with a dislike of dissenting opinion and a strong need for loyalty and obedience from their subordinates. There can be a lack of emotion and maintaining distance from others. Insecurity is at the root of their shortcomings, similar to people born between September 23 and October 22, for instance.

The zodiac sign of Capricorn is associated with the period of December 22 through January 19 or 20. Structure and perfectionism are classic traits attributed to the sign. Yet, are people born at other times of the year also not perfectionistic? Is perfectionism bad? A real world example may be that of the famous movie director Stanley Kubrick, born July 26.[228, 229] Known to demand only the best, his movies are considered pieces of art by many critics. If a scene was not to his satisfaction, he would have it retaken a hundred and forty times if necessary. Still, Kubrick's horoscope has no Capricorn, Aries, Libra or Cancer on the Big Three. While we will not be able to observe Kubrick in action anymore—he passed away in March of 1999—reportedly he was shy and timid, not "real forceful." Considering his accomplishments, apparently being forceful was not necessary to get things done. A similar approach is often cited as a reason for success in sports. Not being reprimanded when a mistake is made and being allowed to take risks can help people grow.[230]

An organization—essentially "a structure through which individual effort can have an effect on a larger scale"—is traditionally considered Capricornian in nature. An organization intends to achieve results in order to survive, hence a need to focus and limit distracting, dissenting opinion. The other side of the proverbial coin is that no organization is static in nature. The economic and political landscape is constantly changing. Therefore, a certain amount of flexibility and adaptability are needed to ensure it can survive the occasional and inevitable storm.

Establishing a foothold, ensuring compliance, and maintaining superiority are three critical elements of a strategy aimed at introducing a new structure in an existing environment. Various methods are at the disposal of those pursuing a victory over the establishment. Methods may be soft as in spreading propaganda and other messages that promote the new person in charge, providing incentives to adopt a new approach, and allowing someone to participate. Hard methods may be the introduction of a new way of conducting business while completely abandoning the old ways, imposing a strict hierarchy, incarceration of opponents and permanently eliminating them.[231] While you may be quite familiar with propaganda as a promotional tool, an initiative such as Mao Zedong's Great Leap Forward may provide a trauma bond equally if not more effective at uniting people behind an idea.[232] Suffering, having to admit to being unable to accomplish a goal on one's own, losing relatives, these can be visually and emotionally powerful instruments of indoctrination and assimilation no matter their original intention.

Principles such as self-justification and "birds of a feather" can similarly enforce the Stockholm Syndrome[233] effect: "I helped with the new project yesterday, and while we were not successful, maybe today will be better"; not being able to escape a situation; celebrating a victory over a common enemy; receiving a reward for compliance with the new regime; or striving to overcome challenges together may instill a camaraderie that keeps the dominant leader in charge. When these elements are in place, it may be very attractive—or simply a matter of following the path of least resistance—to set doubt aside.

Along similar lines, many societies over the course of human history have come and gone. Many an insecure ruler has implemented harsh measures to eradicate dissent if the history books are a guide. And yet, is history not always written by the winner? What do we know about those who lost their lives fighting what they considered to be a just cause? We may be bearing the emotional scars of what our ancestors went through and have limited knowledge of what really happened to them.

One highly contentious issue in America, for instance, is the issue of slavery, and specifically the extent to which free people owned slaves. On social media, posts may surface that suggest only 1.6% of the population in the United States of 1860 owned slaves, whereas a closer look at the origins of such a statistic appears to indicate the number was closer to 5%.[234] What does that say about the conditions free people enjoyed at the time such as the workers in the New England textile mills?[235]

At the same time, what can we learn from those who fought for the abolishment of slavery? Their humanistic perspective must have gained the upper hand, or the perpetrators may have seen the light. The economic reality may have changed, or a combination of these and other factors may have contributed. While history books and articles may point in a certain direction, we have no other way of finding out but by reading the accounts of others. We may never know what was done to counteract slavery in America by those who did not participate, and by those who openly opposed the institution, if anything was done at all besides the reported political discussions on the subject.

How did some former slaves, freed after the American Civil War, feel about the opportunity to return to Africa and establish a new country, Liberia? Only speculation may be able to shed light on what transpired, but those in government appear to have facilitated the forced labor[236] of the indigenous population of the land that the new Liberians settled. It has been suggested that the regime of William Tolbert, the twentieth president of Liberia, contributed to the chaos that ensued upon his assassination, plunging the country into civil war and subsequent suffering under Charles Taylor.[237] Taylor's horoscope reportedly has Aries as the rising sign of his horoscope, while Tolbert's chart is alleged to have had Capricorn as the Ascendant. A proud Leo Moon and a determined Taurus Sun sign must have given him the impetus to defy the voice of the opposition and stifle dissent. Upon Tolbert's death, Liberia descended into chaos and war.[238]

Slavery as a form of institutionalized narcissism—that is, suggesting that another human is worth less than oneself therefore it would be permissible to take the lesser human as property—has been around for millennia. Some of the earliest records of a slave trade date back to the Code of Hammurabi in Babylon in the eighteenth century B.C. Bias and lack of access to information may be reasons some are less familiar with the cultural elements that were conducive to slavery for societies the world over in the past. What people have been able to glance from historical records and have since published in books and posted online may be our only guide. And yet, how does the emotionally traumatic memory of an ancestor's victimization not play a role in one's identity today? A certain African tribe may have had slaves from another tribe as in the case of the famous Queen Nzinga of the Ambundu Kingdoms.[239]

In all, reportedly twenty-eight million African slaves alone have been traded in the Muslim world over the past fourteen centuries,[240] while North Africans captured white Europeans between the Mediterranean and the English and Irish coasts as slaves—known as the Barbary slave trade[241]—during the same period when Northern Europeans sent African slaves to the Americas.

The raid on the village of Baltimore on Ireland's southwest coast is reportedly one of the more horrific acts performed by Barbary corsairs. In June 1631, over two hundred armed pirates landed there and pulled the sleeping inhabitants of the village from their beds. The men, women and children were taken as slaves to Algiers. It is said that slaves in Barbary could be white, black, or brown and of any religion—Catholic, Protestant, Orthodox, Jewish, or Muslim. In *Christian Slaves, Muslim Masters: White Slavery in the Mediterranean, the Barbary Coast, and Italy*,[242] historian Robert Davis writes that, "One of the things that both the public and many scholars have tended to take as given is that slavery was always racial in nature. [...] But that is not true." This may sound controversial, yet Davis continues by claiming that white slavery has been minimized or ignored because academics "preferred to treat Europeans as evil colonialists rather than as victims." Allegedly, the slave trade did not cease on the Barbary coast until European governments passed laws granting emancipation to slaves.[243] Were the actions of the Barbary pirates a "karmic" response of sorts to the European slave trade or vice versa?

The Roman Empire is perhaps most well known for having relied heavily on slaves from conquered territories as a source of cheap labor. Today, we are still witness to the ongoing need to have someone provide a service or make a product for less. China, for instance, has extensive manufacturing and warehousing operations in Africa as part of their Belt and Road initiative[244] because domestic Chinese labor is considered cost prohibitive to some local businesses.[245] Moreover, people frequently work for free when their contribution benefits a cause they believe in such as providing housing for poor families, the mission of Habitat for Humanity.[246] But the latter type of labor is "voluntary," of course—or isn't it, when behind the volunteer's back, investment bankers wreck the economy and conspire to deprive workers of a livable wage so that they can no longer buy decent accommodations with their paycheck?[247,248,249]

Throughout history, the practice of slavery has been adopted and outlawed in accordance with the ethics of the time and place. The mindset that leads to one person taking advantage of another, whether through slavery or unfair labor practices, is another issue altogether. A volunteer labor force may be no less subject to restrictive, demanding and unfair treatment than paid workers are: being underappreciated, experiencing emotional burnout, unresponsiveness from the community and inadequate resources and support are some of the areas reported in connection with volunteer work.[250] When people with a utilitarian perspective run amok, their utopian and dystopian philosophies may rise to the very highest levels of society, embedded in labor and welfare policies and regulations.[251] In the meantime, for the average citizen, life is still just that: real life.

"Everything can be taken from a [hu]man but one thing:
the last of the human freedoms—to choose one's attitude in any given set
of circumstances, to choose one's own way."
—Viktor Frankl, MD, PhD

REAL LIFE IS "REAL"

"Every interaction is a reflection of the
state of our mental health"—Anonymous

A Nobel prize winning economist, Daniel Kahneman recently passed away after a successful career in economics and psychology.[252] Together with others, Kahneman established a cognitive basis for the most common human errors that arise from heuristics and biases. Heuristics is defined as the process in which humans use mental shortcuts to arrive at decisions. For example, I am being introduced to somebody. If I tell this person what kind of job I have, their brain will immediately categorize me. This is a very fast process that relies on the bias they have towards the type of job they *think* it is if they know anyone in my field, what has been reported in the news about the industry, and any other details they may have picked up regardless of their validity. Unfortunately, it doesn't stop there.

The moment just before I was introduced, my new acquaintance may have been in conversation when they heard something negative or positive, had a specific mood and may have been thinking about something. These three things, and possibly others, have been shown to affect how they feel about me even though this is totally out of my control. As a final point for now, the very wording used to introduce me to this person will reportedly affect how they think of me from that moment forward—another factor over which I have absolutely no influence. Kahneman lived for bias and he identified several that may be useful. Anchoring bias is one—when we rely too heavily on the first piece of information about someone or something.

Alternatively, when we hear several things, we may only remember the first and last item even though those in the middle may carry more weight. People who try to guide us to a decision that works best for them may purposely arrange the options in a particular order hoping you won't notice. Availability as a bias presents as our ability to picture an event determining how likely we think it is that it will happen. Confirmation bias makes us appreciate information that confirms what we already know, while we underestimate the validity of information that contradicts our belief. When I own something, the endowment effect makes me value it more highly than something I don't possess, even though the item I don't yet have may be more beneficial for me.

Here are a few other types of bias that can jeopardize our judgment:

- When someone describes something I need, I am more likely to agree to acquiring it if is presented as having an eighty-five percent chance of matching what I already own, versus there being a fifteen percent chance that I won't like it, according to the *framing effect*.[253]

- *Hindsight bias* tells us that we believe an event had a higher likelihood of occurring after rather than before the fact. It is important to acknowledge that a situation may be more complex than we are willing to admit. [254]

- When we have greater confidence in our abilities and in our judgment than we should, it is called *overconfidence bias*.

- A brain shortcut that facilitates judging the probability of an event happening is called *Representativeness heuristic*.[255] It tricks us into discarding logical, statistical information and opt for what we think we know instead.

When it comes to finding and living our purpose, events and the agenda and opinions of others may throw us completely off course. Those who face continued hardship may feel as if they can never get a break. On the other hand, let us not forget that life may not always be as short as insurance actuaries would have you believe. Live long enough and your purpose might change, perhaps even many times and spread across different places. The day you decide to learn something completely new and different, or when you suddenly get an opportunity to branch out into a new field, you may surprise yourself. Still, what can we do when we feel stuck in a rut?

A Few Good Cardinals

I did not wake up one morning with the thought, "Hey, I would like to hear a police officer lie under oath in court today," but that is pretty much what happened. One balmy late summer evening in September, I went to pick up my mail like I had done many times before. On my way back, I would drive past two intersections. As it so happened, at the second intersection was a Boulder County Sheriff's patrol car waiting to make a left turn from the main road into my street. There was just one other vehicle at the intersection, a pickup truck on my left that was waiting at a red light and for me to cross the main road. From the first intersection, it would take about twenty-four seconds for me to reach the next, provided I traveled at the maximum allowed speed. In that time, my light would have turned red long before I reached it. With this in mind, I approached the intersection like always: prepared to come to a full stop.

The officer in the patrol car apparently had another idea. For some reason my traffic light remained green. Still, I stopped because in Colorado people run red lights when their patience runs out. After looking left and right, I proceeded to cross three lanes while making the turn. Meanwhile, I noticed the light turn yellow and then red by the time I reached the other side of the road. After a few hundred yards, just as I get ready to take the onramp for US 36 South, I see not just a pair of headlights in my rearview mirror, but also flashing blue and red lights. Must be going to an incident, I think. As I pull over, I notice the cop is pulling over as well…

"You can't ask me any questions about the reason I pulled you over," I heard the officer say. Keeping in mind that memory may not always be my most reliable friend, I reconstructed the incident that led to a ticket for "disobeying a traffic safety device" with the generous help of the local County Road Supervisor. In court, the officer described how she had been waiting to make a left turn when she saw the car I was driving run a red light. People must do it all the time, I thought, committing traffic violations right in front of a cop. But that would be in clear daylight with lots of traffic around. This was eight o'clock in the evening on a dark, deserted road. In the Denver metro area, people joke that they get a ticket "just for farting." Others may be entrapped with far more serious consequences. Yet, how is it not the principle that matters—someone in authority taking advantage of their position to make a quick buck for the county? The ticket I got on that September evening in Colorado inspired me to write this book.

Why discuss a simple traffic violation when we could be dissecting the far more impactful actions of a litigious District Attorney in a murder case? It seems that society, to a large degree, runs on dramatic effect. The media gets our attention with big headlines, many of which are not nearly as "big" as they claim to be once you click on the link to read the article. Drama releases cortisol in the brain.[256] A simple story, in contrast, does not have quite the same effect—yet it does set a thinking process in motion that encourages the brain to reflect on its implications.

If "my" traffic light had indeed been working correctly, as the officer claimed, it would have been red a full fifteen seconds before I reached the intersection. In those fifteen seconds—which can feel like an eternity—the officer would have had to wait for just one vehicle to pass before making her turn. In other words, in "real" life, statistically speaking the officer would not have observed me "running" a light no matter what color it might have been. As anyone who has ever been falsely accused of anything by a police officer can testify, trying to convince a judge of one's innocence without a witness as back-up is pretty much impossible—especially because the court has no obligation to consider evidence, whether circumstantial or factual.

Nothing may happen by chance alone, especially when I feel that someone is lying to me. It seems that the act of lying starts out small—not just when children lie for the first time to their parents, but also with regard to the nature of the transgression. How is the first lie not a test of, "Can I get away with this?" Isn't it funny how experts suggest that we tell our children that "lying is wrong",[257] but that it may be necessary sometimes? Narcissists seem to know what a lie is, yet also that the rule meant to discourage lying does not apply to them. Psychology distinguishes shame and guilt as two distinct mechanisms for handling a lie. Narcissists experience shame and project it onto others. They literally hold another person accountable for their own actions. They also seem to cover for each other in the act of lying.

What happens when the number of narcissists were to exceed a certain tipping point? How much different would society become? It seems we only have to look as far as Russia, China, India, much of Eastern Europe and quite a few countries in Africa. Lies tend to become bigger and bolder as the perpetrator finds acceptance for her of his version of the truth. People appear to support each other in maintaining a perverted image of the truth often because their role in the community depends on it, they can gain a prolonged, perhaps lifelong advantage over others. The question, "Is a lie a lie when I don't believe it to be so?" could be an easy way out for someone with a more flexible interpretation of truth, or for those who think that you can't handle the truth. How can we potentially identify this individual without having to resort to cumbersome fact finding missions or worse, hoping for the best?

A community can spend a significant amount of taxpayer money on training and equipment of law enforcement personnel. If people commit crimes, law enforcement may consider their presence justified. But what if people "see the light" (pun intended) and treat each other with respect? What if the economy is doing so poorly that people simply have no money to spare for traffic tickets or worse and therefore commit fewer infractions and crimes? Law enforcement personnel may be looking for that "feel good" reward we explored earlier just as much as anybody else. A little bit of it might come from issuing tickets for imagined or petty offenses. The concept of self-justification might rear its "ugly" head here as well: "I did it once, it worked and nobody noticed. It seems perfectly okay to do it again," as two police officers in Florida once tried as an excuse to issue bogus tickets to drivers they allegedly never pulled over.[258]

When we join an organization dedicated to uphold a specific standard, we need to fit in, or we need to have enough leverage to make a change. Most rank and file members may opt for the former. When we feel protected, we may stretch our interpretation of what is acceptable behavior. For givers, self-justification doesn't appear to be a good reason to commit a transgression or a crime. For takers, on the other hand, self-justification *is* often the main reason. Somewhere in between stands truth without a capital T.

What makes truth such a powerful weapon? Is it because deep down each one of us wants the truth above all else? Many people seem unable to handle the truth. *Homo sapiens* was created before any concept of God, religion or philosophical doctrine existed yet we have always attempted to make sense of our existence. Cave and rock drawings, stone tables hieroglyphs, extensive monuments and other relics are powerful testaments. Throughout history people have made attempts to explain their existence and that of the world in which they live. You may have noticed that some who claim to have *the* answer seek to convince others while rooting out the opposition by any means possible. In an attempt to maintain unity, followers of a particular doctrine, be it a political or a religious one, may seek to ridicule those who disagree, persecute or condemn and perhaps also eliminate—all because of an insecurity complex.

Life is full of compromises. As we ponder the consequences of compromise, we sometimes stumble on behavior that we consider inappropriate, but that others justified in light of their beliefs. Consider reported abuse on Indian reservations in the U.S.[259] In Montana, *The Missoulian* reported in 2011 that the church has been a focal point of religious life in the Mission Valley since the 1830s. Yet, one resident may have said it best when he summarized the feelings of parishioners as follows, "People hate us belittling our town and our church" because "they don't know what hell we went through." The Oregon Province of the Society of Jesus, also known as Jesuits, were forced into a bankruptcy organization after reported abuse by Jesuit priests and nuns starting in the 1950s at boarding schools and parishes on remote reservations and villages in the Pacific Northwest and Alaska.

How can events taking place in a specific context (*i.e.*, perpetrated by those of a religious order) that appear to run counter in such a fundamental way to the basic premise of the underlying doctrine take place at all? It may be because nobody can truthfully translate the books on which today's religions are based without falling prey to political influence. It may further be because many people besides those committing crimes in the name of their religion ignore the fundamental tenet of morality, fairness and human decency for personal gain. The question subsequently emerges, how much spiritual progress have we made as humans with regard to the truth and respecting another for their truth?

When a certain behavior is tolerated or ignored, and when the truth is dismissed by more than one person for the sake of the health of the community, nation or society, we could call it institutionalization. Bureaucracies exist because of the need of efficiency and expediency. Court systems and financial systems were developed, for instance, to speed up the processing of criminal convictions and investment transactions. Bureaucracies by their very nature imply efficiency though usually not for their customer. A bureaucracy exists to serve a purpose, generally that of those who instituted it—which tend to be the ones in power. When a discrepancy exists between your version of the truth and that of the bureaucracy, the latter tends to win because it's considered not very efficient to have to sort out your side of the story. As such, bureaucracy, no matter the constitution that supports it, tends to introduce something that I would call institutional marginalization of individual rights. This is a big term for something as simple as my giving up my personal rights for that of the larger whole.

With this conundrum in mind, might we have arrived at what could be a familiar concept to some: karma, or "what you reap you sow," or maybe even more familiar, "do to others what you would have them do to you?" [Matthew 7:12] As institutions appear to diminish our individual rights, the question turns from sharing our personal truth and respecting the personal truth of another, to improving human relations in general by being more truthful.

Narcissism may be a healthy, necessary stage in life. It apparently serves us during our toddler and teen years because it tends to give us an inflated sense of confidence that enables us to leave the security of the parental bond to explore the world. Children growing up in a nurturing environment may reach the end of their narcissistic explorations with an integrated sense of self and awareness of the separateness of other people. However, if children are traumatized or are insecure in in relation to their caregivers at these crucial stages, they may not "graduate" from the school of narcissism and consequently become "toxic people" who view others merely as extensions of themselves without separate needs and feelings.

You may encounter narcissistic people every day without understanding why they are so rude, have an unfounded sense of entitlement and seem to have boundary issues. Many of us have been raised in families that pass down narcissistic vulnerabilities. As a result, we may have become easy prey to narcissists who are always on the lookout for people who can be manipulated into serving them.

There is a good argument to be made for accepting life as it comes—for always being a good person, giving your best and being the most respectful individual one can be. There is no doubt in my mind that this is a solid way of life. And yet, I am very conscious of the fact that once I am no longer ignorant of something, and if have discovered something that could benefit many, I may have a duty to share it.

Giving someone the benefit of the doubt and expecting someone's behavior and attitude to change for the better are a moral duty. Certain people and situations can bring out the best in all of us. Similarly, certain other people and situations can arguably bring out the worst in us, especially when we have been stressed out or haven't been getting enough sleep. Using the psychological approach, it may take a while in figuring out why someone lashes out. Was it because of an argument with his wife last week where he didn't feel heard and now he is taking the opportunity to vent? Or was it because his father always gave him a hard time and he has bottled it up all those years?

An alternative would be to find at least one of the three personal points. How close could we get to being able to say:

1. If this person gets into a stressful, demanding situation, he may just wing it.

2. He is going to fudge the data to look good.

3. He may create a crisis to cover it up.

4. There is too much at stake here.

People who can apply focus and determination have been known to be at the forefront of significant advancements in society. What do you know about the "second greatest Briton of all time,"[260] Isambard Kingdom Brunel, born April 9, 2806? Still, others have arguably made for breakthrough contributions in science at least at a similar rate. What we need to keep in mind is that inventors, leaders and statesmen are few and far between among the numbers of the general population. Context and company seem everything. Being successful may alleviate a few negative side effects of narcissistic behavior, or it may enforce it. It appears to depend on how evolved the individual is.

Charismatic and ambitious narcissists such as Elizabeth Holmes, born February 3, 1984, of Theranos infamy[261] and Robert Mugabe, born February 21, 1924, of Zimbabwe[262] were once running "free," wreaking havoc on both a small and large scale—the former misrepresenting the capabilities of a revolutionary method to draw blood, the latter for destroying the economy of his country. Mugabe was praised as a revolutionary hero of the African liberation struggle, while critics accused him of being a dictator responsible for economic mismanagement and widespread corruption and human rights abuses, including crimes against humanity, and genocide.[263]

Scientists tell us that merely observing a phenomenon has the potential to change its characteristics. If the status quo in government and large organizations needs to be changed, it isn't going to happen overnight. Perceived injustice has been addressed and attempted to be reversed and righted for as long as there has injustice has been perceived. Wanting to right a wrong seems an integral part of human nature. How the approach we explore here is different from others is that it aims to offer a better understanding of how you and I look at it versus a narcissist.

A narcissist may:

- ignore or dismiss any suggestion you make because they didn't come up with it themselves; and,

- they may purposely intimidate their audience (*i.e.*, you) with jargon.

- When questioned, they may brush off a request for clarification because they would be hard pressed to explain what they just said.

They may do it because somebody else did it to them and they adopted it not knowing any better.

LIVE AND LET DIE

"The most important factor in survival is neither intelligence nor strength but adaptability"—Charles R. Darwin

Survival of the fittest is a concept most often associated with Charles Robert Darwin.[264] He reportedly coined the term to describe his theory of evolution. While his research and the results he achieved are duly noted, it appears that there are some gaps in his line of thinking regarding one species in particular: Darwin's own.[265] Allegedly, he became aware of this and prepared to publish an update. Alas, Darwin passed away before he could finish it. As we continue to morph our social structures and pursue an ever increasing lifespan, what happens with our bodies—do the remnants of a natural drive to survive dictate our potential, or did we evolve past our animal ancestors to develop a hybrid, unique survival instinct?

While some parents go to any length to make sure (most of) their offspring survive into adulthood, others don't mind having their young raised by others. In nature we call them brood parasites. Arguably, we live in nature despite our efforts to cover the connection up by surrounding ourselves with electronics and virtual reality. What seems to set us apart from the rest of the natural world, though, is our ability and propensity to reason. A bird who discovers that she has been hatching eggs from her cuckoo neighbor may be upset.[266] The cuckoo may "argue" that it was her natural instinct that made her do it. Regardless, there is no government or charitable organization available to provide assistance to the Eurasian reed warbler raising a cuckoo chick, nor does the cuckoo offer to contribute to food supplies—or the rent for that matter.

However many parallels there may be between behavior observed in nature and human behavior, there is no doubt that we set ourselves apart with our inclination to rearrange the furniture, as a manner of speaking. For example, while beavers manipulate their environment as well, sometimes with dramatic consequences,[267] *homo sapiens* do not just make changes in their environment out of an instinctual drive—other than perhaps for the need to have a protective roof over their heads. Humans have shown quite capable of manipulating life in many different ways, including in the reproductive system. In fact, humans reportedly make so many changes that overpopulation due to increasing control over natural predatory factors seems to have become a real issue—the malaria mosquito and its effect on productivity perhaps being a good example.[268] Widespread ignorance and denial regarding the consequences of human interventions in the natural world have scientists and interest groups crying crisis the world over.

If human behavior finds its origins in nature, is it to be condoned? It seems to be a sensitive subject because generally, in this day and age, the one with the biggest gun and the most political influence generally sets the rules. Unless we get together and decide we have had enough of the "senseless" killings, the oppression or whatever else bothers us, we are bound to repeat history.

Until about twenty years ago, many psychologists denied that animals communicate with each other. We didn't even know elephants "talk" to each other until we picked up their low-frequency acoustic signals called infrasound.[269] Maybe one day we will discover and decipher how zebras tell lions to back off. Until then, we will have to do with the most recent theory: the handicap principle. The handicap principle was first proposed by Zahavi in about 1980, and has only in the past few decades become widely accepted as a central unifying theory explaining many aspects of animal signaling and communication.[270]

Apart from the question who is right about something at any point in time, there is the eternal, philosophical consideration of why life happens the way it does. Then there is the age old question of past karma, if it exists at all and how we should rectify that. One could argue that at some point a tipping point of narcissism may be reached, when the options of turning the corner become increasingly, let's say, less well defined and fewer in number. The Western Roman Empire, for instance, reached such a point in about 376 A.D. What exactly was the last drop in the proverbial bucket may never be certain. It could have been collective lead poisoning,[271] or the cumulative effect of a gradual weakening of society through the influx of large numbers of outsiders.

Survival of the fittest is our specialty. Still, just like microplastics, narcissists seem to be everywhere. If we accept reincarnation as a concept, maybe narcissism is a natural part of the cycle of human life: one starts as a narcissist, learns the ropes, runs into a few obstacles. After a few lifetimes, slowly but surely experience turns into expertise followed by wisdom. Through cause and effect, much can be learned. One starts loving the neighbor a bit more. One ponders the needs of the body in order to survive better and longer: "If lions eat meat, why not me?" may be a question asked not just by a vegan.[272]

One becomes respected in the community helping and teaching others. Narcissism appears to occur in every culture and society. Meanwhile, human ingenuity seems to know no bounds—almost every day there is another breakthrough allowing a small or big problem to be solved with a unique solution—kind of like the principle of "ask and you shall receive."[273] How do we deal with all this as an individual? How much impact do we have? It has been suggested to follow one's feelings[274] in order to pursue one's mission: feelings that originate in the gut and the heart.

Denial of feelings can have consequences. As humans we are a social species and our life is complex. We rely on others for our survival especially in our early years as infants and toddlers. The information that we receive from our caregivers often stays with us for our entire life. It pays to critically examine the validity of the methods used and nutrition provided to help us reach adulthood. You may have been raised in a household with an alcoholic parent, or somebody may have suggested that certain drugs would not be harmful.

To *not* be a slave of circumstance and custom requires knowing oneself, which idea takes us to an ancient bit of wisdom from Socrates: "the unexamined life is not worth living."[275]. Knowing ourselves well enough to not be a slave may require making conscious decisions. Decisions which may not be so easy to make when one lives in the emotional fog created by cognitive dissonance, bullying and other trauma leading to cPTSD. And yet, some who have "been there" encourage us through the words they left behind to keep following our feelings[276] and our *conatus*—the "Will to Live."[277]

Much of what happens before you buy a new pair of jeans or when you shop around for a new dentist occurs outside of our awareness and long before we have to make a decision about either. When I put on new clothes, I may not think about whether they can catch fire easily or if they fall apart after a few washes. Depending on the price I paid, I have certain expectations as to how long they will last. And in terms of them being fireproof, there is a lot of negotiation and testing between the government, the textile industry and experts in materials science going on before the retailer can sell them—under ideal circumstances, that is. What is the principle that governs expectations? Trust. There is another, legal term for it: "good faith." It is used to describe how we hold expectations.

When I go to a dentist, my visit and payment for services is an act of good faith on my part that the dentist has my best interests in mind for my oral health. Have you ever asked a friend for a recommendation to a good dentist? That is an act of trust. Honestly, I have never pressed anyone as to their definition of "good." Without very much information being exchanged, I trust that my friend will provide useful advice. The dentist, continuing our train of thought, works at the end of a production line of an oral health "industry" that extends all the way from the people who study nutrition and chemistry through the manufacturers of dental practice equipment and the makers of toothpaste to the dental chair I will soon be sitting on. That is an impressive chain of cause and effect. Yet, if you have as much time as I did for these things before writing this book, you may not give it much thought either.

The oldest known record of the "sugar for oral health" seems to date to about 2,500 years ago. The remedy is apparently called "Zhin-he-tong" ("sugar from the white tree") in Mandarin and is used for cavities and gum disease.[278] The Chinese appear to have known about xylitol, as it is known in English, for a long time. So did the Native Americans as they cleaned their teeth with wood from birch trees. In Russia and Alaska, people swish the sap from birch trees, while grocery stores sell xylitol for baking and regular use. Wal-Mart in Beijing reportedly has drums full of xylitol gum at every checkout, but try finding it in Arkansas and you might be out of luck. What happened in the rest of the United States and Europe?

Successful scientific pursuits generally go like this: trial and error leads to invention which, in turn, leads to adoption and mass production—provided that there is an investor or two who believe in the product, and a business person who knows how to sell it. What happens if someone stumbles upon a solution to a problem I always expected my dentist to fix, a cavity for example? What if that solution prevented a cavity from forming in the first place? Who would be the first to tell me? Take mercury fillings. Dentists don't call them mercury fillings because the toxicity of the compound is so widely known that they want to avoid the negative connotation. The solution is to give them a different name:

A Few Good Cardinals

"amalgam" or "silver."[279] What would be the best way to prevent them? I often have to remind myself that today's internet search engine comes in handy.

With the introduction of artificial sweeteners, xylitol was almost relegated to the dustbin of time. Re-discovered during World War II, it replaced table sugar when that was scarce in Europe. The health benefits of xylitol were observed and duly recorded: children eating xylitol had almost fifty percent fewer ear infections while cavities practically vanished. How long did it take for xylitol to make a comeback and replace silver fillings as a treatment protocol? It never did. Laser treatment has become the solution of choice instead, an invention originally from Scotland.[280] Fortunately, thanks to Finland which introduced the world to xylitol sweetened chewing gum in 1951, we may "chew our way to dental health."[281]

It happens in every branch of scientific inquiry and in daily life—the research never stops. Most days it is like kaizen, the Japanese principle of continuous improvement, yet occasionally it is more like a massive breakthrough. Some discoveries happen simply by accident. Some are the result of years of tireless research. Nevertheless, their impact can be significant. When a prior invention has managed to attract an audience and a market, it may take a while for a new one to gain traction. Decades may pass even. Do you know about the dangers of asbestos?[282] There are a number of potentially fatal diseases related to inhalation of asbestos fibers including mesothelioma, asbestosis, interstitial fibrosis, and lung cancer. Before we knew this, they used to put asbestos in the filters of cigarettes. Doctors used to be featured in cigarette marketing.

In the meantime, in the field of health care clinical studies may be carried out in a haphazard fashion. Data may be fudged to favor one product over another. Researchers may simply deny that the new discovery has any commercial value because they can't *believe* what they are seeing. There are many ways that new inventions can be kept out of reach of the consumer.

On a personal level, money and influence may not be the common denominator that stops progress. Instead, the most common obstacle to escaping from a situation we no longer desire appears to be a stubborn inability to release. When I faced a stressful situation as a child, such as my mother scolding me for venturing outside the house even though it was raining and "don't you have homework to do", I used to react emotionally by feeling hurt. Physically, feeling hurt happens through the release of adrenaline. I quickly learned to hide my emotions because expressing them was not a "manly" thing. After a while, I started having trouble sleeping or I would vomit inexplicably in the face of overwhelming stress. Nobody saw the connection with suppressed emotions.

The body apparently records how emotions are managed. Reportedly, it has to deal with the presence of adrenaline as well, just like an animal that faces the threat of a predator checking out their chances for dinner. Yet unlike the animal that physically releases the emotional response when the threat subsides and whose body processes the associated hormones,[283] as humans we appear to have lost that natural instinct. Fortunately, there appears to be a solution pioneered by Lester Levenson: an exercise in which one visualizes the release of tension while asking oneself a series of specific questions as described in *The Sedona Method*.[284]

Whatever our current situation, we may not have to be a slave to it. While accepting reality may be one form of empowerment; becoming more open minded may be another. The possibilities may be endless when we are open to a change of perspective. When the opportunity comes to make a leap of faith, would you be ready? This is the very short story of a tool that traveled many tens of thousands of years through time to be with us still: the axe.[285] After roughly 20,000 years of production and use, how could we still improve on it? Someone in Finland did exactly that. Heikki Kärnä invented the Leveraxe,[286] a safer, easier and faster way of splitting wood. The design of this axe gives it thirty-five times the hitting force of a traditional axe.

TELL *YOUR* STORY

"If you love what you do, the only exit strategy is death."
—Larry Gagosian

How is life not similar to painting—start with a blank slate and add layer upon layer of paint as one gets older and hopefully wiser. People who were born into negativity and difficult circumstances may start off with a darker layer than those born into a nurturing, supportive environment. There is character in every layer. Now imagine that one does not really start with a clean slate. Instead, the location, the culture we are born into, and the actual moment of birth also may contribute something. Was it summer or fall, is the community isolated or is it a big city, what is the history of the people?

How fascinating and multi-dimensional the birth of a human being can be. No wonder we are so different and unique. The history of the environment we are born into may be shared with us in the form of a story. In the absence of one or both parents, those who took their place may fill in the blanks for us, or we may be on our own having to figure it out by ourselves. For some, their story becomes their life and truth against which they compare everything else. For others, their story is one of many and they welcome yours. Stories can also help us make sense of unexplainable events. Is the story difficult to digest, or may our audience judge us if we tell the truth? It may be best to rephrase our story in a context our audience can relate to. Many cultures explain their presence and pass it on to the next generation in the form of myth, folklore and the written word of the divine.

It is no secret that quite a few cultures have reportedly lived and perished throughout history, and whose descendants have merged into another. Their stories may have been lost in time or survive as myths. People who identify with their culture generally identify also with a particular location. While migrations, either by force, or as a survival strategy, have shifted people all over the continents on a fairly regular basis, island dwellers similarly didn't shy away from venturing outside of their habitat. In addition to exploring the world in peace for the purpose of trade, there have been "a few occasions" when a blood thirsty leader convinced his followers to wage war and expand the territory. The story of their conquest often speaks of the righteousness of their cause, the crimes of their adversary, and the freedom and prosperity that resulted. In the midst of the chaos of war, the fruits of peacetime and everything in between, some people sought to safeguard ancient knowledge. Libraries the world over were—and some still are—filled with books whose words I may never have time to read or will ever get access to. The stories and wisdom they contain will most likely remain a mystery. And yet, life goes on. Every day a new story is being written, this time in mostly electronic form. Once someone pulls the plug or updates the operating system, yesterday's story may be lost forever. Still, a story is more than the recorded word—there may be emotion, trauma, loss, pain and gain.

In ancient times, it is probably safe to say that people did not have access to electronic mail. Imagine that you sent a letter to a friend a hundred and fifty miles away. It had to be hand delivered on horseback if you could afford it, a journey that might take two days, or less if the messenger was lucky and you paid enough for the horses, their feed and the messenger's rations, the weather was accommodating and the land not too unforgiving. If your friend was home, instead of, let's say, on a hunting trip, you could reasonably expect a response withing about a day—provided (1) they felt inclined to answer promptly, and (2) you had supplied sufficient funds for the return trip rather than making your friend pay for postage.

While you were waiting, you had plenty of time to think about all sorts of things, including about what you should have said instead of the words your friend might misinterpret. Who knows, they might get into a jealous rage, breaking off the friendship or worse. But let us not dwell on the negative. Besides, who wants friends who might become fearsome enemies at the drop of a hat? Whatever we do today is (partially) the result of everything that came before. Whatever we do today, is also, partially, the result of everything we *expect* to happen and do in the future. These two concepts culminate in this moment of the present—which is, it seems, a powerful observation to make, until someone decides to change the story…

For some people, having an epiphany or profound realization doesn't seem to change anything, at least not right away. For them, the realization that they acted like a total jerk, for example, may change something for about two minutes while they assure you that they didn't mean to hurt you, that they have changed, that everything will be better now. They may beg you to understand where they were coming from, and to forgive them. Of course you do. In fact, you tell them they can stay. The next thing you hear is, "Great! Now, do me a favor…" For others, having a profound realization means they give up what they fought for because they see how futile it was. Their story no longer matches up with reality. They apologize for the wasted effort and give thanks for whatever little has been accomplished. Then they create something better.

Imagine that everything that has been, is now and will be is exactly the way it is supposed to be. There is no wrong or right, no utopia, no better, best or worst. Everything just is and we let life evolve and change as it happens just like it has done for millennia. What does that look like? Can you imagine a scenario where the path you take and the decisions you make are yours? Now think back to a time long ago, to your very first memories. Do you remember thinking about the future then?

If you are a bit like me, you may have had a dream about what you wanted to be when you "grew up." When I was little, people were my source of entertainment and books were a source of inspiration. Just before the first Moon landing in 1969, we got a black and white television. When I saw Neil Armstrong and Buzz Aldrin walking around on the Moon I was instantly hooked: I wanted to go to space. I annoyed my fourth grade teacher in elementary school to no end when I had to give a five minute presentation about a favorite topic. Whereas my classmates chose to talk about their pet, I "entertained" them for twenty five minutes discussing how we went from simple rockets to the Space Shuttle.

How has life changed since then? Today's one year old may already know how to swipe a smartphone, while a one and a half year old tells her grandmother that she wants to go take a nap. In day care, a young one slaps a child in the face because she wants to show who is the boss—without ever having watched another person hit someone else. Apparently, we adapt our actions and behavior to others—in order to fit in or to save ourselves the effort. How we express ourselves emotionally may be similarly the result of the example set by our environment: caregivers, neighbors and people we see on television or in social media clips. In other words, if I like your presence, I might choose any one or more of a number of options, including physical contact and speech, to bring the message across. But what if I need something? That seems to be a different category of communication altogether: I may need food in order to survive.

The dark side of getting our needs met surfaces when we deal with people who seek to get their way at any cost. Charm and a respectful yet convincing argument may not be their strong point. Do we adopt their style, escape the situation, or submit to their demands? They may use any one of a number of tools to get attention and cooperation.

Psychologists tell us that the development of a human life is dependent on how a child is raised, the nurturing and direction it gets from its caretakers and the feedback it receives from its environment. How does a child raised by a domineering parent not turn out differently compared to a child raised by a nurturing, supportive parent?

What happens when we cause harm to another? Experts who study narcissism appear to suggest that the condition makes someone less capable of knowing what harm is. Carl Tavris and Elliot Aronson devote a significant part of their career to writing about people who deny that they did anything wrong in *Mistakes Were Made (but Not by Me)*.[287] Considering how much suffering appears to exist in the world, we may be at a crossroads.

Some parents want their offspring to be the next celebrity genius, actor or billionaire, while their child may have very different aspirations. Some may be so impacted by the demands placed on them, they seek to gain dominance over others at any cost just to feel better. What is their story?

We started with the premise that life may be just the way it is supposed to be. What do we do when we perceive injustice? We may join forces with others to do something about it. What if nobody agrees there is a problem? I may have to hold on to my concerns until a tipping point is reached. Sometimes, if I let destiny take its course, a problem "magically" corrects itself. Destiny may be referred to as time.

WHO IS YOUR FRIEND?
A FRESH LOOK AT TIME

*"I hope our wisdom will grow with our power, and teach us that the less
we use our power, the greater it will be"*—Thomas Jefferson

For as long as people have been looking up at the night sky there has been a sense of wonder and awe as to how we fit in. How our fascination with the stars started may eternally remain a mystery. Yet, it is no secret that people the world over have tried to associate the movement of the planets and the stars with events on Earth for thousands of years. Civilizations may have come and gone, while their archaeological remains testify to their ingenuity or lack thereof. Meanwhile, Earth keeps making its rounds and so do the other bodies in our solar system.

As a twenty-first century human who grew up watching the Apollo space program and the NASA missions to Venus and Mars, I can't imagine how it started. Someone must have been really curious at one point, and they must have been really good at math. Associating the bodies we call "planets," meaning the Sun, Moon, Mercury, Venus, Mars, Jupiter, Saturn, Uranus, Neptune, and Pluto, with twelve Zodiac signs, Pisces, Aries, Taurus, Gemini, Cancer, Leo, Virgo, Libra, Scorpio, Sagittarius, Capricorn and Aquarius, and somehow connecting this to human behavior seems simply fascinating. Today, we know that his approach doesn't just rely on observation and association, there is real statistical analysis involved.

If you think of astrology as a tool to predict events, I can't help you because I haven't had much luck in that arena. What does fascinate me about astrology instead is how it can be used to analyze behavior and relationships. Oftentimes, I think people behave a certain way because of their social status, how much money they have or what family they grew up in. What can also play an often significant role is intergenerational dynamics. A therapist who dedicated his life to helping people unravel unhealthy family dynamics is Anton (Bert) Hellinger (born December 16) who developed a concept he calls Family Constellations.[288] Through his work with an entire group of people at once, he helps individuals come to terms with the emotional trauma in their family's history. Interestingly, how much success people have in overcoming their trauma has been known, in my experience, to relate at least partially to their horoscope.

While the above mentioned and other factors can certainly play a role in determining someone's future, they don't seem to fully explain why some who acquired or inherited great wealth contribute to a greater cause than their own, while others seek outsized control over others in order to secure and further advance their position—as if they know how vulnerable they really are. An example of the latter may be John D. Rockefeller (born July 8) who converted his oil wealth to the development of allopathic medicine.[289]

They say life is an illusion—a pretty darn good one, with real dreams, emotions, good food, and bullets… Shattering illusions is what life can be: shattering dreams, plans, and hope. Some people are considered determined, ambitious, or "stubborn" in their outlook on life. They seem to have no trouble manifesting their dreams. Earlier we identified three different behavior modes: Visionary, Designer and Builder. The Designer's primary strength seems to be in making highly focused decisions that propel them forward. Such decisions are beneficial foremost to themselves as the principal character in their life. The key to understanding how people function is recognizing that each of us may have one or more of the modes in our personality.

In my case, my personality is centered around the mode of the Visionary. As I go through life, learning, growing, and relating, everything I do is focused on sharing new ideas, cultivating the future and planting the seed of renewal— the latter mostly figuratively. The mode of the Designer is meant to take an idea from the Visionary and run with it. They forge a path in the physical world, give structure to a concept and promote. The next step is for the Builder—taking the blueprint from the Designer and turning into something tangible and useful.

The horoscope of Apple's Steve Jobs (born February 24, 1955) had two Visionary elements and one Designer on his personal points.[290] Jobs was reportedly known for his vision, a drive to get things done and a penchant for perfectionism. Time and moments for reflection appears to have given him an opportunity to learn from mistakes, to integrate those lessons and adjust his behavior accordingly. The Designer element appears to be the most challenged in this regard. When we are in the company of someone who is challenged like this, we may need to guard ourselves against optimistic expectations. Let's start with the presumption that context determines behavior. Context meaning:

- how we feel,

- what our responsibility is,

- what our expected contribution is,

- what our goals and objectives are, and

- how much authority we have.

Add to that how much affection and respect we need, what our family's standing is in the community, what we have done in similar situations in the past, and we end up with a broad palette of factors that could affect how we act in any given situation.

The result of these factors influencing each other simultaneously might be virtually impossible to determine, but that hasn't stopped psychologists, anthropologists and other experts from doing their best to find out. While some situations seem to bring out the worst in people, some people seem to want to make the worst out of potentially good situations.

Life appears to be a cacophony of perspectives. You may empathically consider it best for someone to wear a warm coat when you feel cold. The other person may say they feel just fine, but you dismiss their response. One person thinks abortion should be allowed, but their neighbor disagrees. Societies make rules and laws to make order out of chaos. People form "families" and "tribes" to amass political and financial power and use that to rule over others. Yet, there always appears to be someone with a different perspective: the proverbial outsider.

Some differences in perspective seem to stubbornly persist. Not surprisingly perhaps, scientists have determined that people tend to behave differently, or to make different choices, depending on the kind of information they have at their disposal and, more importantly, depending on context and circumstances.[291, 292]. Let's say that I have been wanting to ask my boss for a promotion for months. I am ready for it, my numbers are great and I know the rest of the team will support me. With clients, I am a confident negotiator. Yet, every time I want to bring it up with my boss, some seemingly insignificant interruption stops me in my tracks—my boss takes a day off, walks out to get coffee, things like that. I never seem to have the courage to go with the flow and ask my boss when would be a good time. In other words, I use these interruptions as an excuse to postpone dropping the question. "I can do it tomorrow," I tell myself. "Obviously, this is not the right time." I may attribute my procrastination to insecurity. The reality is that confidence did not come naturally for me.

Confidence is something everyone needs and its seeds are sown in childhood. An overbearing parent, an absent parent, and a controlling parent are scenarios that may inhibit confidence. As we saw, the primary rule in life is that we all learn by example, and that everything has a cause and an effect. As it so happens, one of the most important tools for building confidence in children is proper role modeling.[293] Did it help that my mother had a dominant personality at home yet acted submissively to most strangers? Not so much. In a case like this, therapy can do wonders it seems. The personality who is most likely to take advantage of low confidence in another person appears to be the Designer. With the cards stacked against the Builder and the Visionary, what may be the best strategy for them to up the ante? Getting to know themselves better, discovering how seemingly insignificant things trip up their best intentions, and allowing themselves enough time to integrate a more confident style.

This brings us to the gist of our exploration in that there may always be someone who, instinctively, may criticize or reject what we bring to the table simply because they did not think of it first. Imagine that you are looking at two babies. Which one seems to cry all the time? If not food, they need attention. Perhaps it is because they are more insecure than the other. This very basic type of behavior, perhaps rooted in a sense of deep insecurity, may carry on into childhood, adolescence and eventually adulthood. It appears to dictate human behavior for some individuals to such an extent that it impacts every aspect of their lives. They need control, they need people to do their bidding, or they need people to admire them. We appear to accept the consequences of this attitude everywhere primarily because we have not quite identified where it comes from, yet we know not everyone behaves like this.

To compensate for this behavior, we may have adopted various rules, regulations and laws. And yet, it seems that the people who behave according to the principles of the Designer don't feel they should have to obey the rules. Any rules for that matter, and especially when it would be inconvenient. Just like you and I, they come into the world full of hope and expectation. Yet, they quickly act as if they own the place. They may charm you into believing they have the answer to your problems—sometimes without even bothering to question what your problems are.

If they don't like what they see, they yell and scream until you give them what they want. No challenge is too much for them, they simply "blow up" whatever blocks their way and let you deal with the mess. Actually, they blame you for it. Maybe you are their partner in "crime." You love them because they remind you of you when you were younger. The zeal, the boundless enthusiasm, the drive to achieve at any cost. Their innocence and passion are contagious until you realize they don't like you to share in the rewards. You might take revenge or…, no, you know better than that. You have been there, done that, and you paid the proverbial price.

Sooner or later, they take up a cause, just like any self-respecting human being is expected to do. It could be the support of the family, a creative idea, technology, it could be the environment, or a political ideology. There are some who, because of their upbringing or beliefs—whether religious or not—may develop a grudge against someone else, an organization or a principle and build their entire life around said resentment. You might not forget an injustice, but to forgive, is that possible? For those who can't, a grudge may, under the "right" circumstances develop into something bigger: a grudge against a religion, against a culture, or against a people. How big does a grudge need to be for it to turn into something horrendous?

The Designer appears to see the world from the perspective of lack. The Builder appears able to distinguish the nuance between lack and abundance. The Visionary, on the other hand, sees abundance and fulfilment, recognizing how the perspective of lack simultaneously undermines the sustainable wellbeing of self and community. Where there is mostly lack, there is restriction. Where there is uncontrolled exuberance, the future is squandered. Where lack and exuberance live side by side, responsibly managed by vision, there is progress and good fortune. What would society look like if people were allowed to flourish in positions and situations that provided them with an experience according to the presence of Designer, Visionary or Builder mode in their horoscope?

A historic case against bullying might be that of Herman Webster Mudgett.[294] Also known as Dr. Henry Howard Holmes, Mudgett was a con artist and serial killer. Born on May 16, 1861, his horoscope has no Personal Point in a Designer sign except for ambitious Capricorn on the Ascendant according to simplified chart regression. Mudgett's behavior was likened to that of a dictator. The Moon in his chart, indicative of his needs, was in Leo—associated with a need for attention or validation. Another dictator, one with even greater ambitions, we remember as the man who took Nazi Germany to war against the world. Both he and Mudgett were born under the Zodiac sign of Taurus, a sign that is known not to stop once it gets going. Both had Capricorn on a Personal Point. For Mudgett it was the rising sign, for the other it was the Moon—the need to control.

Allegedly, Mudgett was bullied around age six. I have yet to encounter a horoscope with a Designer sign on the Ascendant whose owner did not fall victim to some form of bullying or violence at an early age. Unfortunately, they also appear to have a strong need to take revenge for perceived wrongdoings against them or against a cause they believe in. The majority of bullying victims with a Designer sign on the Ascendant I spoke to admitted to having bullied or acted violently against others including siblings.

If Mudgett needed a context to plan his ultimate revenge, the bullies of his childhood seem to have provided it quite willingly. The human mind can not be expected to speak up or even retaliate against victimization instantly, especially at a young age when the brain still has years of emotional maturation ahead. We see it in sexual assault victims who may hesitate to come forward for sometimes decades, and who, at a young age, appear to have no recollection of their trauma at all. From an astrological perspective, in Mudgett's case there must have been careful planning of his actions thanks to the Taurus mindset, arrogance from the Leo Moon—and a keen sense of death from the placement of the Moon in the Eighth house, associated with death and rebirth. Did Mudgett seek to fulfil the need to be reborn through the death of his victims? Did he seek fame through Moon in Leo—which was conjunct Jupiter, linked to success in any endeavor, especially when it comes to fulfilling a need?

When raised in a predominantly Designer influenced environment, one of the main challenges Builder and Visionary children face is that they are psychologically forced to overcompensate for their shortcomings. The Designer parent sees no difference between the capabilities of child versus adult and tends to make unrealistic demands accordingly. The resulting psychological trauma experienced by the child can reportedly lead to post-traumatic stress disorder. The result may be over-performing in what for normal people would be routine tasks, and an individual who tries too hard to please others.

In the right context, people with Designer influence in their horoscope contribute in a substantial and often beneficial way to life. Still, Designer sign influence on the Moon and Ascendant appears capable of distorting the impact of the Builder or Visionary mode on the Sun sign. The behavior may be dominant, overbearing and self-aggrandizing.

Life is based largely if not solely on negative and positive polarity. Observing people and their culture, religious beliefs, socioeconomic status etcetera and how they act, I can't help but conclude that all differences are simply a smokescreen for this very simple yet profound fact. Out of this observation came an equally profound realization: there are fundamentally just two kinds of people. In addition, it appears that in the process of gathering and synthesizing experience in life, one kind of person evolves gradually from one end of the spectrum to the other. We might even go as far as to conclude that those who have made it to the "other end" of this spectrum are here to help the ones who have not yet completed the journey, but that may go beyond the observable scope of our awareness. This arguably begs the philosophical question, who is right, and does it matter?

Ever since Sigmund Freud's efforts[295] at analyzing the mind, people have wanted to be able to identify others. Personality tests like Myers-Briggs[296] and DiSC[297] are among the more established[298] that were created for this purpose. How many personality tests are designed appears to ignore that personality is to a large extent determined at birth. Fortunately, research is ongoing as to how the complex interaction of, among others, early childhood memories, trauma, education, exposure to role models or lack thereof, nutrition and physical development and exposure to harmful pollutants affect neurological development and thus behavior.

A good example of something that has emerged recently may be the concept of neurodiversity.[299] It is a way of acknowledging that there is (much) more to diversity than skin color and gender. At one time, I worked for a company that introduced this concept with much of the usual excitement that commonly accompanies new corporate initiatives: consultants were brought in to give lectures on the topic, materials were distributed and posted on the company's Intranet, and people walked around with that warm fuzzy feeling after one of those seminars where people sat in a room with their eyes closed for three minutes observing their mindfulness as if a new world had opened up for them. At least, I did for the simple reason that I had seen it all before.

In the late seventies and into the nineties, finding oneself was a popular thing to do for members of the executive suite in many corporations. Top executives would trot the globe in search of the latest mindfulness, corporate wellbeing and purpose-driven workshops and retreats. I was involved with several of the conference centers that hosted these workshops and got to meet the people who came to deepen their understanding emotions and spirituality, and how it could ultimately benefit the bottom line.

Neurodiversity is a broad concept. If someone is sensitive to light and performs best in an office where the lights are dimmed, accommodations may need to be made, for instance. If another person has a traumatic history of loudly arguing parents, they may be more sensitive to the lively discussions about a new product launch, especially when there is disagreement. With the introduction of neurodiversity, we learn that people are not robots. It is an opportunity to identify barriers to optimal productivity, collaboration and success.

How we perceive others is determined by our own unique perspective, which may change over time. Perspective is based on a situation and our own, very personal interpretation of it. The documentary *Brain Games* provides many excellent and fun examples of this.[300] If we see ourselves as honest, we may one day encounter a situation that challenges that perspective. In *(Dis)honesty – The Truth About Lies*, Dan Ariely shares that research participants cheated less on an exam when their perspective was adjusted by being told in advance that the school had a policy against unethical behavior—even though such a policy didn't actually exist.

What may seem to be fairly innocent, albeit frustrating, differences between people in one setting can easily become multi-million dollar problems in another. Some may see government as an "evil empire of bureaucrats ready to suck the life out of every undertaking." Ideally, government is a representation of the people it serves. The laws and regulations that government sets are the result of a process of negotiation that aims to define what is best for the people. What is best inevitably changes over time. For instance, when the first mass produced cars were introduced, the global population was around 1.7

billion[301] Air pollution from car exhaust gases may not have been on the mind of many.

Still, that didn't stop the invention of the battery powered car. Between the gas and electric powered car, which type got the first speeding ticket? The latter. A taxi in New York City got the distinctive honor of allegedly going a speedy 8mph. About a century later, more than seven billion people call Earth home, many of whom drive gasoline powered cars. The government decided that it needs to do something to combat "climate change." One car manufacturer whose name shall remain anonymous came up with a solution for this dilemma: a tool called "defeat device." It consisted of a software trick that could detect when the car was being tested for emissions in a laboratory setting.[302]

Behavior may be adopted by others because it is seen as the norm. The question becomes, who sets the norm, and who gets to challenge it? This is how each of the three modes considers survival:

Designer - survival of me (A)

Builder and Visionary - survival of the collective (B)

Watch for those who hide their own characteristics by temporarily adopting that of another. There is a term for it: Acquired Situational Narcissism.[303] Maybe a situation challenges us to choose between two perceived evils. Maybe we call our choice the "best" and vilify everyone who chooses differently. Maybe we sometimes get to justify a choice before friends or business associates. How do we react when they claim we may have made a bad choice: by digging in, or by being flexible?

The argument has been made that great leaders have flexibility as a character trait, and that those who eventually sink the ship do not. Sometimes we may not have all the information at our disposal that would allow us to make a perfect decision. Yet, life must go on so we choose based on what we know. The moment to change direction might come when new, substantially more relevant information becomes known that would not only benefit us now but also in the future. Not only do top executives deal with this kind of dilemmas, many of us deal with these kinds of situations on a daily basis—especially on a tight budget. Astrological indicators of limited flexibility in decision making as shown in the horoscope may be the Moon in Aries (focus on self, associated with a need to be number one); the Moon in Gemini (when stressed, being too critical of others), the Moon in Libra (social detachment), Taurus rising (single minded, determined), Scorpio rising (tenacious, "still waters run deep"), and Aries Ascendant (takes the initiative and discourages anyone who is too slow, "shoot first, no need to ask questions").

How does somebody with a Designer sign amidst their Big 3 experience frustration? This is the story of a person with Gemini Sun, Scorpio Moon and Aries rising: "I just came out of a six year relationship with a Pisces—Pisces Sun and Moon, Taurus rising. The relationship took a severe emotional toll on me, leaving me at psychological rock bottom. This is what happened…

1. Breakdown in communication: In the beginning, we had deep conversations about our interests, family, and life goals. After a few months, the effort faded on their end. I kept pushing for connection. They withdrew emotionally, and after a few years, it felt like they weren't even present in the relationship anymore.

2. Emotions over logic: Most arguments were about them processing things emotionally while I relied on logic. Even when I didn't fully understand their perspective, I listened. If I ever expressed emotions in a way they didn't like, it became a problem. There was a lot of gaslighting and dismissal of how I felt.

3. Withdrawal: They were completely detached, cheated on me and ghosted me. They would disappear for long periods without explanation, and when I eventually asked about it, their responses were vague.

4. Apathy: Unable to confront problems directly. Whenever I brought up a concern, they got defensive. If the issue repeated itself and I pointed it out, I would get a half-hearted apology before we fell back into the same dysfunctional cycle.

I loved their creativity and empathy, but I suffered deeply at the hands of their neglect." —*Anonymous*

How should we interpret this? The rising sign for everyday living is more important than is often acknowledged. When we wake up, our rising sign is how we face the day. The Pisces partner had a fixed rising sign: slow, and stubborn or determined. Aries on the rising sign for the subject means an energetic, initiative taking side of the personality. Communication in a relationship involves needs (Moon), wants (Sun) and that all important rising sign, which, for all intents and purposes, is practically invisible to ourself—that is, the Pisces partner may not have known how stubborn they were.

Scorpio Moon goes deep—it needs to control through knowing. Our Gemini Sun subject sought balance in a partner with lack of fire, but that balance came at a cost. A second factor is that Designer signs speak a different "emotional language." That may sound strange, but people who do not have a Designer sign on their Big 3 can't fully comprehend what somebody with at least one Designer sign on the Big 3 is saying. There is always something getting lost in translation.

In addition, Pisces is Water and Gemini is Air. Pisces men tend to feel uncomfortable with all that feeling they are doing all day long. There is a lot of information they are processing in addition to words and visual cues. Gemini is much more direct and to the point. Our Gemini Sun subject was right in teaming up with Pisces for the other "half" of the data in the environment, but for the other reasons mentioned it sounds like it was tough keeping up with our subject.

History is full of examples of the contribution the Designer personality makes: a great spirit of invention, especially Aries. Driven to an extreme, the Designer may be quick to argue that the solution their competition offers is weak and should be ignored, while secretly adopting the most useful features others have come up with. The result may be social disharmony, discord, economic strife, and war. At the foundation of these and other social struggles is fear—fear of lack, fear that someone will take something away. It is not that this fear is entirely baseless: you may build something, and nature may take it away through the emergence of a pest, fire, flood, tornado, earthquake and similar disasters. How could we possibly cope with these scenarios? There is one industry that figured it out. One group of people that combines the power of money with the principle that we who are willing help out when our fellow citizens have met Mr. Misfortune can do so pretty much effortlessly: the insurance industry. Still, they are not alone.

There is another mechanism through which you can help your fellow citizen in need: charity. You may generously help someone in need or you may donate to an organization that exists to fulfill this very specific desire that characterizes us as human. And yet, there is charity by you and then there is charity by "them." What is the difference? They may purposely create circumstances that deprive you of wealth. They may deceive you and make it appear they have the right solution and therefore attract the business you both aim for.

Take the case of William (Bill) Gates, co-founder of Microsoft Corporation. Accused of abusive trade practices, in *United States v. Microsoft Corporation*[304] Gates was challenged to put his company back on a straight, lawful path of business. For years, Microsoft appeared to create buggy software that people bought because it was cheap—all the while making Bill Gates a very rich man. Microsoft was accused of operating a monopoly, of undercutting competitors and of manipulating the code of its flagship Windows operating system so that competitors' products would be deemed inferior in the eyes of the consumer. Some familiar with Microsoft's practices allegedly said: "…remaining dominant and monopolistic after the trial, [Microsoft] had continued to stifle competitors and innovative technology."[305] During the trial, Microsoft Chairman Bill Gates was called "evasive and nonresponsive" by a source present at a session in which Gates was questioned on his deposition.[306] He reportedly argued over the definitions of words such as 'compete', 'concerned', 'ask', and 'we.'"[307] It seems best to consider Bill Gates, with a Scorpio Sun and Moon in Aries and Cancer rising in his horoscope, a Designer with a mission. With the Sun in a Builder sign, his mission does appear to have taken the path of the innovator.

Those in the financial industry, as we learned from recent economic setbacks, may know "better."[308] If their hiring practices attract bankers who spill money on prostitutes or drugs while getting themselves out of sheer arrogance and miscalculations into failed deals, they may not sue the drug dealer, they may just call the Treasury Department.[309] After the 2008 financial crisis, "The Obama administration's demands suggest it learned nothing from the financial crisis, which was caused partly by 'diversity' mandates and affordable housing mandates that encouraged lending to people with bad credit scores who later defaulted on their loans. Banks were under great pressure from liberal lawmakers to make loans to low-income and minority borrowers. For example, "a high-ranking Democrat telephoned executives and screamed at them to purchase more loans from low-income borrowers," *The New York Times* noted.[310]

Psychologists warn us that children who are the subject of unjustified ridicule or worse suffer harm. Studies appear to show the long term psychological damage to confidence, the ability to feel safe and to trust and to hope.[311] In addition, children who grow up in these types of circumstances may grow up suffering lifelong post-traumatic stress disorder similar to what soldiers may experience upon a return from war. There are theories that take this a step further, suggesting a transgenerational influence of stress on our DNA. Not to be dissuaded, Anne Ferguson-Smith, a geneticist at the University of Cambridge, UK, who co-led a recent study, decided to do some experiments on herself.[312]

The qualities of the Designer signs do not appear to discriminate. The Designer attributes are in the most fundamental and true interpretation of the term equal opportunity "employers:" they focus on the task at hand, they assemble the required people and resources and charge ahead. We can find their expression in people of all ranks of society regardless of financial means or spiritual accomplishment. Because of the amount of effort they often consider themselves to be making, when they have adopted narcissistic traits they may cultivate a climate in which they take most if not all of the credit.

Someone with a Capricorn influence—or a strong placement of the planet Saturn in the horoscope—may display a need for control. Capricorn Sun exerts control, withdraws, and comes across as the natural expert while hiding any lack of knowledge or experience. They may be ruthless and quietly ambitious. The person with the Moon in Capricorn needs control—whether over money, resources or you. The Ascendant in the sign of Capricorn may come across as a natural authority, as ambitious, ruthless and controlling, while failing to understand why the world around him pushes back because they mean well from their Sun sign. Saturn—the ruler of Capricorn—when it is in the first house can bring an element of control to the personality for any sign on the Ascendant.

With the Sun in Capricorn, it could be an individual who never takes "no" for an answer and who will walk right over anyone who thinks of uttering the word. As if any narcissist ever takes no for an answer anyway. Saturn in the first house may hide the true nature of the sign on the Ascendant as any Saturn placement brings both insecurity and need for control, discipline and structure. In its extreme, Saturn is also linked to outright abuse.

"I was sexually harassed and bullied multiple times by my peers and older adults from the moment I started working at a department store in town. The bullying was aggressive. After that, I worked many other blue collar minimum wage jobs. They were almost all the same: a very sexually charged environment. I remember getting approached casually by a male coworker who showed me a photo of his penis on his phone and asked if I wanted to hook up on our break.

When I said no, he insulted me. This happened at other jobs too. It's like an initiation process when the "new girl" comes along, all the guys (and also some women) want to have sex with you. I see why blue collar jobs have a very bad reputation and get very little respect. The hypersexuality and how they disrespect women is really bad and it is the reason why I will never work at them ever again. It's not safe at all because the coworkers get upset if you turn them down."
—*Anonymous*

HOW TO DEAL WITH A (TOXIC) NARCISSIST?

"We clicked very well. I think he probably knew that I was lying, but I think he liked that too." – Simon Napier-Bell, describing how he introduced himself to movie director Michelangelo Antonioni (born September 29) [313]

What is the difference between a dead narcissist and one who is still alive? I am sorry to disappoint you, but this is not a joke. A live narcissist can still change their attitude, pretend there has been "an accident," wait until a better moment to strike (again), or they may simply manipulate the situation and any "innocent" bystanders into convincing us we are wrong. In the case of a dead narcissist, all we have is an account of the situation most often as described by someone who also wasn't present as a witness. When we consider historical figures, how easy is it not to consider Napoleon Bonaparte a psychopath responsible for the death of about three million when we don't like him, and how easy is it not to paint him as the heroic figure who reformed France when we do?

As we saw earlier, the narcissist distinguishes themselves with focus: they concentrate on themselves and their project, whatever it is. Their critical advantage over an empath is that they are not troubled by setbacks and challenges like the latter can be. For the narcissist, there is less wasted time reminiscing over what went wrong because they easily blame someone else or a situation. If they feel guilty, it may hurt them just as much as anyone else unless they mastered the art of blame shifting by moving further on the sliding scale of narcissistic spectrum disorder towards psychopathy, from healthy to toxic narcissism.

What we feel when things are not going our way or when our purpose is out of alignment with the demands of others is tension. While men and women may each respond differently to tension—men by expressing anger when they have trouble self-regulating, women by talking it out with a trusted friend or by lashing out in public—narcissists differ in who they target. Let's explore with an example what happens when we get close enough that we can sense tension. Someone well known on the motivational speaking circuit as the "Ice Man" is Wim Hof, born April 20: "He ran a full marathon without training or water in a desert then rehydrated with beer."[314] Iceman Wim Hof is allegedly best known for his superhuman feats of enduring cold with twenty-six world records to his name including staying submerged in ice for almost two hours.

In the course of our lives, we may meet people who seem to have traits that set them apart from others: unusual confidence and affability, great moral rectitude, an intimidating intellect and, most importantly, a saintly aura. Only if we really pay attention and take a step back from their charismatic behavior may we notice an ever so slight exaggeration to these traits, as if the person is the main character in their own movie. Empathy may be used by the narcissist to gain your favor. Generally, it distracts and hides their narcissistic traits from public view.[315] In the case of Wim Hof, as an outsider we may be enthralled by the subject's demeanor and accomplishments which baffle and astound. Wim's immediate family, unfortunately, apparently is not so lucky. In a recent article, the Dutch paper *de Volkskrant* reported that his family suffered domestic violence.[316] It can happen to anyone and in any family situation. Who to believe and how to adjust our perspective are critical questions when deciding how to deal with a toxic narcissist.

Narcissism can be healthy (adaptive) or toxic (maladaptive). The narcissist can be grandiose (overt) in their expression, or vulnerable (covert), hiding the traits. Three additional types of narcissism that are often recognized are antagonistic narcissism, communal narcissism and malignant narcissism. How to deal with a narcissist is a question clients ask me a lot. To answer it, it may be best to revisit the definition of narcissism. Once we have done that, it may be best to consider whether we need to deal with a narcissist at all—or if we should rephrase the question like this: "How to deal with toxic behavior?"

If we define narcissism as "a personality disorder which gives the subject an unreasonably high sense of their own importance, resulting in the need for constant attention and admiration,"[317] it may seem that we cover far too many people. Areas where narcissists may be particularly active would be social media, the entertainment industry, politics, and finance—any field where frequent brain stimulation and circular conversations can provide a "feel-good sensation" that introverts and empaths reportedly have no explicit need for.

Narcissistic traits can easily mesh into a group or organizational culture so that it becomes very difficult to distinguish them from the practice of setting health boundaries perhaps a bit too aggressively. Not shying away from pushing back when someone seems to act in a narcissistic manner may be a quick way to resolve an issue. If the person immediately responds in a constructive fashion, recognizing that they may have come across as overbearing or inconsiderate, a concern could be immediately relieved.

Overt or grandiose narcissism may express itself as an abundantly outgoing personality, venturing into arrogance, entitlement, having an exaggerated self-image, needing frequent praise and admiration, showing exploitative and competitive signs, and overall lacking empathy. Covert narcissism, on the other hand, correlates to behavior that expresses low self-esteem, anxiety, depression, and shame. The person may be introverted and insecure, or suffer from low confidence—although these traits can be easily misinterpreted with victims of abusive behavior whose coping strategy was fawning, while introversion in and of itself is of course never to be considered a standalone narcissistic trait. The covert narcissist may also be excessively defensive, avoid confrontation, and have a tendency to feel as if they are the victim—or to play the victim.[318]

Malignant narcissism may be seen as a more vindictive and sadistic form of narcissism characterized by increased aggression when dealing with others, being paranoid, or by having increased anxiety about potential threats. When any form of toxic narcissism takes on a long term or institutional nature, we may consider it morphing into what is considered strategic narcissism. This may have a serious adverse impact on a local, regional, national or even international stage, implicating the interests and security of many stakeholders.[319]

The research that appears to have been conducted to date on the neuroscientific aspects of narcissism appears to show that the gray matter in the brain of the narcissist is not functioning in the same way as it does for the empath. In addition, the cerebral cortex—the thinking and reasoning part of the brain—appear to show abnormalities as well. Both these structures are considered involved in compassion for others.[320] As mentioned in the disclaimer, I am not an expert in the field, nor am I a licensed medical professional. Nevertheless, how can I not pose the question, What part of the brain may be considered causative—or at least correlative—for the disorder and to what extent—if we consider that narcissism presents as a spectrum. While the experts debate this question, let's see what we have to deal with on a virtually daily basis:

1. How the narcissist deals with reality appears to be fundamentally different from how an empath approaches life; when presented with an option they didn't consider, a narcissist is more likely to deny or even ridicule it.

2. Life is not a laboratory setting. Empaths and other narcissists have to deal with narcissism and toxic behavior on a virtually daily basis without the guidance of an expert.

3. Even if we knew that the brain is causally related to narcissism, how difficult if not impossible would be it be to restructure society in such a way that we keep narcissists, or at least toxic people, from making too many impactful decisions going forward?

Narcissism can present anywhere from a very personal obsession that otherwise does no harm—on the moderate end of the spectrum—to sociopathy at the extreme end of the spectrum. Narcissism can be immediately obvious in someone's behavior, or it can be difficult to detect such as with covert narcissism. The narcissist may like us and do no harm, or they may not. How toxic a narcissist is going to be is often difficult to predict. For several years I did volunteer work as a chef and catering manager for an organization. The organization had been started by an artist with a great vision: to combine creative workshops, personal development and nature. An old farmhouse in a quiet farmland setting had been converted by an army of volunteers. People from all over the country came to take classes and enjoy the peaceful surroundings. They attracted teachers from abroad and gained a reputation as one of the best educational facilities of its kind in the country.

Unfortunately, the long hours and heavy workload eventually took a toll on the founder despite having had a lot of support. A fund was established by the people who had been managing the financial aspects of the organization. This fund wanted to buy the property and take over the business. Negotiations ensued. Suddenly, the changed her mind. She became more involved in the day to day running of the organization than before. Her demeanor changed: she became more critical of everyone's contribution. Finally, the news broke: she refused to sell the property and the business to the fund. Instead, without telling anyone, she had accepted a bid from a private buyer. The organization was to fold: it was all over. The founder's birthday: April 3.

Reflecting on the founder's motivation, the consensus was that she had been unable to come to terms with the possibility that her brainchild was going to be more successful after she had let it go. The need for control and the want for recognition seemed too strong—she could not fathom letting anyone else share in that. It was heartbreaking for the many people who had contributed so much.

Antagonistic narcissism is considered a subset of narcissistic behavior that can involve callousness and aggression. These people tend to be excessively concerned with their own success coupled with a strong sense of entitlement which they defend in an aggressive manner. Antagonistic traits can manifest differently depending on the contexts—from aggressive behavior to using manipulation or coercion tactics over an extended period of time. Gaslighting is a term that is often used in this context.[321] When antagonistic traits verge into the realm of a social context, we can say that someone displays communal narcissistic traits—people who may become easily morally outraged, describe themselves as empathetic towards a specific demographic, and who react strongly to what they perceive as injustice without giving much thought to the broader picture or how much impact their actions (can) have.

If the toxic narcissist perceives life as a theater of war that they need to control, how does the healthy, adaptive narcissist consider life? The adaptive narcissist, and the cognitive empath, may see life as an adventure, whereas the somatic empath who is capable of feeling what others feel, and the affective empath, who responds to people's emotions, may see life and all of its manifestations as a big puzzle to be solved. These differences in perspective can have major implications as to how people solve problems on a day to day basis.

Whoever said that it costs nothing to be kind, seems to have never met a narcissist. Why confront someone who seems ignorant of the consequences of their actions? Reflecting on the principle of learning by example, the toxic person may have an extremely strong sense of how things need to be done. They may need very little exposure to make their way in the world. Their brain does not seem to work the same way as that of the empath—the cues it picks up from the environment serve only themselves. A good example of this may be the case of David Geffen, the ambitious music and movie executive who established

Geffen Records and DreamWorks. After a questionable start in the business, Geffen quickly rose to considerable fame in the music industry.

In 1970, Geffen co-founded Asylum Records. It was intended to be fair to artists while offering them career and artistic support. After a few years and having achieved considerable success, Geffen turned around and sold the label to Warner Communications without any prior indication he was going to let all his talent down. They were back to square one, at the mercy of the predatory tactics so common in the industry.[322] David Geffen was born February 21. His horoscope appears to have Cancer as the Rising sign, acutely in tune with his environment while occasionally feeling abandoned in personal relationships.

The behavior of the narcissist may only be corrected through instruction and command, with success being dependent on how much leverage one has. If you have ever dealt with a narcissist over an extended period of time, you may have had to communicate a need which they frequently ignored and perhaps ridiculed. On occasion, you may have had some success in getting the narcissist to briefly pay attention. A toxic narcissist may persist in ignoring you using any excuse they see fit. What might be the best strategy, confronting the person or the behavior? If we confront the person, their ego may feel threatened, possibly triggering retaliation. If we confront the behavior, we may signal that the person is not "bad" while simultaneously leaving them in control as to how to correct themselves. If they choose not to correct the behavior because they deny they are at fault, the next logical step may be to sever the relationship at the earliest opportunity.

When someone's behavior and attitude affect us, the narcissist may be considered to have turned into a toxic person. Yet, how do we know if we are affected? When we meet someone for the first time, we may have a gut feeling about them. When we start a new project with someone we already know, they may behave differently if it requires a skill they don't have. When we go on vacation with someone we only know in familiar surroundings, they may have a completely different attitude because they have never been there and they don't speak the language. When someone gets a promotion, they may start behaving differently because they feel pressure to perform. In other words, there are many ways in which people may behave differently from how we know them or expect them to behave.

If you are concerned that the psychiatric profession is leaving you hanging when it comes to predatory people, you are not alone. Dr. Karen Mitchell, Ph.D., wrote in an X post on June 28, 2024 that:

> "[m]any, many psychologists and psychiatrists are narcissists / psychopaths / predators" who "LOVE the control and power it gives them over people, the way they engage in manipulation, the ability to apply sadistic behaviours, all without being suspected and with the added delight of being able to use their professional role against the client if ever challenged or exposed."[323]

Leaving an issue with a toxic person unaddressed, experts appear to suggest, may have long term negative effects on our own psyche.[324] This long-term effect on the mind is reportedly potentially more harmful and debilitating than the impact a sudden, unexpected tragic event can have. Therefore, consider some of the reasons why we would want to confront an issue with a toxic person as soon as we are aware of it:

1. the alleged effect of emotional trauma on the brain as a result of interactions with a toxic person;

2. by ignoring the issue, we may lock ourselves into a state of learned helplessness;

3. the financial cost of treatment, including spending time being less productive, having to take time off due to burnout;

4. the effect of narcissistic behavior and the possible crimes committed by toxic people lowers the quality of life of ourselves and of the community; and

5. overall, the actions of a narcissist may contribute to significant personal and organizational costs.

When the mentality of the toxic person invades our place of work, we may witness what could possibly be best described as a marginalization of our rights as an individual because only they and their interests matter at the end of the day. The most commonly suggested remedy is to simply avoid them—to disconnect, disengage and to go no-contact. Experiencing stressful situations with a narcissist who turned into a toxic individual may not always be avoidable. The person may be part of your team and contribute critical skills, or they may be a family member. The number of narcissists in your situation may have passed a tipping point: their grip on the organization is so strong and pervasive that no-contact is a virtual impossibility unless you quit your job or move away.

> "White collar jobs often involve complex office relationships because everyone is sitting close to each other, which gives off the impression that everyone knows each other and all the stuff in their lives. [When sex is involved, i]t is no longer just a casual hook up; it defines you and builds a construct for your whole work experience. Hooking up with a coworker in a white collar job is tantamount to getting engaged; everyone at work will not only know all the ins and outs, but is also granted the privilege of open commentary at all times. Done once, condemned forever." —*Anonymous*

Contractual obligations can keep an empath attached to a toxic individual. When disengaging is not an option, let them seek another victim. Self-empowerment may be your best option and a logical approach your best bet. In my experience, any interaction with the toxic person must be accompanied by confident body language and proper phrasing of what needs to be said. This might be along the lines of, "It seems best to avoid making a decision because we don't seem to have all the facts," or, "How can we justify this since we have rushed to conclusions in the past and it has hurt us?" Giving someone the opportunity to reflect on your statement and own it may present an opportunity for cooperation. Many books have been written about dealing with narcissistic and toxic people, yet if you are a bit like me, you may think outside the box and appreciate an unexpected gem on negotiation tactics such as Chris Voss's *Never Split the Difference*. Voss presents his trials and errors in dealing with hostage situations, turning them into a remarkably useful method for dealing with difficult people in general.[325]

Because we can't always address the situation when we first become aware of it, let's see what happens when we hold a toxic person accountable at a later stage—after the damage has been done. A narcissist may throw anything plus the proverbial kitchen sink at us to advance their cause. A common technique used by narcissists is gaslighting. Therefore, it doesn't really matter how well prepared you are. What does matter is:

    A. how we conduct ourselves;

B.   which constructive arguments in our (and our organization's) favor we present, while stressing quality over quantity—repeating the high quality argument ad nauseum if necessary; and

C.   how well our language respects their position.

Avoiding terms such as "should" and "need to do" may help us prevent getting bogged down with the toxic person, while words such as "it seems best to…" may facilitate progress. The important thing is to let the toxic person's self-centered mind reach the conclusion that the decision is theirs—even though we planted it in their mind.

Examples of what NOT to say in a discussion with a narcissist:

- Let's focus on [person's name] solution
- You/We should behave more like/do this…
- The organization needs to go this route…
- I don't want to do this
- I don't feel like discussing your concerns right now

Examples of constructive dialogue with a narcissist:

- It is best to avoid … if we don't want to …
- It does not seem to be the right time to discuss this
- It seems best if we postpone our discussion until later [when things have calmed down]

How can we best coax someone to adopt a particular course of action? Inserting the word "because" seems to be a very successful approach. When you need more money for a project, try this with a boss who always objects: "We need to spend more to get this to work, because we are not going to meet the deadline. How can we get $10K more right now?" Be creative and practice with different reasons why you need the money, including one that may be entirely unrelated. In the reverse situation, when a toxic person pressures us to go along with their idea, they may use literally anything we say against us. Rather than arguing at length why we can't oblige, may be better off saying no more than we have to in order to get our argument across.

How to deal with the emotional aftermath of an encounter with a toxic person is another story. One day I suggested to a friend that music can be great therapy. Their response was less than enthusiastic if not outright condescending. If you ever consulted a career counselor and heard, upon sharing what your aspirations were, that it would be best to pursue a career path along lines you would never ever consider (without explaining why), then you know that not all experts are empathic to your cause. Immediately after a challenging encounter, I may feel down and deflated. I may try to justify a statement and convince the other person that I made a valid point. Or I may decide to get back at them next time when they make a suggestion.

Neither of these tactics have ever worked in my favor. Unfortunately, I learned something else: people can be incredibly set in their ways and averse to any information that challenges their position. The best way to handle a relational setback like this seems to be one or more of these options: avoiding off-topic conversations, reducing the frequency of interaction with the person, and disengaging altogether.

It may be difficult to identify a narcissist at first because they prefer not to be known as such. The covert narcissist may disguise their true intentions until they have got us under their spell. There is nothing wrong with working for and learning from a narcissist as long as we keep our sanity. We all have bills to pay. Make sure to have a healthy outlet for pent up stress and don't put too much strain on our family. But what to do when the tables are turned, when you are paying someone for a service? Anyone can potentially fall victim to the spell of a toxic narcissist. One such a scenario is an emotional one—wedding planning. She was well-presented in social media. Her Web site featured all the important aspects of a beautifully organized wedding. People had left positive reviews while prospective customers were invited to come see the venue where she was going to organize the next event. In other words, nothing seemed amiss. Still, in the north-eastern English town of Hull, Dana Twidale would proceed to defraud reportedly more than a thousand brides and grooms who were eagerly anticipating the most important day in their lives together.[326]

Telling you to watch out for red flags is easier said than done. Narcissists learn from each other's mistakes too. A birth date is not always available as a way to gauge who you are dealing with. Trusting your gut instinct may be a last resort. What if you checked for red flags and the offer seems just right? Ask yourself again, is it "just right" or "too good to be true?" The swindler does not necessarily go for large amounts, at least not at first. As a wedding planner, Dana Twidale offered a service that suited a low budget. However, for the couples who were anticipating that magic moment, even seven hundred or so in the local currency for decorations, tables, and a tent was a lot. For those who "splurged," the result was just the same: their entire savings was lost.

Just when they needed her the most, Twidale skipped town for a beach vacation. While Twidale was on the beach, her clients were confronted with venue reservations that Twidale did not follow through on, with caterers who did not show up and other disasters. How did they deal with it? People chipped in from everywhere at the very last minute. Many had their wedding day "saved" by the contributions from generous strangers. Even though Twidale went to prison for the fraud she committed, no money was recovered. The only one to get "compensation" was the state: the opportunity to keep a bad person off the streets for a few years. A victim of this kind of abuse is literally left to their own devices—live and learn.

Earlier we met someone who pretended to be an empath only to get carried away with an obsession for a perfect society while ignoring the skeletons in the closet. As a politician, Olof Palme appears to have had widespread admiration for his vision of justice and fairness. Born January 30, 1927, his horoscope reportedly featured an Aquarius Sun, while the Moon and rising sign were in Sagittarius. As you can tell, there was no Designer sign on the Big Three, but there are two fire signs demanding our attention.

Who else has two fire signs? Neil Armstrong, the first man to set foot on the Moon comes to mind—a very different life with very different aspirations. For Armstrong, the air quality in his chart shows up in the rising sign: Gemini. Fire in his chart presents as Leo for the Sun and Sagittarius as the Moon. Both men had a need to be respected for their opinions. While Armstrong wanted a "stage" to perform—which he got as the star of the first Moon landing—Palme wanted social change. For Armstrong, Gemini rising is associated with an intellectual connection to others. In contrast, the fire sign on Palme's chart's Ascendant made his enthusiasm shine through and relatable for a country used to long, dark winters.

Where did it go "wrong" for Palme? The fire element on the rising sign is like a fire breathing dragon—and many times impossible to switch off in combination with an equally fiery, needy Moon. In other words, if you ever run into someone who won't take no for an answer and keeps going down a particular path of destruction no matter what, despite having displayed good intentions at first, chances are there is some fire in their horoscope. Their mission may just have to run its course. Despite having made solid political connections in the Soviet Union and South Africa, it was not just the CIA who reportedly wanted Palme out of the picture. His communist allies allegedly wanted him gone too.

Empathy can be a powerful antidote for the damage toxic narcissism can wreak on society. Yet, the toxic narcissist may weaponize even that. In fact, the toxic narcissist may use any positive character trait against their target. Empathy has become a popular theme of late. In light of increasing social anxiety, alienation and exaggerated differences, it is no longer differences of opinions that get some into fierce arguments. Hate is quickly becoming a focus of policy makers of those who seek to address prejudice.[327] This is an interesting development, especially when we consider the many victims of domestic abuse whose cases have increasingly been ignored—albeit in a different part of the United Kingdom.[328] Law enforcement and the judiciary have a limited capacity to deal with societal problems. How does the toxic narcissist take advantage of this?

Compassion may be a solution even though empathy is the buzzword. Let's make clear that being an empath and having empathy are two different things. Anybody can have empathy, the question is how deep it runs. An empath may sympathize with a cause and have compassion for their fellow human. Healthy empathy means recognizing healthy boundaries. An empowered empath does not facilitate lawlessness, weakness or an "anything goes" attitude. Instead, the hallmark of the constructive empathic approach is to recognize limitations, the rule of law and the existence of contracts, and responsibilities. Empathy recognizes the root of narcissistic behavior as much as the plight of the victim. Narcissism ultimately only benefits the narcissist. The empath who supports the narcissist in their quest may thus ultimately not be an empath, but a toxic narcissist in "sheep's clothing."

Whatever the outcome, powerful forces are at play. Forces that challenge our technological ingenuity, our compassion and our resoluteness. Do we hold the psychopaths who concocted the Covid-19 vaccination fiasco accountable? Do we tackle electric vehicles before they get a chance to do even more damage to the environment than they have already? I am referring to mining for precious metals and pollution from car tires and toxic brake dust.[329] What is the truth about power generation, and how soon will nuclear fusion be online to make a meaningful difference? The good news is that practically not a day goes by when yet another "miracle" development is announced in energy storage and transmission, especially when it comes to the discovery of chemical and material properties suitable for use in the field.[330]

What stops innovative leaps in technology from becoming mainstream? Apart from unforeseen technical challenges that take longer to be overcome, prove insurmountable, or are trumped by even more efficient and economically feasible alternatives, vested interests, obviously. It takes courage to take the next step and abandon what appears to lack in suitability prematurely. A kaizen or continuous improvement mindset intrinsic to Japanese society may be one solution, recognizing the critical contribution of inventors who have the best interests of society at heart may be another. Toxic narcissism should not have a role here.

Another, more insidious factor preventing an invention from reaching the production stage is (industrial) espionage. For the outsider, accurate birth data may be hard to come by. For our investigation, it seems best we turn to one of the most notorious spies in recent history once again: Kim Philby. We met Philby earlier when we reminisced on the implications of intelligence operations around and after World War II. We already know that he was born on January 1. Now we are ready to add the year and location: 1912, Ambala, India. Thanks to accurate record keeping by the British, we also know that his time of birth was reported to be 2:30pm. This gives him the chart presented in Figure 2. If you follow PurposeDay on Reddit, you may have seen one or two of our posts on relocated charts. The topic of relocation is outside the realm of our discussion here, but if you are interested there is a bit more information on this in the epilogue. A relocated chart would arguably add nuance to the interpretation of Philby's natal chart and life, except we are not discussing the merits of his life, we are primarily interested in his motivation as shown in the Big Three: Sun (wants), Moon (needs) and Ascendant (mask).

Figure 2. Birth Chart of Kim Philby[331] (Koch Houses)
January 1, 1912 – Ambala, India; 2:30p.m. local time

Harold Adrian Russell "Kim" Philby had an illustrious career as a journalist and spy, traveling the world and mingling with the rich and powerful. Philby's horoscope's Big Three is all Earth—ambition, determination and bold, in-your-face charm thanks to the Moon and its aggressive conjunction with the planet of war, Mars. Saturn is in the twelfth house, associated with being very comfortable operating alone. Venus in the seventh house of one-on-one relationships facilitated the charm he radiated with Moon on the Ascendant, which means being very attuned to one's environment and displaying emotional receptivity to others.

While Philby's chart's Moon on the Ascendant may have given him psychic abilities, Venus on the Descendant made it appear as if he held others in high regard without any effort on his part: Venus in the seventh house is associated with sacrifice of one's values to others. Venus "rules" the chart as a result of Taurus being the rising sign which gives this planet additional significance. In addition, Venus rules the chart's sixth house of employment in Libra. Negotiation and relationships featured strongly in Philby's professional life. With Mars so close to the Ascendant—albeit just over one degree in the twelfth house with this birth time—we could argue that he was capable of charming someone one moment and kill them the next. The target would never have seen it coming from a twelfth house Mars, a placement associated with all things hidden from view.

Alternately, Mars in the twelfth house tends to be correlated with working behind the scenes and not being able to properly judge the effect of one's actions. Whether his professional recognition comes from Saturn in the twelfth, associated with his Sun sign, or Mars, how appropriate wasn't it that it came after his death when his face appeared on a Soviet postage stamp in 1990? As karma would have it, that was one of the last official acts of the communist regime as it collapsed shortly thereafter.

Moon in Taurus tends to give the individual an introverted nature while its placement right on the Ascendant, as we saw, connotes an easy rapport with the environment. As we look further, we see that Philby's chart radiates all the right elements necessary for a career that has elements of being an outsider or eccentric with the sign of Aquarius on the cusp of the tenth house (MC), using unusual or hi-tech means to get the job done while being exposed to sudden changes of plan and location while on the road—Uranus in the ninth house. In short, very much a James Bond type of career that required resolve and discipline in high stakes negotiations. MI6, his primary employer, was allegedly heavily infiltrated by Soviet spies which gave Philby plenty of coverage for his clandestine spying activities for the U.S.S.R. He was recruited by the Russians in 1934 and did not come under official suspicion until 1951 when he publicly resigned from British intelligence.

In 1949, Philby was transferred to Washington, District of Columbia. His contact within the CIA was reportedly also a Soviet spy. Philby was exonerated from any wrongdoing he was accused of behind the scenes by the U.K. Foreign Secretary in 1955. He ended up in the Soviet Union in 1963 after finally having been unmasked. He died there in 1988 having enjoyed twenty five years of peaceful retirement. Was this Capricorn the only one successful at manipulating public and professional opinion in his favor? The more politically correct question would be, was this Designer sign the only one?

―――――――――――――――――

"I am not easy. I am difficult, sarcastic, stubborn,
independent, emotional, and a pain in the ass at times. But *if
you treat me right*, I am also the most loving, supportive, fun,
understanding, naughty, humble and loyal person you will
ever find." —said an anonymous Capricorn; emphasis by the
author…by the way, who defines "right"?

―――――――――――――――――

Let's jump back into the mundane, a situation where we are more likely to
personally encounter the Designer influence. The power-hungry manager may
prevent a staff member from doing their best work. If you work in an office, or
know someone who does, how often do you have to ask colleagues to be quiet
so that you can think? The open office floor plan was borne out of the idea that
cubicle walls and offices might be downright "fascist." The spaciousness and
flexibility of an open plan, architects like Frank Lloyd Wright thought, would
free office dwellers from the confines of what they considered boxes. Many
companies saw an ideal opportunity to use the new design as a way to pack as
many workers as they could into an ever shrinking amount of floor space per
worker, in theory saving a nice bundle that could be passed on to the equity
incentive bonus pool for the decision makers.[332]

Some consequences of more than a hundred years of exposure to unwanted
and unwarranted noise from colleagues, insults from managers howled at the
unwitting employee from across the floor, and others, are still poorly understood
yet alone accepted: conflict, high blood pressure and increased staff turnover.
While research into the effects of the military drill exercise equivalent of
perceived productivity boosters is ongoing, what we know so far suggests that
open, flexible, and activity-based spaces make people more visible and more
agitated at the same time. Rather than fostering increased meaningful
interaction, there is less of it while more staff than ever opt to work from home
in order to avoid both visual and auditory distractions—as well as the physical
presence of their micromanaging, toxic-narcissistic boss.[333]

Neurodivergence is a concept that has gained significant traction in recent
years together with diversity, equity and inclusion initiatives. While the latter
has since been exposed as highly discriminatory towards a certain demographic
and is on its way out, the former does not appear to discriminate in and of

itself—rather, it takes a toxic narcissist to make life miserable for people who are (especially) sensitive to noise, redundant and unrelated visual stimuli, toxic behavior and other workplace distractions.

People who feel naturally insecure and intolerant of those who need peace and quiet, for example, to perform at their best, may be more inclined to deprive another person of that which they can't do their best without. The timekeeper or manager who insists on talking to everyone on speakerphone, preferably at the highest setting because they (a) need to emphasize to the team how important they are, or (b) they deny that they are losing their hearing, is not just a nuisance and may be best sent packing, they are usually also a drain on the bottom line, directly and indirectly due to an increased error rate in the work of people who are in their line of sight and the resulting reduction in productivity.[334]

Loud people are known to hide inadequacies because a booming voice can be not just a physical attribute, but also an offensive weapon: how does it not instill fear in many a subordinate? Addressing the issue respectfully and effectively before it makes the most competent employee quit may be the best option. Using proper language, choosing a proper location to sit down with the offender, and timing are three critical elements in resolving the problem. The most well-respected managers speak softly, choose their words wisely, and know when someone needs an additional push or encouragement. How else can we limit the damage that the "commanding officer" of the open floor plan a.k.a. the boss?

Some companies, including law firms whose work often demands confidentiality and privacy, have eagerly followed the open space idea in order to save on real estate costs. Noise mitigating paneling has found its way into the most modern of offices. What effect does it seem to have? Apparently, none whatsoever other than increased job dissatisfaction. Timekeepers and their secretaries, professional staff and support staff alike complain about the distractions of working in the office. The culprit of the latest and "greatest" in open, participatory floor plan design are managers—not revenue generating employees—whose mandate it is to save costs rather than increase productivity.

How do they deal with the stress and associated health issues? Mounting workers' compensation claims, increased absenteeism, turnover and presenteeism, and "quiet quitting" may be some of the consequences. Yet, there appears to be little experimental research investigating the effects of office noise on things like cognitive performance, physiological stress and mood. The results of one study using heart rate, skin conductivity and AI facial emotion recognition, appears to show the effects that distracting noise has is real. A significant causal relationship between open-plan office noise and physiological stress was reportedly discovered.[335, 336] Unless business owners and managers start taking the issue seriously, employees may continue to suffer under the burden of the toxic attitude that led to the current state of affairs in many companies.

"We have always done it this way" may not be the best argument for maintaining the status quo. "Always" is relative, very relative. The industrial revolution is only a few hundred years old. People have been around for thousands longer. We are only now beginning the understand the physical and emotional context in which the human mind thrives, recognizing simultaneously that we are all different with different needs and sensitivities, which may vary over time and depending on the contract we have with them.

> *"If people base their identity on identifying with authority, freedom causes anxiety. They must then conceal the victim in themselves by resorting to violence against others."*
> —Arno Gruen

THE RULES AGAIN

"C-PTSD is associated with intrusive flashbacks, feelings of panic, overwhelming feelings of rage, debilitating feelings of hopelessness, chronic feelings of shame, a harsh and unrelenting "inner critic," and a lack of trust in other people." —Arielle Schwartz[337]

Before we look at the next step, let's revisit that one thing that prevents chaos and brings order to our universe: the existence of rules. When rules are broken, the trauma inflicted may be different from what you and I acknowledge as a logical consequence. Physical trauma is widely recognized by the legal system. Emotional, mental and spiritual trauma seem much further behind in being acknowledged. Post-Traumatic Stress Disorder (PTSD) is well documented, but what about the effects of ongoing stress inflicted by a manipulative parent, spouse or boss: being less able to concentrate, suffering from poor sleep, being inexplicably emotionally triggered, or often being in flight, freeze, or fight mode. These are things that can adversely impact your wellbeing, career and relationships.

There is a term for it: Complex PTSD[338] (or cPTSD), reportedly coined by Dr. Judith Herman of Harvard University in 1988.[339] The three traditional coping mechanisms of fighting a threat, fleeing or freezing are well recognized. Pete Walker[340] appears to have been the first to recognize a fourth trauma coping mechanism: fawning, or giving the impression of cooperating with the perpetrator.[341] To this day, fawning seems severely underestimated in the therapeutic arena—and perhaps even frowned upon—though it appears to be most effective in facilitating a broader insight into the perpetrator's motivation. Possibly, fawning may also lead to a better remedial, prevention or exit strategy. Dr. Glenn Patrick Doyle reminds us that children may be especially vulnerable to adopting fawning as a coping mechanism when he says:

> "Kids who gr[o]w up in complex trauma very often go
> through life feeling we missed the chapter on 'how to human'

in the user manual every other person seemed to get. So we've been making it up as we go along, hoping for the best—but worried we're gonna get found out."[342]

A factor that adversely impacts behavior—often quite strongly yet imperceptibly—and that gets very little attention may be prolonged exposure to stress.[343] Stress can result from exposure to people who break the rules intended to maintain order. Perhaps in effect similar to cPTSD, long-term stress seems to have a strange way of affecting the mind: it can make me tune out things I have become accustomed to due to repeated exposure, while it may make me act irrationally angry at a new, unexpected trigger. I may have become conditioned to tolerate certain stress factors, yet when I least expect it, I might still be caught off guard when an amygdala hijack strikes in response to an unexpected "threat."[344]

"Amygdala hijack" is a term originally coined by psychologist Daniel Goleman[345] to describe an immediate, overwhelming emotional response out of proportion to the initial stimulus because it has triggered an emotional threat disproportionate to the stimulus. The amygdala perceives a threat and triggers a fight-or-flight response before the cortical centers can fully assess the situation. In essence, the amygdala "hijacks" the rational response process. This tends to lead to impulsive reactions to perceived—that is, not necessarily actual—threats. Afterwards, we may feel guilty, ashamed or embarrassed.

What effect can nutrition have on our capacity to deal with stress? A few years ago, Jules Bernstein of the University of California set out to answer this question. Soybean oil is a widely used additive in many processed foods. In fact, it is considered the most widely used compared to all vegetable and seed oils allegedly associated with the international, Western health crisis. "The hypothalamus regulates body weight via your metabolism, maintains body temperature, is critical for reproduction and physical growth as well as *your response to stress*," said Margarita Curras-Collazo, a University of California at Riverside associate professor of neuroscience and lead author on the study (emphasis mine).[346] What implications might this study have? While mice are generally used for studies that aim to replicate the effect of a compound on humans, it is important to note there is no proof the oil causes disease or that the findings may be applied to humans. As a cautionary note, the researchers stress (pun intended) that the findings do not apply to other soy products or to other vegetable oils.

Attempts at avoiding the stress associated with poor health may backfire. The need for doctor visits, managing one's diet and earning enough to pay medical bills may have an effect on our behavior in every other area of our life. Arguments about finances with loved ones may lead to separation and divorce, followed by loneliness and decreasing life satisfaction. Dr. Chris Knobbe, founder and president of the Cure AMD Foundation—a nonprofit dedicated to the prevention of age-related macular degeneration—appears to suggest that seed oils are the unifying mechanism behind westernized chronic diseases like heart disease, obesity, cancer and diabetes.[347] What is behind the proliferation of seemingly inappropriate food additives such as soybean oil? It seems someone was looking for a way to address the nutritional needs of an ever increasing population.

The negative effects of soybean oil may not have been known at the time it was first used, but what should health organizations do now? They should perhaps reverse course and alert us at the very least. But that would mean admitting they may have been asleep at the proverbial wheel, possibly as a result of lobbying from the vegetable oil industry. The rule that stipulates soybean oil is incompatible with human health has been broken. Health organizations may fear risking their reputation. Instead, as recently as 2017, the United States Food and Drug Administration (FDA) authorized a health claim for soybean oil.[348,349] While international organizations such as the World Economic Forum alert us to the beneficial effect of a healthy diet, little research appears to be carried out on the effects of the most prolific of food additives in general—fats:

> "Over the last decade, a growing body of research has shown that diet can have a huge impact on our mental health. In fact, a healthy diet may even reduce the risk of many common mental illnesses." A November 7, 2022 article focuses on fermented foods and fiber instead.[350]

Reportedly, about one third of managers harbor unconscious fear which has been suggested to equate to a $36 billion productivity loss in the United States alone for failing to follow the rules—fear that higher ups will criticize them, or worse, if they don't meet a production or sales target.[351] Failure to follow the rules can have direct financial consequences as well. In business this is called non-compliance. An area where the consequences can be particularly grave is in money-laundering, when people who don't follow the rules against the distribution of illegal drugs, for example, seek to reintroduce illicit financial gains back into the official, legal financial system—for which another set of rules exists.[352]

Arguably, in any financial system that has ever existed there may have been some kind of deviation from the rules—a black market, corruption, bribery, and together, fraud. Currency can be an extremely efficient means of transferring value from one party to another. When I want to buy some meat for my family, I don't have to speculate or barter with the seller what they would like to exchange it for. Yet, the biggest challenge in any trade is establishing value—this challenge is not eliminated by substituting currency for tangible goods. The introduction of an increasingly global economy as a result of the expansive trading practices of the Europeans back in the late 1400s has led to a substantial influence of their culture and technology on the rest of the world. With it came a rapidly increasing expansion in the field of fraud—an expression of inefficiency in the economy and someone acting on a difference in perspective.

After the establishment of the original thirteen colonies in America, there appears to have been a desire to establish a more humanistic society respectful of individual rights. People worked hard to produce food, make tools and clothing, and to live in freedom despite an ongoing struggle with the British Crown and the original inhabitants of the land.[353] Craftspeople were well respected; every craftsperson was an expert in the full production process. For instance, a cordwainer (shoemaker) would personally execute all the steps necessary to create a pair of shoes. With the advent of the Industrial Revolution in Britain, manufacturing in America would not be left behind. In the 1830s, a new set of rules applying to business was introduced pertaining to profit, pricing, market expansion, innovation and risk. Piracy at sea is a phenomenon well established throughout history. With the introduction of the industrial manufacturing process, accompanied by national and international marketing, all of a sudden piracy of goods and intellectual property also became lucrative.[354]

The introduction of industrialized manufacturing brought a monumental change for trades and craftspeople alike. No longer would production be handled by a single person, skilled in their craft initially through years of apprenticeship and working as a journeyman. Each production process would be divided into carefully orchestrated steps, each to be carried out by a specialist whose wage could be carefully managed and controlled. The humanistic approach largely died out alongside this development. Rather than being performed in a small shop in the local community, production would now be concentrated in large factories outside of town and out of sight of anyone who had an interest in the welfare of the worker.[355] Free market competition for labor ideally ensures that any benefit from optimized production methods improves the lives for all, except perhaps when management takes a utilitarian approach whereby labor is expendable.

Rather than exploring the many nuances of labor practices over the past two hundred years and how they affected government policy, let us reflect on the far end of the spectrum of worker welfare: communism. When a mechanistic (read, narcissistic) approach in a capitalist society takes the upper hand, the engine of the economy—the worker and consumer—may suffer. Consequences may include:

1. substituting safe, high quality ingredients in food production for cheap, toxic versions that harm the health of the worker;

2. cutting corners in the production process and skimping on safety measures;

3. manipulating the cost of doing business by maintaining separate books for different stakeholders; and

4. paying workers less than the cost of living demands.

Environmental pollution can present another significant burden for the worker and the consumer alike. This burden often benefits the health care industry which is known to heavily lobby politicians.[356]

The capitalist system relies largely on government to remedy any harm done while stakeholders negotiate their way through a maze of legislation and fines. In an effort to remedy this power imbalance, communism seeks to level the playing ground. Unfortunately, without a reasonable mechanism to root out corruption, it too eventually succumbs to the realities of the market, power dynamics among the elite, and inefficient decision making. Meanwhile, a more egalitarian approach to economic inequality—for example, such as discussed in a recent paper on hyper-globalization[357]—is often dismissed by those who see it as a threat to their lifestyle or philosophy.

We may have to go back at least three thousand years to find a society that managed to handle climate change and economic crisis with any success.[358] An examination of two documented periods of climate change in the Middle East, between approximately 4,500 and 3,000 years ago, appears to reveal evidence of resilience and even of a flourishing society despite climate change. It seems that the success of every attempt to satisfy the needs of one group of stakeholders or another depends on their leverage of resources—economic, spiritual or military—and political power. Both can be manipulated through misinformation, the motivation for which eventually resides in the ever present personality attribute of fear.

An infamous enemy of capitalism, Karl Marx, for example, argued— reportedly without verification—that product value is proportional to labor time. Allegedly, he simply defined it to be true.[359] If only all economic uncertainty could be resolved as easily. No matter what political or economic model we choose, rules exist to prevent chaos. No matter the model, those who deny that the rules that maintain order apply to them seem to be the greatest danger to fair progress, economic success and sustainability. Then again, life is not supposed to be fair, or is it?

A Fair Tale of The Disgruntled Politician, in Three Acts

ACT ONE
in which a child receives a lesson from his father

FATHER: Son, listen to me.

CHILD: Yes father.

FATHER: Life is not fair. Never forget that.

CHILD: Yes father, life is not fair.

ACT TWO

in which the child turned adult runs for public office and loses the election;
he is told his opponent cheated

ADULT: [Expletive deleted] I will get the bastard!!!

ACT THREE

in which the adult wins the Presidency on his promise to "end the war"

ADULT: [Still remembering that lost election years earlier and his father's wise words] I will show the bastards, bomb that country to pieces. I will show you what's fair!

ACT FOUR

this was just added; karma came calling…

ADULT: I am not a crook!

———————————————

WHAT'S NEXT?

"People have GOT to know their limitations"

—Adopted from Clint Eastwood's character in the movie *Magnum Force*[360]

Imagine that you are in charge of beverages for a big party. When the guests arrive, for simplicity's sake, let's pretend you are serving just one drink but it has to be done right. The host has decided it will be a mixed juice drink. One ingredient will be just a splash and it has to be added after the glasses have been poured. If there is too much of it, you can't see it, but the drink will taste bitter and the guest will not like it. You practice with your team on a few glasses and it seems you have got this. Unfortunately, within ten minutes after serving the welcome drink, some people complain. You are embarrassed. You quickly give these people a new drink. Hopefully they won't tell the host.

A few years ago, a similar situation unfolded for the manufacturer of a vaccine. Except this time, the subjects were too young to tell if anything might be wrong. The result was not a bitter taste in the mouth, it was death for many babies within three days of having been administered the diphtheria-pertussis-tetanus (DTP) vaccine from Wyeth Laboratories (Wyeth). Fixing the situation was not possible—it is not possible to bring a dead baby back to life. Preventing a recurrence might have been. Instead of destroying the remaining vials from the bad batch, though, executives appear to have had a much more sinister solution.[361]

Who doesn't want to save money when the budget is tight? Which manager does not want to make their profit and loss statement look better for the quarterly presentation? While the manufacturer agreed to recall the lot of affected DTP vaccine vials, "their [next] concern was more about splitting up the vaccine lots to promote 'maximum variety of lot numbers'." That's right, the solution to save money and not destroy the affected vials was simply to distribute them over a large population so that people "might not notice a correlation." If they were caught, any government imposed fines would apply to a budget cycle far into the future, when revenue from product sales would have been long accounted for. In a letter from Alan Bernstein at Wyeth, dated August 27, 1979, the following statement introduced the plan:

> "After the reporting of the SID [Sudden Infant Death
> Syndrome] cases in Tennessee, we discussed the merits of
> limiting distribution of a large number of vials from a single
> lot to a single state, county or city health department and
> obtained agreement from the senior management staff to
> proceed with such a plan."

The strategy was aimed at improving public perception of Wyeth and its DTP vaccine. Our concern here is with the mindset behind executive decision making. If what happened at Wyeth would have stayed at Wyeth, we might just have left it as a historical footnote. Unfortunately, along came Fauci. Dr. Anthony Fauci allegedly fought to keep a variety of treatments for AIDS off the market in order to promote the deadly and ineffective drug AZT, aimed to treat HIV. AZT appears to have, to a degree, a lot in common with patented COVID-19 medications.[362] Fauci was reportedly born December 24, 1940. In his horoscope, the Sun would be in the ambitious sign of Capricorn.

The principle of *equipoise*[363] is an integral part of research ethics. It states that a clinical trial is ethical only if there is valid uncertainty that an intervention is more effective than the current standard of care. There seems to have been no standard of care to test against an experimental COVID-19 vaccine other than a placebo. Manufacturers took advantage of this and confidentiality agreements with governments the world over to protect their interests.[364] Dissecting the intricate web of corporate and government interests may be an impossible task for us as individuals. What we can do is examine individual behavior and see how it scales up once embedded into a bureaucratic hierarchy.

He became a popular author after a life full of intense experiences. He confessed to being a not so nice person to many, including to his ex-wife whom he loved until his final days. He mingled with the Hollywood elite as a producer, hosting many parties with his wife. Then he covered the misdeeds for those same elite as a writer for *Vanity Fair*.[365] Drugs, alcohol, depression, major life changes, they reportedly were part and parcel for this Scorpio. His horoscope had Moon in Aries—a placement that we earlier saw associated with a virtually insatiable drive for the next project, and with having a "need" to be validated, to be number one. His name was Dominick Dunne.[366] In the biographical documentary *After the Party*[367], he expresses the late-in-life realizations about his personality. By that time, his ex-wife was no longer alive.

How can we come to terms with how our behavior impacted our relationships earlier in life? What can we learn from the feedback we receive from others? Therapy seems to focus on overcoming childhood trauma just in time so that we can have full and unhindered access to our faculties. As far as I know, those who suffer with complex PTSD in particular can have a hard time with trust. Is a trauma aware, empathic therapist always available when we need them? Will we recognize a helpful book on the topic when we see it and start the journey of recovery? Dunne, for instance, describes how his father used to take it out on him as a little boy with severe corporal punishment for the slightest infraction. He suggests that he always felt an outcast in his family.

Dominick's life appears to have had some dramatic twists and turns. The first half was apparently marked by narcissistic behavior. Several important people disappeared out of his life while this and other circumstances forced him to reflect on his will to survive. Dominick confesses that his behavior had been reprehensible, and that he had arguably offended and hurt a lot of people—especially people who had been very dear. He tried to escape from his demons into the world of drugs. True to the nature of Scorpio, he came out again roaring, starting a second life as a successful writer and social commentator.

Moon in Aries, a fire sign, and its associated "need" for validation—and to be number one—may challenging for an outsider. As a Designer sign, its modus operandi is associated with a utilitarian perspective and an excellent focus on the task at hand. It may propel the subject to pursue an endless variety of projects and interests without much regard for the needs of others. Like Dominick Dunne's, the horoscopes of Steve Jobs and Tim Cook, former and current Chief Executive Officer at Apple, Inc., respectively, reportedly also feature an Aries Moon. As leaders of their respective ventures, their inner need for recognition does not stop them from fostering a climate of intense achievement each in their own way. In the case of Jobs, as history appears to show, it did not prevent the occasional clash with other contributors. Jobs's run-ins with Apple's Board,[368] and the commotion around the birth of the Macintosh are two indications of a fiery personality.[369] Strong pushback from people who stand their ground may channel the aspirations of an Aries Moon personality—though a high level of self-confidence may be required as well as a good sense of timing.

People with Aries as a rising sign are known to consider anyone showing up on their proverbial doorstep as a challenge to their authority. Rash, blunt, and arrogant are keywords associated with this placement. When we know who we are dealing with, a laid back yet self-confident response may be all that is needed to calm the tensions. Stoics may have an advantage here. Having the right response to each zodiac sign's expression as a Sun, Moon or Rising sign may be a matter of trial and error. It goes without saying that those who cannot adapt, retreat and recover will be forever at their mercy unless they go no contact altogether.

Project focused as Aries as a zodiac sign can be, the Sun sign seems to thrive in a setting that challenges them frequently. If they don't get enough pushback from their own endeavors, they may seek it from others. This is how we see Aries occasionally venture into the political arena where they can easily do more damage than good because, well, with the fire of Aries in their proverbial belly they may not be too well known for their diplomatic skills. Curiously, Libra, the opposite sign on the wheel of the Zodiac, similarly seems to thrive in inventions and politics of any kind. This zodiac sign, especially as the Sun sign, thrives on "balancing"—yet not in the sense that most empaths define it. When there is peace, count on Libra to start a war. If there is a war, count on Libra to bring parties together and establish consent. Aries and Libra Sun sign personalities like Barbara Walters, Martina Navratilova and Olivia Newton-John, and inventors like Dean Kamen[370], Isambard Kingdom Brunel[371] and Alfred Nobel[372] are duly noted for their contributions to society.

How people manage their relationship with celebrity Aries and Libra signs may be very different compared to those with less well known individuals. Politicians and celebrities tend to have leverage unlike anyone else, even compared to business people where the nature of the relationship may be quite different. Let us look at an example of how one person's leverage managed to obscure his criminal actions over an extended period of time.

The late Robert Durst was born on April 12 as the eldest son of a prominent New York real estate family. Trauma for this Aries came at an early age when his mother committed suicide. His father made him watch through a window, helpless and unable to cry out to her. Even though Bob was the eldest,

A Few Good Cardinals

real estate isn't exactly the dynamic environment Aries often longs for. His father appears to have had a keen sense of what his sons were capable of because he dismissed Bob as heir to the throne in favor of his younger brother, Douglas.

Bob's horoscope shows that the Moon was in Cancer at the time he was born. Zodiac signs manifest differently as a Sun, Moon or Rising sign, as we saw in the chapter *The Essentials*. Cancer as a Moon sign tends to be very protective of one's emotional state. Contrary to Cancer as a Sun sign, it is not very conducive for success in the cutthroat world of business because it seeks someone to blame for everything perceived as wrong. The frustration of being left out of the family business, possibly combined with the subconscious abandonment and horror around his mother' death, appears to have led him towards a path of revenge. The documentary series *The Jinx*[373] shows the viewer how Bob handled himself in his first marriage, and how he killed two other people besides his first wife. What was Bob's contextual framework that diverted his life from that of corporate success to crime?

Bob was born in New York City in 1943. He grew up in the tony New York City suburb of Scarsdale as the eldest son of real estate magnate Seymour Durst and his wife, Bernice Herstein. He worked in his father's firm and expected to succeed him at Seymour's eventual retirement. His paternal grandfather, Joseph Durst, was a Jewish tailor from Austria-Hungary who immigrated to the United States in 1902. He went into real estate and founded the Durst Organization in 1927. Bob had three younger siblings Douglas, Tommy, and Wendy Durst, of whom Douglas would become his father's favorite.[374] Bob claims to have witnessed his mother's suicide, asserting that moments before her death, his father walked him to a window from which he could see her standing on the roof. But in a March 2015 interview in *The New York Times*, his brother Douglas denied that Robert had witnessed the incident. As children, Bob and Douglas reportedly underwent counseling for sibling rivalry; a 1953 psychiatrist's report allegedly included a mention to "personality decomposition and possibly even schizophrenia."

Bob earned a bachelor's degree in economics in 1965 from Lehigh University, where he was a member of the varsity lacrosse team and the business manager of the student newspaper, *The Brown and White*. Later that year, Durst enrolled in a doctoral program at the University of California, Los

Angeles, where he met Susan Berman, who became his best friend, but eventually withdrew from the school and returned to New York in 1969.

Resisting the rigors of corporate life, Bob opened a small health-food store in Vermont. In late 1971, he met dental hygienist Kathleen McCormack. After two dates, he invited her to share his home in Vermont, where she moved in January 1972. After his father pressured him to resettle in New York to work at the Durst Organization, Bob and Kathleen closed the store in Vermont and returned to Manhattan. They married on April 12, 1973, his birthday. Almost twenty years later, in 1992, Bob's increasingly inappropriate conduct led to his father breaking with tradition and appointing Douglas to take over the company. Bob claimed that Douglas had stolen what was rightfully owed him, leading to his estrangement from the rest of the family. In 2006, he was bought out of the family trust for $65 million, but not before he had killed his first wife, Kathleen, his best friend Susan Berman and a neighbor, Morris Black.

Karma tends to have a strange way of catching up with us in my experience. Some therapists appear to suggest that people may be living the karma of their ancestors and that it is possible to play out the dynamic of previous generations in a therapy setting in order to get closure. Hindsight is inevitably twenty-twenty. As an onlooker, having the advantage of being at least one step removed from the drama, it goes without saying that watching someone like Bob Durst express himself in *The Jinx* with a strange facial grimace—as if he is forcefully trying to hide what his subconscious really is trying to say—it is easy to blurt out, "He's guilty, he did it." The filmmaker eventually resorts to a dramatic tactic at the end of the first part of the series.

While Bob was acquitted in the 2003 trial for the killing of a neighbor, Morris Black, he was not so lucky when he was tried for the murder of his friend and confidante Susan Berman in Los Angeles. At the Black trial, psychiatrist Milton Altschuler diagnosed Durst with Asperger syndrome, suggesting, "His whole life's history is so compatible with a diagnosis of Asperger's disorder." On March 14, 2015, Durst was arrested by FBI agents at the Canal Street Marriott in New Orleans, where he had registered under the false name "Everette Ward." Finally, on October 14, 2021, Bob was sentenced to life imprisonment without the possibility of parole for the murder of his closest friend Susan Berman. Robert Durst died in prison at the age of at the age of seventy-eight, after more than three decades of leading people on, lying about his whereabouts, his finances and his identity.

Having a will to live and feeling like life has meaning may be all one
needs to keep going. The challenges life inevitably throws at us may be
opportunities to grow, for knowing oneself better, and to learn even if we don't
know what we are learning for. In a Western style society, are people more
fulfilled, happier and prosperous after abandoning the hunter/gatherer days? Are
they more in tune with their purpose and with divine provenance? If we go by
the attempts of psychologists, theologians, philosophers and government
statisticians alike, these appear to be questions that haunt many of us.

As we saw earlier, it appears that the extreme focus and concentration of
the Designer signs can lead to important discoveries and inventions.
Unfortunately, it may also lead one to judge the contribution of another as
inferior or to dismiss it altogether. The range within which this utilitarian
perspective presents is referred to as narcissism spectrum disorder (NSD). There
are natural and learned narcissists. The latter generally seem to adopt the
behavior of a narcissist only to survive a narcissistic environment. We
discovered that research appears to point to a connection between date of birth
and narcissism: people born between September 23, and October 22, for
instance, seem to display the behavior when deprived of a good role model and
a loving and supportive environment in childhood.

Likewise, people born between June 21 and July 22, between December
21 and January 20, or between March 21 and April 19 may also present on the
scale of the narcissism spectrum. Imposter syndrome may be a practical

manifestation of their insecurity. There appear to be at least two other criteria involved in determining whether someone may be a narcissist. I used a very specific aspect of the ancient science of astrology, used by the elites to interpret life events, to find them: the rising sign (Ascendant), determined by a person's time and location of birth, and the sign of the Moon at the moment someone is born.

It goes without saying that trauma is, unfortunately, a fact of life. You are going to say I am a misogynist and that I ignore the abuse of women, but there are three things that pertain to men in particular that seem to not have changed very much over time. One may be considered the tolerance of sexual exploitation by religious elders of young boys. A second would be genital mutilation, while the third factor affecting men seems to be the credo of "manning up" when one objects to men expressing their emotions. Women seem to have a valid argument that they don't feel safe no matter where they go if statistics of rape, domestic violence and other abuse are any indication. But if you were to ask me directly, how could I not paint a different, perhaps highly distorted picture for you based on my own experience?

While trauma has remained mostly omitted from our exploration for the very reason that I am not educated in the field nor licensed as a psychotherapist, it appears that it may significantly impact behavior. According to the experts, trauma of a physical or emotional nature may result, in case of a single event, PTSD, or, due to long-term exposure, in complex post-traumatic stress disorder, cPTSD. We looked at bias and how it can contribute to traumatic experience when a utilitarian perspective results in decision making that abandons common sense and discards warning signs. But what are we supposed to do when a utilitarian habit grew out of a situation that has long since been forgotten in the annals of history? Perhaps it would be best revisit the topic of bias by illustrating how it can take root via the example of a millennia old, often disputed practice: genital mutilation. Women and men, as parents, in some cultures appear to find it perfectly acceptable to circumcise their baby boy or girl because at some point in time somebody felt it was just "better" or "God wants it."

In today's day and age when some cultures encourage the questioning of everything and anything, the discussion around the topic can be heated, settled or non-existent. What gives parents the right to determine, at an age when an infant cannot make a conscious decision on the issue, that their perspective on bodily hygiene, cultural norms or religious preference is correct? Is genital mutilation a personality issue, in other words, one that arises out of a desire to exert control and dominance? Those who first practiced it arguably are no longer around to tell us why. Perhaps it was simply a case of miscommunication regarding a health issue. How can I not wonder what God thinks of the practice when he could have sworn to have created his offspring as perfectly as possible? Later we will revisit the issue of personality in the sometimes stubbornly persistent practice of certain activities despite new information suggesting it may be best to abandon an established custom.

Considering the reportedly considerable divisions or outright animosity between the sexes in many cultures, how certain are we that there is no connection or at least not a significant one between circumcision and disrespect from one gender to another? While the psychology profession claims expert insight into what the emotional consequences are of forced bodily mutilation, which they tend to hide from the general public, most laypeople appear to simply lack the same knowledge let alone the willingness to understand it. Besides, when it comes to male circumcision, there appears to be no conclusive medical evidence at this point in time, as far as I know, that objectively includes all risks and psychological factors involved in the practice.[375] Psychologically, it is difficult enough for a man to accept that he does not have the same body as his mother, even though she may love him as much as a daughter.

The exercise here is not to justify, judge or confront abuse. What we know is that significant abuse occurs between the sexes. There may be abnormalities in brain development manifesting in a personality disorder that experts consider to be at the root of at least some abusive behavior. Our exploration into this realm is merely to observe and obtain some tools to perhaps improve our chances to address objectionable situations.

How is "perspective" not at the root of all thought? The bad news is that a perspective may be skewed. I may be so traumatized and "locked up" into one way of thinking that it is unfathomable to consider a different angle or two. Perspective may be skewed from birth. Some children are abused before they are even born. The father may be upset with his pregnant spouse. The expectant mother may not want the child. While these may sound like very innocent arguments against the unborn, how do they not represent rejection and possibly emotional abandonment nonetheless? If a nurturing, loving environment indeed prevents narcissism as a personality disorder, when should we start nurturing?

Perspective may be skewed not just because of trauma suffered in the womb, but, as we saw earlier, perhaps just from being born on a certain day, at a certain time and at a certain place. When information becomes available that conflicts with our perspective, how open minded are we to consider it or to accept it? From the 1970s on, a movement towards something that people referred to as *empowerment* seems to have emerged.[376] Consider it, in its early days, a harbinger of the diversity and inclusion initiatives of today. People attended workshops so they could have the tools and psychological awareness to make something of themselves regardless of their upbringing, early childhood trauma and psychological makeup – as long as they drank the proverbial Cool-Aid from the "gurus" of the time.

Empowerment seems useful to ensure that we don't find ourselves in objectionable adversarial situations. Empowerment could mean having the wherewithal to withdraw before harm can be done, and to maintain a state of calmness. Empowerment can involve allowing yourself to refrain from being dictated by circumstance, and to retain self-control. How can they harm you when you are not present to cooperate? When his army was at its weakest, this approach seems to have been quite effective in George Washington's effort to win the War of Independence for America, for instance.[377] Empowerment could thus be defined as the *acquisition of tools that allow us to maintain our personal integrity, to live our life in peace, and to confront potential abuse at the best possible place and time before the prospective perpetrator has a chance to violate the sanctity of life.*

Denial, as we have seen, appears to be a powerful tool for some to ignore a plea for change. Using constructive language may "force" the person who denies that I was wronged to reflect on their own contribution to the situation. I may be able to not only ensure my survival, I may be able to also gain respect at the same time. Self-empowerment means I seek to improve the way I communicate, that I consider the effectiveness of the words I use to address abuse, and that I adapt my overall behavior accordingly.

Just because some things *appear* to be set in stone, why should they dictate your life forever if their usefulness has expired? Knowing which rules matter and which keys can unlock your potential are two critical success factors. Let time be your friend. They say that for every narcissist, there are signs[378]. Yet, who wants to see only the bad in others? Reciprocation used to be a noble act. These days, it doesn't seem to be so "popular" anymore. How close are we to a tipping point[379] after which respect for each other is gone "forever"?

A big concern for many these days seems to be suicide. Many countries wage a "war on drugs" without making too much of a fuss of the drugs readily available at the local pharmacy—drugs used to end a life of misery. When we see another human, what is the first reaction: "That person means harm," or "That person wants what I want"? Notice that I did not use a label: enemy or friend, competitor or collaborator. Imagine that the soul exists just before birth? What if the soul is assigned a human body in order to experience a specific life? How is life then—given that the human body appears to have an expiration date—not a suicide mission in and of itself?

Wishing or mandating that somebody *not* commit suicide, consequently, may possibly be a narcissistic exercise in control—the legality of it notwithstanding. If bullying, victimization, and the institutionalization of ever diminishing individual rights are the equivalent of winter for the spiritual growth of the soul, challenging the "victim" to bring out their best qualities in preparation for spring, when is it supposed to end? Information on suicide is of course available online where a search may be more anonymous than a consultation with a physician. While suicide is still considered a crime in many places, the practice is highly stigmatized and discouraged pretty much everywhere.[380]

How do we compare someone's story to our own experience? What qualifies as abuse to you and a reason to consider ending it all, may be a "life lesson" from the perspective of another. This is how abusers at religious-run schools in Ireland may have considered it. Reportedly, approximately 2,400 allegations of sexual abuse were recorded by three hundred and eight schools run by religious orders between the early 1960s and 1990s. The allegations were made against eight hundred and eighty-four alleged abusers. The allegations of abuse in schools span twenty-two counties in Ireland. It took so long for the accusations to be taken seriously that over half of those accused are estimated to be already dead.

> "Over 180 survivors, the "overwhelming majority" of whom were men, spoke about their experiences. The report heard from many survivors who said that 'their childhood stopped the day the abuse started.'"[381]

There appears to be a significant difference in suicide rates between men and women—there are about four male deaths by suicide for each female death. Still, there are apparently about three female attempts for every male attempt, while there are approximately 750,000 suicide attempts in the United States each year in all. An estimated five million living Americans have allegedly attempted suicide.

Considering that suicide is highly discouraged or even illegal, does anyone actually believe these numbers? Is there a reward for reporting an attempt? The source of these data is reportedly the Centers for Disease Control and Prevention,[382] the same people who allegedly insist on the benefits of the flu, Covid-19 and every other vaccine laced with toxic metals that slowly kill us according to Gennady Ibraev.[383] Of course, suicide affects all countries and may be influenced by mental disorders, depression rates, and life satisfaction. In 2019, Lesotho reportedly had the highest suicide rate at 72.4 per 100,000, followed by Guyana, South Korea, and Kiribati. Belgium has a high suicide rate, possibly influenced by its policies on the doctor-assisted version. South Korea's high suicide rate is attributed to factors like elderly isolation and academic pressure among students, whereas in China suicide is reportedly the fifth leading cause of death. Communism is apparently not as successful at encouraging people to stay alive as authorities want us to believe.[384]

Sensitive children like Helena and I are often seen as outliers even though they are technically the canary in the proverbial coal mine of life. She suffered from abuse which she was told to keep quiet about. By age thirteen, the family doctor put her on valium. Not once did a prescriber tell her it should not be taken longer than a month. At age twenty-two, battered and bruised from years of abusive relationships and physically unwell with something that wouldn't be diagnosed until she was forty as "fibromyalgia", she was told by her doctor that she had a chemical imbalance in her brain—Prozac would "help," it was suggested.

Helena wasn't aware of the lawsuits being settled in America for the people who had killed themselves taking this drug.[385] Instead, she was very happy with the weight loss Prozac seemed to give her. However, soon after she shares that she started developing terrifying panic attacks and ferocious headaches. Eventually she was allegedly told to stop taking it—and then all hell broke loose. Helena entered the psychiatric system and became trapped there and on the psychotropic medication that was to destroy her life; physically, mentally and spiritually over the next thirty years.[386] Where were the empaths in her life?

Sometimes it is not as complicated as Helena's story. Health experts recently started calling for stricter regulations for the use of sodium nitrite, a product commonly used for meat curing, following its link to suicides. Because the substance is easily accessible and can be mistaken for table salt, people may also "unknowingly overdose," Yub Raj Sedhai, an assistant clinical professor at Virginia Commonwealth University, and colleagues noted.[387] What drives somebody to consider suicide may hardly be the same motivation that drives somebody to fight in war such as it did for Lieutenant General Sir Adrian Paul Ghislain Carton de Wiart—born May 5, 1880 in Brussels, Belgium. He reportedly joined the British Army in 1899 during the Second Boer War. He enlisted under the name "Trooper Carton," claiming he was twenty-five when he was "not older than twenty." During his military career, he was allegedly shot in the every part of his body and even tore off his own fingers. De Wiart reportedly survived multiple plane crashes and managed to tunnel out of a prisoner-of-war-camp. He became a legend, a man with "war in his blood."[388]

What might astrology tell us about suicide? The element of water in the chart can allegedly be an indicator of depression. For example, the chart of Robin Williams (July 21, 1951) has three water signs on the personal points of Sun, Moon and Rising: Cancer, Pisces and Scorpio, respectively. Water is an element of emotional sensitivity. Robin's fate was the task to understand the role of emotions and use it in his work.[389] "Don't wait for the storm to pass, learn to dance in the rain," suggests Vivian Greene.[390] It may be that a prevalence of Builder ("fixed" in Western astrology) signs on the three personal points can prevent one from moving on after a traumatic challenge, making one focused on one path only and ignoring a way out of being stuck.

Bruce Geller and Tom Cruise may be on to something with *Mission: Impossible*.[391] Much has been made of the concept of the Garden of Eden and that it may be somewhere here on Earth. Maybe all of the planet together is the Garden of Eden. What if life is not just an exercise in mental and emotional toughness, but just as much, if not more, a challenge to find all the elements that would make life eternal—together, the proverbial Holy Grail? If you are concerned about microplastics, for example, the news that there may be a solution for that[392] may give hope.

The toxic narcissist appears to have a habit of turning the tables on their target. How they do this may in part be their reliance on accepted rules and conventions while ignoring gaps in our understanding. One such gap may be the concept of false memory. Memories may seem to be a solid, straightforward accumulation of who people are, evidence suggests that memories are much more complex, subject to change, and occasionally unreliable. Memories of past events can change we age. People may recall childhood events differently than they actually occurred, or they may omit important traumatic events altogether. Conversely, others may suggest that a certain event occurred because "it makes sense" and underwrites their beliefs—this is called confirmation bias. Through suggestions and other methods, it has reportedly been proven that we can even create new false memories.[393] When a person in authority, or with a charismatic persona, tries to convince us of their version of the truth, how likely are you to challenge them successfully?

Countering a narcissistic move at the first opportunity to avoid an escalation may be a tactic you might pursue unless there is a threat of physical violence. Unfortunately, bullies tend to be acutely aware that their victim is best intimidated and controlled by sudden and unanticipated action. Every interaction with another person triggers a hormonal release in the brain. Some people make us feel good, others make us feel excited or anxious.

In a sense, life could be considered as a venue where we learn to process traumatic experiences while exercising our willpower and emotions. The question arises, naturally, how the legal and educational systems of society should be structured to facilitate and promote healthy behavior. If a woman cannot reasonably expect to be treated fairly and respectfully when she has been victimized, how can a man expect her to respect him when it is obvious he has no intention to call for reform?

If there is anything more critical to be aware of than simply the possibility of being deceived, it may be the concept of cognitive dissonance.[394] We looked at future faking earlier. As a psychological tool, cognitive dissonance may be the next most surreptitious of all in the arsenal of the utilitarian individual. There seem to be two reasons for this: (1) due to how the mind processes data, and (2) because we cannot observe dissonance. If I tell you something that conflicts with what you know or perceive to be true, your mind will go through an intensive, energy draining process of resolving the conflicting information.

At some point during this process, the narcissist may take advantage and effectively hijack your *emotional* commitment to the cause at hand. They may follow up with an unambiguous and clever solution to the conundrum they made you face, while successfully "implanting" in your mind a picture of them as the proverbial hero who saves the day. True empaths would never manipulate another person in this way it seems. When you find yourself in such a situation, give yourself time to recover—and rather than confronting, maybe step away from potential trauma if you can.

There are moments when we may simply not feel up to making an important decision or doing a particular activity. Someone who did an extensive, very accessible study on this is Daniel Pink, the author of *When*.[395] Knowing yourself[396] and mastering control over one's emotions may be the best solution for countering pressure from others. People may deceive, push or otherwise manipulate someone into acting in the moment, and even threaten them with the consequences if they don't proceed. Procrastination is the term the narcissist most often uses to make others feel guilty.

How did NASA fare after they reorganized their management structure in the wake of the 1986 Challenger disaster? In our exploration of the cause of the explosion on January 28, 1986, we discovered that a dysfunctional culture had reportedly contributed to the incident that resulted in the loss of life for seven astronauts. The fleet of Space Shuttles, originally slated to fly two missions per month, was subsequently grounded for almost three years while NASA management underwent drastic change. In 2003, unfortunately, complacency and a dysfunctional organizational culture once again led to a fatal incident, this time for the Shuttle Columbia when it reentered the atmosphere with a broken heat shield. The orbiter caught fire and disintegrated over Texas killing all on board.[397] It was to be the final nail in the proverbial coffin for the Shuttle program. Similarly, Thomas Bouch,[398] who had designed the Tay Bridge which collapsed as a result of poor engineering practices, saw his reputation badly damaged when other works of his were found to be likewise lacking. His forte may have been similar to NASA's approach at the time of the Space Shuttle program: cheapness. By the time a crisis wakes people up or galvanizes support for change, chances are the narcissist has already left their calling card.

In the context of the utilitarian perspective, we looked at several bridge engineering projects because they are complex undertakings that affect our lives one way or another. A bridge is something many take for granted, yet they are known to let us down at just the wrong moment. Shortcuts may have been taken during their construction or lack of maintenance may be the culprit, but a fatal incident and a bridge being out of service can wreak major havoc. Are such situations always the result of narcissistic behavior? And how can the decision making process that led to shortcomings in bridge design teach a lesson for others?

Let's take a final look at the complexities of engineering and the unlikely connection between pigeon excrement and five and half billion U.S. dollars: "misplaced priorities." In the years prior to 1983, in the State of Connecticut the authorities were running low on funds for highway maintenance. The federal government provides funds for interstate highway maintenance which the State government in Connecticut did not take advantage of. Instead, they opted to charge a toll for the Mianus Bridge,[399] making Connecticut no longer eligible for the federal contribution. The I-95 interstate runs from Florida to Maine, passing through Cos Cob and Riverside while crossing the Mianus River. The Mianus Bridge—constructed from steel—fulfills an important function for this busy transportation corridor.

Steel bridges require regular inspections for rust, cleaning and maintenance. The state government had drastically scaled back its funding for such work in light of a general economic malaise. At the time of the collapse, Connecticut had allegedly just twelve engineers tasked with the inspection of almost three and a half thousand bridges. After the collapse of a section of the Mianus Bridge, Connecticut all of a sudden had $5.5 billion available for bridge inspection, repair and other transportation projects. Before the collapse, there was not enough money to remove a twelve-year buildup of pigeon excrement on the bridge, which excrement prevented inspectors from properly assessing rust damage to a critical component that failed the night of the incident that killed three people.

A crisis can be a turning point in any stagnant or challenging situation. Mental health issues affecting the perpetrator of a mass shooting, patients dying of medical errors, cars plunging off bridges and astronauts falling to their death in the ocean, all these situations and many more may be preceded by the pleas of those who care to prevent disaster instead of allowing it to happen. The counterargument is that a catastrophe can provide significant insight into issues even those who warned of its potential could not have foreseen. It could also bring a paradigm shift in organizational dynamics. How big, then, should the disaster be before we are willing to change our ways?

When we looked at the rules that govern our lives, we did not really examine the conflict between rules that prevent something versus rules that govern the remedy. Our health seems to hit closer to home than anything when it comes to control, prevention and remedy. Without good health we can't be there for someone in need, we can't work to the best of our natural ability, and we can't be there for our loved ones after we die—prematurely. What tools do we have at our disposal to avoid the worst? John D. Rockefeller was reportedly known as a ruthless businessman. As we saw earlier, before 1908 traditional natural medicinal cures were the standard of care, while Dr. Forrest Shaklee opened a window towards preventive options in 1915. Then, the Rockefellers established allopathy: "A system in which medical doctors and other health care professionals treat symptoms and diseases using drugs, radiation, or surgery."[400] Fast forward to 2024, let us review some numbers in the United States:

- Medical billing errors reportedly cost Americans US$210 billion per year;

- Approximately twelve million Americans appear to be misdiagnosed per year; and

- Medical errors cause an estimated two hundred and fifty thousand deaths in the United States per year.[401]

Rockefeller used chiropractic and homeopathy for himself and his own family, while using his influence to prosecute many homeopathic physicians for offering their services to others. He wanted to gain control of education, including the medical education systems. He reportedly did just that with the help of Fred Gates.[402] Rockefeller was allegedly obsessed with control, rooting out natural and homeopathic competition in medical hospitals with the same tactics he used in the oil industry. Abraham Flexner assisted with his *1910 Flexner Report*—also called *Carnegie Foundation Bulletin Number Four*. Flexner assessed every single medical school in the US and Canada:

> "Many aspects of the present-day American medical profession originate with the Flexner Report and its aftermath. While it had many positive impacts on American medical education, the Flexner report has been criticized for

introducing policies that encouraged systemic racism and sexism. Colleges for the education of various forms of alternative medicine, such as electrotherapy, were closed." [403]

What connects Rockefeller with modern day health care providers? It may be the question of whether medicine is more of an art rather than a science. The American Stroke Association[404] reported that almost eight hundred thousand Americans suffer a stroke each year. Stroke is a leading cause of disability. A 2014 study on medical treatment outcomes noted that the "implementation of a national quality improvement initiative was associated with [...] lower in-hospital mortality [...] along with an increase in the percentage of patients discharged home."[405] For the consumer of medical services, this means that hospitals which use a standardized approach appear to lower the chance of death and disability for patients the most.

Conversely, hospitals that allow physicians to base their admitting orders on personal preferences seem to offer a disservice instead. In fact, a study among eight hospitals in various countries demonstrated that when physicians rigorously adhere to a set of protocols in the operating room, medical errors were cut nearly in half.[406] The problem seems to be that while doctors have access to evidence based guidelines and rules, they simply choose to ignore them.[407] Like with John D. Rockefeller's alleged obsession with control, personality can apparently dictate clinical health outcomes. The question of medicine as art or science is a debate that you as a patient may not even know is taking place behind the scenes. Even the way your trusted primary care physician listens to you and observes scientific discipline may determine whether you live or die.

A disaster that evolves over time may be just as impactful as one that happens instantly. When we arm ourselves with negotiation tactics, high self-confidence and all the leverage we can muster, it may still not be enough to change course. For decades, everywhere people have been encouraged to recycle plastic. Unfortunately, the massive effort by consumers to help the planet excused the plastic producers from their contribution to the problem in the first place.[408] Besides materials scientists who dedicate their lives to discovering environmentally friendly substitutes for plastic and to removing existing plastic pollution form the environment, not many meaningful efforts have been introduced. A report from the Center for International Environmental Law[409] has allegedly revealed the legal means to hold corporations accountable.

History seems to be replete with individuals who stirred up the imagination and support of many for their cause—a cause that may have sounded noble at the beginning, but that may have turned disastrous for one party or another. We saw how Napoleon Bonaparte became complacent and overly confident after a number of victories, then tried to compensate for an "unexpected" loss against Spain and its allies by taking on an enemy greater than his proud army could muster: Russia. Between two and a half and three and a half million soldiers are estimated to have died in the course of the wars Napoleon instigated.[410] But what about the history of mental health?

You may have heard of Sigmund Freud (born May 6, 1856)[411] and possibly of Carl Gustav Jung (born July 26, 1875),[412] yet John B. Watson may not be as well known. John B. Watson (born January 9, 1878) was a revolutionary psychologist whose groundbreaking experiments paved the way for the school of thought known as behaviorism. Born in Greenville, South Carolina, Watson's curiosity about human behavior allegedly led him on a journey of scientific inquiry that forever changed the course of psychology as we know it. Watson advanced his theory on human behavior through a 1913 address at Columbia University titled *Psychology as the Behaviorist Views It*. He conducted research on animal behavior, child rearing, and advertising.

Watson conducted the controversial "Little Albert" and Kerplunk experiments, the latter demonstrating the ability to turn voluntary motor responses into a conditioned response.[413] In the controversial yet influential "Little Albert" experiment,[414] Watson conditioned a fear response in a young child by pairing a neutral stimulus with a loud, frightening noise. This study demonstrated the principle of conditioning and the malleability of human behavior, which continue to be applied the world over to make populations accept psychopathic authority.

The institutionalization of narcissism and abuse may not take place when opposition is strong and justly motivated. It takes a crisis, a critical number of followers, or both as the tipping point for denial of rights and violation of morals to take root. Victims of sexual abuse by caregivers, clergy and others, displaced refugees caught up in war, and illegal immigrants falling for repatriation schemes and human smugglers wait for a solution perhaps just like those who believe in climate change, fossil fuels and processed food.

Many famous people throughout history have lacked confidence at times, or they were abused, imprisoned, and faced other extremely challenging situations. After reading and watching many biographies and documentaries, it became obvious to me that history does seem to repeat itself—except that technology has changed so dramatically. Through film, photography, and online social discourse we can expose the abuses and the victories of the past in ways not before possible. So, after all that, how do you like your soup?

"Human beings have a demonstrated talent for self-deception when their emotions are stirred."
Carl Sagan, *Cosmos*[415]

EPILOGUE

The key takeaway may be that narcissism has always been with us, will always be with us and may never be fully addressed. In our daily lives, the healthy narcissist sets an example for the younger generation by setting healthy boundaries that may otherwise not be set by someone too empathic for their own good. Toxic narcissism, on the other hand, is our main concern. Conditioning—through daily exposure from people around us, social media, advertising and other online and offline channels—together with "future faking" seem to be the most powerful tools in its arsenal. Avoiding exposure and having compassion for ourselves may be our boldest response.

We saw a few historical figures and their birth dates pass our radar screen. Not all had a birth date within one of the four date ranges associated with an elevated risk of toxic narcissism. When we look at their horoscopes, we may find that Napoleon Bonaparte had a Capricorn Moon, Josef Stalin a Libra Moon and Pol Pot an Aries Moon (if his birth date of Mary 19, 1925 is correct)— qualifying for narcissism through the Moon sign. In modern days, some people may want to know what Erdogan's chart says, the President of Turkey. Reportedly, with a February 26, 1954 date of birth, his Sun and Moon are in a Visionary sign, Pisces and Sagittarius, respectively, but his rising sign is Capricorn—a clear indicator of narcissistic behavior potential.

Another figure in the news is Nicolas Maduro of Venezuela who just cheated his fellow citizens in a presidential election. His chart for a November 23, 1962 birth date shows the Sun in Sagittarius and Moon in Libra with Cancer as the rising sign. Obviously, when he took over from Hugo Chavez (Leo Sun, Moon in Cancer), he endeared himself to the public with the Cancer Ascendant providing a "nurturing" and familiar feeling to the populace. Unfortunately, Nicolas wants a type of Sagittarius freedom of expression that is hard to come by in his position, while his admiration seeking Libra Moon feels shortchanged. Libra as a Moon sign makes the individual cold and calculating in social settings, attributes which Maduro seems to have displayed quite dramatically in the course of Venezuela's downfall. The communist regime took the country from its position as one of the wealthiest countries in the world to impoverished beyond recognition.

No stranger to controversy, Luiz Inácio Lula da Silva is another South American president who stole an election. If Libra Moon needs admiration, the Sun sign wants that and harmony. Lula has both. Libra Sun wants to be known as the peacemaker. When there is peace, they will sow discord just so they can come to the rescue and restore the proverbial balance. For a contemporary figurehead across the Atlantic, look no further than Vladimir Putin who seems more than happy to eliminate any sign of disruption to his own carefully orchestrated version of peace.

An emphasis on Builder (fixed) signs on the Big 3—or two or more fire signs—may have a similar effect on the personality as that of the Designer (cardinal) signs.

In our mundane daily lives, birth dates for work colleagues and fellow members of a social club may be more difficult to obtain than for politicians and celebrities, but that doesn't mean we should let an opportunity escape us. Social convention precludes premature bias, but as we noted, trauma can be inflicted quite early in the process of getting acquainted with someone. The toxic narcissist will bait the empath to see how easy it is to manipulate them. In fact, they may be able to gauge their target just by looking at your posture and facial expression—when in Russia, don't forget not to smile.

Just as psychology is remiss in revealing what exactly it knows about the roots of narcissism, astrology as a science appears to be holding back some useful information as well. What astrology hides does not necessarily pertain to narcissism, though, rather it is a type of institutionalized narcissism in and of itself. I am referring to three distinct elements of astrology: (1) retrogradation of planets; (2) the impact of hard aspects to the lunar nodes; and (3) locational astrology. With regard to the latter, of you have had the privilege of travel or relocation to distant places, you may have noticed that you felt different or that your life took an unexpected turn. That was not an accident.

Astrocartography is the art of interpreting your natal chart for any location at least about 200 kilometers or miles away from the place of birth. The new chart is called the relocated chart. It acts as a layer on top of the natal chart, which continues to function in the background. It is as if you are living two lives at once.

In the event that Neptune is transiting your relocated tenth house and your natal seventh, challenges in the career may be present in addition to confusion or abandonment in personal relationships. With astrocartography, the natal chart is projected onto the globe. This is merely for display purposes because only through the relocated chart will you be able to determine what a destination may hold in store.

The second aspect that astrology does not necessarily talk about it is aspects to the lunar nodes, and more importantly hard aspects: the conjunction, opposition and square. If you ever hear an astrologer say that aspects to the nodes may be ignored, run as fast as you can. The opposite is in fact true. Hard aspects to the nodes, in particular, can override any constructive contribution that the planet(s) involved may bring elsewhere in the chart. There are Web sites that offer a wide variety of interpretations, as well as books on the topic, one of which is by Celeste Teal: *Lunar Nodes*.

Finally, it seems best to address one of the most controversial shortcomings in astrology today: the omission or disregard for interception and retrogradation.[416] If you were to consult an astrology app, or a Web site like Astro.com, you will notice that an interpretation of your chart will treat every planet the same whether it is direct or retrograde. Direct motion is what most people are used to for the personal planets: Mercury, Venus and Mars. This is because the amount of time that the latter two spend in retrogradation is relatively limited. But even with Mercury's more frequent (around four times per year) retrograde motion, its impact is often neglected.

When Mercury is retrograde in the natal chart, it often represents a speech impediment such as a stutter, being slow in starting to talk, or having difficulty understanding commands from caregivers in infancy. Through progression, which means that the natal chart positions of the planets keep moving after birth but at a significantly reduced rate, eventually Mercury will turn direct. However, it is possible that Mercury will turn retrograde by progression at some stage of the subject's life. In my case, this happened at age twelve. This coincided with my getting glasses and falling behind at school. Mercury did not turn direct again until I was thirty-six years old.

With Venus and Mars, the situation is even more dire because it is completely ignored most of the time. If you have a retrograde Venus and you have trouble relating to people, it is not your fault. Retrogradation essentially means that life is moving more slowly or even backwards—not literally of course. It is as if you are out of synch in terms of what Venus represents and the house that it relates to in your chart. When you compare your perspective of values, love and relating to others you may be in disagreement. The same goes for Mars, except that it may be even more pronounced. After all, Mars is our drive, energy and action oriented side. When Mars is retrograde, it may feel as if you can't get anything done on time. Plans often fall through or are prone to change. Others may criticize the person with Mars retrograde for not picking up a project quickly and taking more time to get organized. It may be that the person with Mars retrograde can't get anything going at all. They may be much more adept at finishing something that somebody else started, or fixing something that needs maintenance.

How is the person with a retrograde personal planet appreciated in society? There is considerable bias towards accomplishment and success. Everyone is expected to produce, but for the retrograde person this may be very difficult if not impossible. In addition, when they do produce something, it is often of a much better quality than what others made because the retrograde person is able to reverse engineer any faults out of the finished product. They may communicate more insightfully, they may have a deeper appreciation of another person, or they may have a better understanding of a project. This doesn't mean that they never make a mistake. Still, they often end up being judged for outperforming everyone else when all they did was live up to their own natal chart's expectations. This may appear to be another form of outcasting similar to what a toxic narcissist does, when in fact it is just a different perspective that can never be communicated to a person who has these planets in direct motion in their own chart.

In similar fashion, Jupiter, Saturn, Uranus, Neptune and Pluto can also be retrograde. The meaning for retrogradation here is that the energy is directed inwards as a spiritual process. With Pluto, it may be that one is less visible and intense in the area of the chart where Pluto resides. With Jupiter, it may be more difficult to obtain worldly success or abundance in the area indicated by Jupiter's placement and aspects to other parts of the chart. With Saturn, it may be more difficult to experience discipline in the material world—one may be unable to fully express oneself or having oddball, round-about ways of manifesting one's influence. It may be that Saturn's influence emerges only later in life after much introspection and adjustment.[417]

With regard to intercepted signs and planets, professional dogma appears once again a major culprit in leaving the public in the dark. Interception does not happen in certain chart types, Whole Sign Houses being the most prominent. If somebody has an opinion that contradicts the experience of another person, it is the toxic narcissistic approach that stifles progress. Let it not be you who prevents someone who suffers from finding respite. Karma can be a b*tch.

In the main text we briefly touched upon what seems to be a challenging situation in Brazil around Alexandre de Moraes's interpretation of Brazil's constitution as an example of a strong-willed personality. What personality characteristics may underlie de Moraes's choice of actions is for the psychological expert to determine. What interests us here is what indicators there may be from an astrological perspective if (1) we otherwise know little about the person first-hand, and (2) we wish to assess what risk we are taking by inviting them on board with us or joining them in their venture.

For this exercise, we ignore how the Builder (fixed) modality or the elements of fire, air and earth may limit empathic expression. There may be others, but at first glance the following chart indicators have been associated with controlling behavior:

1. *Sun* or *Moon conjunct Pluto*—a strong desire (Sun) or a an emotional need (Moon) for control. An extremely forceful individual. An unusually deep insight into the emotional depths of other people which one uses to exert control. An ongoing battle for autonomy may persist well into adulthood stemming from a disharmonious relationship with one or both parents.

2. *Sun square Moon*—a willful and strong-minded individual. There is a conflict between wants and needs. The emotional side does not integrate with the purpose of the individual. A high energy level exists but disharmony between public and private life creates tension.

3. *Sun in opposition to the Moon*—a strong-minded individual.

4. *Sun conjunct Saturn*—Saturn limits the expression of the Sun out of a fear of loss. This aspect is like driving with one foot on the gas and the other on the brakes. Only a purposeful individual can live with this kind of discipline for long. One may reject the needs of others as revenge for one's own experienced limitations.

5. *Sun square Saturn*—ambitious but facing a barrier in self-realization resulting in autocratic, selfish or reserved behavior. A subconscious desire for recognition.

6. *Sun in opposition to Saturn*—a feeling of hostility towards life in general may create resentment towards others. Selfish and autocratic behavior.

7. *Sun square Pluto*—a willful personality intent on being recognized and admired. Compulsive self-aggrandizement may take center stage. Underlying feelings of insecurity translate to egocentric behavior.

8. *Sun in opposition to Pluto*—a strong need for recognition. The personality has strong desires and a compulsion for self-aggrandizement.

9. *Mercury square Pluto*—one becomes extremely focused on ideas of the occult and on one's own intellectual capacity, blending ideas as if they are the only correct ones without regard for the position of others. A tendency to be manipulative in one's dealings with others.

10. *Mars conjunct Saturn*—the expression of actual cruelty and mental manipulation by the violent imposition of one's will is a distinct possibility with this aspect, similar with the opposition to Saturn.

11. *Mars in opposition to Saturn*—one may be controlling and manipulative. There is diminished self-confidence. Subconscious fears may seek an outlet through overcompensation. In extreme situations, one may express actual cruelty by violently imposing the will or by strong mental manipulation.

12. *Venus in opposition with Pluto*—power struggles with a partner or person in authority, depending on the house placement of either, may feature strongly. Manipulation of others is possible. A charismatic and intense personality.

13. *Mars square Uranus*—fits of anger and rebellion may join restlessness and emotional insensitivity. A tendency for dogmatism and pride.

14. *Mars square Neptune*—issues with self-deception or being deceived by others. The individual may strongly influence others.

15. *Mars square Chiron*—anger issues plague the personality who is timid and unsure of themselves, and likely passive-aggressive. Painful experiences with (potential) violence may have scarred the psyche. They may elicit anger from others.

16. *Jupiter square the Midheaven*—an extremely lucky individual in dealing with the public and in one's career, encouraging behavior associated with the stressful aspects noted earlier. Others find the person to be an inspiration, but there can be too much self-satisfaction. Cultivating humility may be an important lesson.

17. *Uranus conjunct the Ascendant*—a strong-willed individual who seeks freedom of movement and independence of mind. Ignores the feelings of others. Tuned in to psychic channels. Impatience and lack of commitment or responsibility.

18. *Jupiter in opposition to Chiron*—the individual goes their own way against the interest of society, seeing no wrong in their own actions.

19. *Uranus in opposition with Chiron*—the individual is challenged to walk the path of honesty and integrity due to the independent nature of Uranus finding itself in conflict with the need for healing.

20. *Neptune in aspect to Chiron*—may take on the pain of others and disappear into one's own fantasy world. Is out of touch with consensus reality.

21. *Pluto in opposition to Chiron*—plunges the individual into the depths of despair and pushes them to the heights of manic madness. Abuse of power.

22. *Chiron in opposition to the Ascendant*—trauma in childhood or a past life make it difficult to accept love from others who are considered the perennial enemy with this aspect. The individual seeks to help others but inner conflict with unresolved trauma prevents this.

ANNEX

Examples of well-known people we have met earlier and some others are, in no particular order of significance:

Steve Jobs (February 24, 1955—Sun in Pisces, Moon in Aries and Virgo Rising)

Kim Philby (January 1, 1912—Sun in Capricorn, Moon in Taurus and Taurus Ascendant)

Amy Winehouse (September 14, 1983—Sun in Virgo, Moon in Capricorn, Gemini Ascendant)

Bernard L. Madoff (April 29, 1938—Sun in Taurus, Moon in Taurus, Leo Ascendant)

Charles Manson (November 12, 1934—Sun in Scorpio, Moon in Aquarius, Taurus Ascendant)

José E. Menendez (May 6, 1944—Sun in Taurus, Moon in Libra and Cancer Ascendant)

Ana Montez (February 28, 1957—Sun in Pisces, Moon in Pisces, Libra Ascendant)

Piers Morgan (March 30, 1965—Sun in Aries, Moon in Pisces)

Donald J. Trump (June 14, 1946—Sun in Gemini, Moon in Sagittarius, Leo Ascendant)

Richard Nixon (January 9, 1913—Sun in Capricorn, Moon in Aquarius and Virgo Ascendant)

Keir Starmer (September 2, 1962—Sun in Virgo, Moon in Libra)

Napoleon Bonaparte (August 15, 1769—Sun in Leo, Moon in Capricorn and Scorpio Ascendant)

Josef Stalin (December 18, 1878—Sun in Sagittarius, Moon in Libra and Pisces Ascendant; Saturn in the first house)

Angela Merkel (July 17, 1954—Sun in Cancer, Moon in Aquarius and Sagittarius Ascendant)

Margaret Thatcher (October 13, 1925—Sun in Libra, Moon in Leo and Scorpio Ascendant; Saturn on the cusp of the first house)

Jimmy Carter (October 1, 1924—Sun in Libra, Moon in Scorpio and Libra Ascendant; Saturn in the first house)

Ngo Dinh Diem (January 3, 1901—Sun in Capricorn; Moon in Gemini)

Mao Zedong (December 26, 1893—Sun in Capricorn; Moon in Leo and Capricorn Ascendant)

Recep Tayyiv Erdogan (February 26, 1954—Sun in Pisces, Moon in Sagittarius and Capricorn Ascendant)

Alexandre de Moraes (December 13, 1968—Sun in Sagittarius, Moon in Virgo and Libra Ascendant*)

Robert Mugabe (February 21, 1924—Sun in Pisces, Moon in Virgo, and Cancer Ascendant*)

Elizabeth Holmes (February 3, 1984—Sun in Aquarius, Moon in Pisces, and Aries Ascendant)

Robin Williams (July 21, 1951—Sun in Cancer, Moon in Pisces and Scorpio Rising)

Kenneth Lay (April 15, 1942—Sun in Aries, Moon in Aries and Cancer Ascendant)

Jeffrey Skilling (November 25, 1953—Sun in Sagittarius, Moon in Leo and Capricorn Ascendant*)

Oprah Winfrey (January 29, 1954—Sun in Aquarius, Moon and Ascendant in Sagittarius)

Bassam Youssef (March 22, 1974—Sun in Aries, Moon in Pisces and Cancer Ascendant)

Ludwig Heinrich Edler Von Mises (September 29, 1881—Sun in Libra, Moon in Sagittarius)

Adam Neumann (April 25, 1979—Sun in Taurus, Moon in Aries and Leo Ascendant)*

Stanley Kubrick (July 26, 1928—Sun in Leo, Moon in Scorpio and Scorpio Ascendant)

Leopold II (April 9, 1835—Sun in Aries, Moon in Leo and Leo Ascendant)*

Herman Webster Mudgett (May 16, 1861—Sun in Taurus, Moon in Leo and Capricorn Ascendant)

Wim Hof (April 20, 1959—Sun in Aries, Moon in Virgo and Leo Ascendant)*

* By chart rectification

ABOUT THE AUTHOR

Carl Vincent is the nom de plume of a dedicated human who has been studying behavior for more than thirty-five years. He has had an avid interest in anything related to personal development from an early age as an emotional abuse survivor with cPTSD, and with a background in industrial engineering. Carl believes in personal responsibility to make the best out of life and in helping others succeed.

Writing for business consultancy PurposeDay, he is the creator of the ROCKET™ personality assessment and human motivation tool. With years of experience providing expertise as a project manager, consultant and business coach to individuals and businesses of all sizes, it is his passion to help people succeed. Educational and volunteer activities, staying young and charting new territory keep Carl motivated.

Stay in touch with PurposeDay on X: @purposeday, and on Reddit at r/1159_TheRule.

The first peace, which is the most important, is that which comes within the souls of people when they realize their relationship, their oneness, with the universe and all its powers, and when they realize that at the center of the universe dwells Wakan-Tanka, and that this center is really everywhere, it is within each of us. This is the real peace, and the others are but reflections of this. The second peace is that which is made between two individuals, and the third is that which is made between two nations. But above all you should understand that there can never be peace between nations until there is known that true peace, which, as I have often said, is within the souls of men.

—Nicholas Black Elk [Hehaka Sapa]

INDEX

(

1

A

Arroyo, Stephen · 65
artificial intelligence · 111
asbestos · 133
Asperger's disorder · 184
Astro.com · 65
Astrodienst · 65
Asylum Records · 158
attitude · 118, 125
authority · 96
Availability · 119
AZT · 180

B

Baltimore · 117
Bamford, James · 29
Bank of England · 19
Bantu · 35
Barbary coast · 117
Barbary corsairs · 117
Barbary slave trade · 117
because · 161
behaviorism · 197
Belt and Road · 118
Berman, Susan · 184
Bernard Madoff · 57
Bernstein, Alan · 180
bias · 97
Big Three · 165, 166
Bill Gates · 150
birch trees · 132
Black, Morris · 184
Blitz Krieg · 26
Body of Secrets · 29
Bonaparte, Napoleon · 205
Bouch, Thomas · 193
BP Deepwater Horizon Spill · 109
Brain Games · 146
Brain structure · 50
Brazil · 30
British Petroleum · 19
bullying · 51, 53

C

Cambridge Five · 27
Cape Colony · 35
Capricorn · 114
Carter, Jimmy · 206
Carton de Wiart · 191

D

E

Ewan McGregor · 113
executive function · 69

F

Fabian Society · 19
fake news · 18
false memory · 192
Family Constellations · 140
Fauci · 180
fawning · 171
Federal Reserve System · 19
field joint · 106
Flexner Report · 196
Flexner, Abraham · 195
Food and Drug Administration, U.S. · 173
football · 22
framing effect · 120
Frank Lloyd Wright · 168
Frederick Taylor · 40
French Revolution · 63
Freud, Sigmund · 206
future · 98

G

Garden of Eden · 191
Gates, Fred · 195
Geller, Bruce · 191
Geneva Convention · 21
genital mutilation · 186
George Washington · 188
Germany · 21
Ghosts from the Nursery · 45, 54
Golden Rule · 20
Goleman, Daniel · 172
good faith · 132
government spending · 17
grandiose · 154
Great Leap Forward · 115
Great Pacific Garbage Patch · 109
Greene, Vivian · 191
Grenfell Tower · 82
Gulf of Mexico · 24
gum disease · 132

H

I

J

Manson, Charles · 205
Mao Zedong · 18, 114
Margaret (Margie) Cantrell · 74
Mariah Carey · 113
Marx, Karl · 176
Matthew 7-12 · 125
McCormack, Kathleen · 184
medieval Europe · 19
Menendez, José E. · 205
mercury · 132
Merkel, Angela · 205
Michael Faraday · 78
Michelangelo Antonioni · 153
Milner Group · 19
Mineola · 74
mirror neurons · 25, 59
Mission
    Impossible · 191
Mission Valley · 124
Misty Griffin · 53
Mitchell, Dr. Karen · 158
Moisseiff · 84
Montez, Ana · 205
Morgan, Piers · 205
Morton Thiokol · 106
motivation · 9, 209
Mudgett, Herman Webster · 207
Mugabe, Robert · 126, 206
Muisca · 11
Myers-Briggs · 10, 145

N

Napoleon Bonaparte · 153, 199
narcissism · 56
narcissism spectrum disorder · 57, 185
Narcissism Spectrum Disorder · 50
NASA · 23, 106, 107, 112, 193
National Aeronautics and Space Administration · 23, 106
National Security Agency · 29
Nayef Al-Rodhan · 48
Neil Armstrong · 163
neonatal intensive care unit (NICU) · 39
Netherlands · 21, 23
Neumann, Adam · 207
Neurodivergence · 168
neurodiversity · 146
Never Split the Difference · 160
New England textile mills · 116
New World · 13
NICU · 39, 40

R

radio · 18
Ranieri, Keith · 11
Representativeness heuristic · 120
reverse innovation · 104
reward · 42
Robben Island · 35
Robert Durst · 37
Rockefeller, John D. · 98, 196, 206
role modeling · 142
Roman Empire · 118
Ronan Point · 81, 82
Royal Dutch Shell · 19
Rudhyar, Dane · 65
rules of engagement · 52

S

Sagan, Carl · 198
San · 35
scurvy · 103
self-justification · 47
self-validation · 37
Self-validation · 38
sexual exploitation · 186
Shaklee, Dr. Forrest · 98, 195
SID · 180
Sigmund Freud · 145
silver · 133
Simon Napier-Bell · 153
Skagit Bridge · 80
Skilling, Jeffrey · 206
skim milk · 49
sociopathy · 56
Soviet Union · 24, 34
soybean oil · 173
Space Shuttle · 106
Space Shuttle Challenger · 23, 107
Stalin, Josef · 28, 34, 205
Standard Oil · 19
Stanley Kubrick · 114
Starmer, Keir · 17, 205
Stephen Ressler · 79
Steve Jobs · 53, 140, 181
Stieg Larsson · 34
stimulus · 45
Stockholm Syndrome · 47, 115
strategic narcissism · 155
structural engineering · 79

Sudden Infant Death Syndrome] · 180
suicide · 189
Sunshine Skyway Bridge · 85
survival strategy · 40
Sweden · 33, 34
Synthesis & Counseling in Astrology · 78

T

Tacoma-Narrows Bridge · 84
Tay Bridge · 79, 80, 84, 193
Taylor, Frederick W. · 12
Thatcher, Margaret · 205
The Brown and White · 183
The Jinx · 183, 184
The Man Who Played with Fire · 35
The Missoulian · 124
The Netherlands · 15
The New York Times · 183
The Oregon Province of the Society of Jesus · 124
The wrongs, harms, and ineffectiveness of torture: A moral evaluation from empirical neuroscience · 48
Theranos · 11, 126
Thiokol · 107
Thirty Years War · 114
Thomas Bouch · 79
Thomas Jefferson · 113, 139
Tim Cook · 181
Tinder · 53
tipping point · 188
toxic behavior · 154
toxic narcissism · 50
toxic narcissist · 164
Transvaal Republic · 35
trauma · 41, 56
trauma bonding · 52
Trooper Carton · 191
Trump, Donald J. · 205
Tyl, Noel · 65

U

U.S. Government Accountability Office · 61
United Nations Declaration of Human Rights · 4
United States v. Microsoft Corporation · 150
University of Cambridge · 151
USS Pueblo · 29
USS Pueblo incident · 29
usury · 19

V

W

X

Y

Z

REFERENCES

[i] Casarella, MD, Jennifer (medical review). *Signs of a Toxic Person.* WebMD, December 18, 2022.

[2] Ruchikabasias. *History of Electricity.* Geeks for Geeks, last updated September 22, 2023.

[3] *Bias.* Merriam-Webster, last visited September 10, 2024.

[4] *Wordnik,* https://www.wordnik.com/words/bias

[5] Payne R.B., *Family Cuculidae (Cuckoos),* pp. 508–45 in del Hoyo J, Elliott A, Sargatal J (eds), 1997.

[6] Madison, Melissa. *Logotherapy: Viktor Frankl's Therapy of Meaning.* PositivePsychology.com, July 28, 2020

[7] *Universal Declaration of Human Rights.* United Nations, December 10, 1948.

[8] *The Principal of Life, Survival and Development.* Committee on the Rights of the Child, arts. 24, 27, 28, 29 and 31. 2006

[9] Graedon, Joe. *Antidepressants Linked to Violence: Rape, Robbery and Homicide.* The People's Pharmacy, October 5, 2015.

[10] *Golden Rule.* Wikipedia. https://en.wikipedia.org/wiki/Golden_Rule

[11] Pathak, Vinay Mohan et al. *Current status of pesticide effects on environment, human health and it's eco-friendly management as bioremediation: A comprehensive review.* National Library of Medicine. Front Microbiol. 2022; 13: 962619.

[12] Karr-Morse, Robin. *Ghosts from the Nursery – Tracing the Roots of Violence.* Grove Atlantic, December 23, 2013.

[13] *Myers-Briggs Type Indicator.* The Myer-Briggs Company.

[14] *DiSC Profile.* John Wiley & Sons.

[15] *Muisca,* Wikipedia - https://en.wikipedia.org/wiki/Muisca

[16] *El Dorado,* Wikipedia.

[17] Metz, Rachel. *Elizabeth Holmes sentenced to more than 11 years in prison for fraud.* CNN Business, November 18, 2022.

[18] *NXIVM Leader Keith Raneiri Sentenced to 120 Years.* U.S. Attorney's Office, EasternDistrict of New York, October 27, 2020.

[19] Ward, Patrick. *Frederick Taylor's Principles of Scientific Management.* Nanoglobals, October 3, 2021.

[20] McLaughlin, Katie. *How can trauma affect the brain?* University of Washington, Stress and Development Lab, 2014.

[21] Griffith, Cynthia. *Did El Dorado Really Exist?* Grunge, December 8, 2021.

[22] *Clog.* Wikipedia, https://en.wikipedia.org/wiki/Clog last visited August 27, 2024.

[23] *Our Corrupt Sense of Fairness.* Steemit, last visited July 28, 2024.

[24] *Summary of The Communist Manifesto by Karl Marx and Friedrich Engels.* Aure's Notes, October 12, 2021.

[25] Smith, G. Vance; Gow, Tom. *A massive, poorly recognized attack threatens to destroy America's vital middle class.* Freedom First Society, 2009.

[26] Walker, Peter; Sweney, Mark. *Starmer says his radical plan to freeze energy bills is needed to cut inflation.* The Guardian, August 15, 2022.

[27] Harris, Katie. *Keir Starmer admits real reason for scrapping winter fuel payments for pensioners.* August 27, 2024.

[28] *Khmer Rouge.* History.com, September 12, 2017.

[29] Reynolds Schram, Stuart. *Mao Zedong*, Encyclopaedia Brittanica, last updated July 13, 2024.

[30] *Is Vietnam Still a Communist Country?* Vietnam War, May 27, 2014.

[31] Boyce, Paul. *Why is Communism Bad?* Boycewire, updated May 8, 2023.

[32] *Pros and Cons of Communism (Guide).* Tag Vault, December 9, 2023.

[33] Yong, Nicholas. *Industrial espionage: How China sneaks out America's technology secrets.* BBC News, January 16, 2023.

[34] *Journalism's First Obligation Is to Tell the Truth.* NiemanReports, Nieman Foundation at Harvard, last visited January 24, 2024.

[35] Tonguette, Peter. *The Fake News of Orson Welles.* Humanities, Fall 2018, Vol. 39, No. 4.

[36] *Usury.* Wikipedia. https://en.wikipedia.org/wiki/Usury

[37] *Jews and Finance.* My Jewish Learning, last visited December 14, 2023.

[38] Naranjo, Roberto. *Medieval Banking – Twelfth and Thirteenth Centuries.* The Ohio State University, last edited 2023.

³⁹ *The Rhodes-Milner Secret Society, the Start of the New World Order.* Maier Files, last visited August 5, 2024.

⁴⁰ https://fabians.org.uk

⁴¹ Betterrightthanwrong. *The Milner-Fabian Conspiracy.* Last visited August 5, 2024. https://milnerfabianconspiracy.wordpress.com/2012/10/13/hello-world/

⁴² Ratiu, Ioan. *The Milner-Fabian Conspiracy.* Free Europe Books, September 20, 2012.

⁴³ *Golden Rule.* Wikipedia. https://en.wikipedia.org/wiki/Golden_Rule

⁴⁴ *1 John 3:4.* Bible Gateway, last visited December 14, 2023.

⁴⁵ Sicinski, Adam. *Understanding the Law of Cause and Effect.* IQ Matrix, last visited December 14, 2023.

⁴⁶ *French invasion of Russia.* Encyclopaedia Britannica, November 23, 2023.

⁴⁷ *Napoleon.* Wikipedia, https://en.wikipedia.org/wiki/Napoleon

⁴⁸ *Operation Market Garden.* Wikipedia. https://en.wikipedia.org/wiki/Operation_Market_Garden

⁴⁹ *Peninsular War.* Wikipedia. https://en.wikipedia.org/wiki/Peninsular_War

⁵⁰ Klemann, Hein A.M. *Did the German Occupation (1940-1945) Ruin Dutch Industry?* JSTOR. Originally published by Cambridge University Press, Vol. 17, No. 4, November 2008, pp. 457-481.

⁵¹ Van Leeuwen, Sacha. *Remembering the Netherlands during World War II: War Diaries and the Role of the Historian in Collective Memory.* EuropeNow, Council for European Studies, last visited December 15, 2023.

⁵² Hansen, Saskia; Zarankin, Julia. *A Founding Myth for the Netherlands: The Second World War and the Victimization of Dutch Jews.* Begemann, 1985, quoted in: De Haan, Ido. "The Construction of a National Trauma: The Memory of the Persecution of the Jews in the Netherlands". The Netherlands' Journal of Social Sciences. Vol. 34:1. 1998.

⁵³ *The Geneva Conventions of 1949 and their Additional Protocols.* International Committee of the Red Cross, October 29, 2010.

⁵⁴ Brischetto, Patrick. *Diego Maradona Hand of God goal: The story of a legendary World Cup moment.* The Sporting News, December 17, 2022.

⁵⁵ *Gamesmanship.* Merriam-Webster Dictionary, last visited August 22, 2024.

⁵⁶ *1978 World Cup Final.* Wikipedia.

[57] Reuters. *Argentine referee accuses player of threatening to kill him.* The Times of India, December 1, 2021.

[58] Pruitt, Sarah. *5 Things You May not Know about the Space Shuttle Challenger Disaster.* History.com, January 28, 2016.

[59] *Chernobyl.* History.com, April 24, 2018.

[60] *Deepwater Horizon oil spill.* Encyclopaedia Brittanica, last visited November 29, 2023.

[61] *Understanding How Deepwater Horizon Affected Fishing Community Decisions.* Gulf of Mexico Research Initiative, January 26, 2016.

[62] Halperin, Demian. *Environmental noise and sleep disturbances, a threat to health?* Sleep Science, December 2014.

[63] Rizzolatti, Giacomo; Craighero, Laila. *The Mirror-Neuron System.* Annu. Rev. Neurosci. 2004. 27:169–92; doi: 10.1146/annurev.neuro.27.070203.144230, March 5, 2004.

[64] Limbach, Raymond. *Blitzkrieg.* Encyclopaedia Brittanica, last updated July 26, 2024.

[65] *Maginot Line.* Crisis and Achievement, last visited August 27, 2024.

[66] *The Drug That Fuelled the Nazi Blitz Krieg.* Sky History, last visited August 27, 2024.

[67] MSW. *French Military Doctrine – 1940.* Weapons and Warfare, August 10, 2018.

[68] Martin, Jonathan. *Spy Web.* A+E Networks, 2000.

[69] *Biography of Kim Philby (excerpt).* AstroTheme, last visited November 6, 2024. https://www.astrotheme.com/astrology/Kim_Philby

[70] *Kim Philby.* Wikipedia. https://en.wikipedia.org/wiki/Kim_Philby

[71] *Amy.* Wikipedia, https://en.wikipedia.org/wiki/Amy_(2015_film).

[72] Toprani, Anand. *Oil and the Great Powers: Britain and Germany, Ch. 7 - From Crisis to Opportunity: 1931-1941.* Oxford Academic; Oxford University Press, April 2019. Ch. 7, p. 67.

[73] Barber, James. *'Blitzed:' How Drugs Fueled the Rise and Fall of Nazi Germany.* Military.com, March 7, 2017.

[74] *USS Pueblo (AGER-2).* Wikipedia, last visited April 11, 2024.

[75] Bamford, James. *Body of Secrets: Anatomy of the Ultra-Secret National Security Agency.* Anchor Books, reprint edition December 18, 2007; Ch. 8.

[76] Schultz, Colin. *The Time the U.S. Nearly Nuked North Korea Over a Highjacked Spy Ship*. Smithsonian Magazine, January 28, 2014.

[77] Saverese, Mauricio; Goodman, Joshua. *Crusading judge tests boundaries of free speech in Brazil*. Associated Press, January 25, 2023.

[78] *Olof Palme*. Wikipedia, last visited July 15, 2024.

[79] *Jewish Wall Street Bankers Funded The Communist Bolshevik Revolution*. State of the Nation, July 28, 2020.

[80] Weber, Mark. *The Jewish Role in the Bolshevik Revolution and Russia's Early Soviet Regime*. The Unz Review, Jan/Feb 1994.

[81] Fetzer, James. *Historical Retrospective: The Jewish Destruction of the Russian Empire*. James H. Fetzer.org, December 8, 2019.

[82] Elie, Marc; Coumel, Laurent. *A Belated and Tragic Ecological Revolution: Nature, Disasters and Green Activists in the Soviet Union and the Post-Soviet States, 1960-2010s*. The Soviet and Post-Soviet Review 40(2):157-165, January 2013.

[83] Team Mighty. *The best Cold War communist military technology was all stolen from the West*. We Are The Mighty, updated August 2, 2022.

[84] Murawiec, Laurent. *The Soviet technology-stealing machine and the loopholes in Western security*. Executive Intelligence Review, Vol. 11, No. 8, May 8, 1994.

[85] Stocklassa, Jan. *The Man Who Played with Fire*. Sky Documentaries, 2024.

[86] Vigne, Randolph; Lowe, Christopher C. *The Delagoa Bay slave trade*. Encyclopaedia Britannica, last updated August 9, 2024.

[87] *Early history of South Africa*. Wikipedia.

[88] *Jan Van Riebeeck Biography*. TheFamousPeople, last visited August 10, 2024.

[89] *Concentration Camp: The Most Shameful British Invention*. WAS, last visited August 10, 2024.

[90] Dickens, Peter. *Debunking the myth that the British invented the 'concentration camp.'* The Observation Post, last visited August 10, 2024.

[91] Michener, James A. *The Covenant*. Dial Press Trade, March 10, 2015. Original publication January 1, 1980.

[92] *Trauma bonding explained*. Medical News Today, last visited March 11, 2024.

[93] *Lewin's equation*. Wikipedia.

[94] Lewin, Kurt. *Principles of Topological Psychology*. (F. Heider & G. M. Heider, Trans.). McGraw-Hill, 1936.

[95] *About the Affordable Care Act.* U.S. Department of Health and Human Services, last visited November 30, 2023.

[96] Messerly, Megan. *Minnesota wanted to curb health spending. Mayo Clinic had other ideas.* Politico, May 30, 2023.

[97] Riggs, Kathy. *Seven Tips for Raising Responsible Children.* UtahStateUniversity Extension, last visited November 30, 2023.

[98] Riskin, Arieh, et al. *The Impact of Rudeness on Medical Team Performance: A Randomized Trial.* Pediatrics. 2015 Sep;136(3):487-95. doi: 10.1542/peds.2015-1385. Epub August 10, 2015.

[99] Kugelman, Amir et al. *Iatrogenic harm to newborns occurs at a high rate in neonatal intensive care units.* GreenMedInfo, sourced from Nephron. 2001 Dec;89(4):433-8. PMID: 18762525. Last visited August 24, 2024.

[100] Ford, Georgina. *Prevalence vs. Incidence: what is the difference?* Students 4 Best Evidence, November 6, 2020.

[101] Clayton, Ph.D., Ingrid. *What is Complex PTSD?* Psychology Today, August 27, 2021.

[102] Marsh, Abigail. *What is the Amygdala, and What Does it Have to do with Helping?* SPSP, September 13, 2019.

[103] *Complex PTSD: From Surviving to Thriving*; Walker, Pete. Azure Coyote Publishing, December 18, 2013.

[104] Bouton, M.E. *Learning and behavior: A contemporary synthesis.* 2007. [MA Sinauer: Sunderland. Archived from the original on 2012-11-27]

[105] Karr-Morse, Robin. *Ghosts from the Nursery – Tracing the Roots of Violence.* Grove Atlantic, December 23, 2013.

[106] *Operation Fortitude.* Wikipedia.

[107] *Stockholm Syndrome.* Cleveland Clinic, last visited August 27, 2024.

[108] Tavris, Carol & Aronson, Eliot. *Mistakes Were Made (but not by me): Why we justify foolish beliefs, bad decisions and hurtful acts.* Mariner Books, April 28, 2020.

[109] *200 Years Ago, Faraday Invented the Electric Motor*; Marsh, Alison. IEEE Spectrum, August 27, 2021.

[110] Al-Rodhan, Nayef. *The wrongs, harms, and ineffectiveness of torture: A moral evaluation from empirical neuroscience.* Wiley online library, Journal of Social Philosophy, §2.2. October 2, 2022.

[111] Rhodewait, Frederick. *Narcissism.* Encyclopediae Brittanica, last updated December 4, 2023.

[112] Lemley, Brad. *The Worst Kind of Milk*. BradLemley, May 15, 2019.

[113] Staughton, John. *4 Health Benefits of Skim Milk*. Organic Information Services Pvt Ltd., February 26, 2020.

[114] *The Essential Guide: how many grams of sugar we need per day*. Tavik.com, December 26, 2023.

[115] Steinmetz, K.A. et al. *Effect of consumption of whole milk and skim milk on blood lipid profiles in healthy men*. The American Journal of Clinical Nutrition, Vol. 59, Issue 3P612-618, March 1994.

[116] *New Study Claims Skim Milk Consumption In Children Can Lead To Obesity*. Medical Daily, March 19, 2013.

[117] Bali, Vinayak. *Skim Milk and Whole Milk Market Report 2024 (Global Edition)*. Cognitive Market Research, Report ID CMR487341, December 2, 2022.

[118] Lemley, Brad. *The Worst Kind of Milk*. BradLemley, May 15, 2019.

[119] Smith-Howard, Kendra. *Pure and Modern Milk: An Environmental History Since 1900*. Oxford University Press, 978-0-19-989912-8, 2013.

[120] Simon, Dr., George. *Narcissism Spectrum*. Dr. George Simon, May 18, 2018.

[121] Nenadic, Igor, et al. *Narcissistic personality traits and prefrontal brain structure*. National Library of Medicine, Published online 2021 Aug 3. doi: 10.1038/s41598-021-94920-z.

[122] *Brain Games*. Netflix. https://decider.com/2015/02/23/brain-games-netflix/

[123] King, Barbara. *Deception in the Animal Kingdom*. Scientific American, September 1, 2019.

[124] Cusack, Joseph; Connor, Laura. *Devastated woman's best friend posed as lover to con her out of £117,000 life savings*. Mirror, April 23, 2022.

[125] McPhillips, Deirdre. *More than 1 million people have died of Covid-19 in the US*. CNN, May 17, 2022.

[126] Feng, John. *Anthony Fauci's China Investments Revealed*. Newsweek, January 18, 2022.

[127] Moniuszko, Sara. *Florida surgeon general wants to halt Covid-19 mRNA vaccines; FDA calls his claims "misleading."* CBS News, January 4, 2024.

[128] Griffin, Misty. *Tears of the Silenced*. https://www.mistygriffin.com

[129] Griffin, Misty. Congress: *We need a Child Rights Act. Child Sexual Abuse is a Public Safety Emergency*. Change.org, last visited January 15, 2023.

[130] Sanyal, Neeti. *How to Manipulate Customers…Ethically*. Harvard Business Review, October 26, 2021.

[131] *United States racial unrest (2020 to present)*. Wikipedia, last visited January 13, 2024.

[132] Karr-Morse, Robin. *Ghosts from the Nursery – Tracing the Roots of Violence*. Grove Atlantic, December 23, 2013.

[133] Hooton, Christopher. *Swedish music festival to be female-only 'until men learn to behave themselves'*. The Independent, July 5, 2017.

[134] Roach, April. *Amsterdam Says Party-Seeking British Men Are No Longer Welcome*. Bloomberg, March 29, 2023.

[135] *Narcissistic Personality Disorder*, Mayo Clinic. Last visited July 3, 2023.

[136] McElroy, Molly. *Babies show sense of fairness, altruism as early as 15 months*. Science Daily, University of Washington, October 10, 2011.

[137] Raskin, Robert; Hall, Calvin. *Narcissism Personality Inventory*. Wikipedia. https://en.wikipedia.org/wiki/Narcissistic_Personality_Inventory

[138] *Enron Scandal*. Wikipedia.

[139] Hayes, Adam. *Bernard Madoff: Who He Was, How His Ponzi Scheme Worked*. Investopedia, March 29, 2023.

[140] Garbus, Liz. *The Farm: Angola, USA*. Gabriel Films; Seventh Art Releasing, 1998.

[141] Robinson, Arthur, Dr. *Children Learn by Example*. Practical Homeschooling, 1994.

[142] *Prince Yasuhiko Asaka*. Wikipedia. https://en.wikipedia.org/wiki/Prince_Yasuhiko_Asaka

[143] White, David. *The Japanese Occupation of China 1937-45: The Divided Opposition and its Consequences*. Open History Society, last visited December 27, 2023.

[144] *Fraud Risk Management: 2018-2022 Data Show Federal Government Loses an Estimated $233 Billion to $521 Billion to Fraud, Based on Various Risk Environments*. U.S. Government Accountability Office, GAO-24-105833, April 16, 2024.

[145] *Bones of Contention: Cadaver-sniffing canine's finds are under suspicion* (ed., original document has been removed)

[146] *Fraudulent Use of Canines in Police Work*, (ed., document has been removed). Daniel A. Smith, Lincoln Park Police Department.

[147] *16 cases mired in dog handler's fraud.* wrongful-convictions, August 30, 2009.

[148] *K9 Fraud! Essential Reading for Handlers, Lawyers, and Judges.* Dog Law Reporter, November 11, 2011.

[149] *An Eagle-Eyed Investigation? Police Dog Is Brought In To Crack A 20-Year-Old Murder*, http://www.cbsnews.com/news/an-eagle-eyed-investigation/

[150] Parker, Harold T. *Why Did Napoleon Invade Russia? A Study in Motivation and the Interrelations of Personality and Social Structure.* The Journal of Military History, April 1, 1990.

[151] Manaev. George. *Why did Napoleon invade Russia?* Russia Beyond, March 6, 2020.

[152] Saw, Charlie. *An Introduction to Western Astrology: Unlocking the Mysteries of the Zodiac, Planets, and Houses.* Finance Geek, July 7, 2023.

[153] *Horoscope.* Wikipedia. https://en.wikipedia.org/wiki/Horoscope

[154] Astrodienst, www.astro.com

[155] Pabilo. *Executive Functions: What are they, and how to develop them?* IQ Exam Blog, March 22, 2024.

[156] Calderon, Johanna, Ph.D. *Executive function in children, Why it matters and how to help.* Harvard Health Publishing, Harvard Medical School, December 16, 2020.

[157] Hall, Michael. *Foster Mother Whose Children Testified in the "Mineola Swingers Club" Case Now Accused of Abuse.* Texas Monthly, November 10, 2013.

[158] Hall, Michael. *'How to Create a Sex Scandal': What you need to know about the new Docuseries.* Texas Monthly, May 23, 2023.

[159] Mehrotra, Kriti. *Margie and John Cantrell: Where are the foster parents now?* TheCinemaholic, May 24, 2023.

[160] *Margaret R. Cantrell.* ClustrMaps - https://clustrmaps.com/person/Cantrell-aqsoa8

[161] Voss, Chris. *Never Split the Difference: Negotiating As if Your Life Depended On It.* Harper Business, May 17, 2016.

[162] David, Larry. *Curb Your Enthusiasm*, S7E10. Home Box Office, 2001-2021.

[163] *Liar's Poker*; Lewis, Michael. W.W. Norton & Company, March 15, 2010.

[164] Perry, Alex. *Oprah Scandal Rocks South Africa.* Time Magazine, November 5, 2007.

165 Tyl, Noel. *Synthesis & Counseling in Astrology*. Llewellyn, 2002.

166 *200 Years Ago, Faraday Invented the Electric Motor*; Marsh, Alison. IEEE Spectrum, August 27, 2021.

167 Cartwright, Mark. *English Civil Wars*. World History Encyclopedia, February 18, 2022.

168 Tearle, Dr. Oliver. *The Meaning and Origin of 'To Err is Human, to Forgive Divine.'* Interesting Literature, last visited December 21, 2023.

169 *Tay Bridge disaster*. Wikipedia. https://en.wikipedia.org/wiki/Tay_Bridge_disaster

170 Ressler, Ph.D., Stephen. *Epic Engineering Failures and the Lessons They Teach*. The Great Courses, last visited December 21, 2023.

171 Peterson, Ph.D., Jillian, et al. *Communication of Intent to do Harm Preceding Mass Public Shootings in the United States, 1966-2019*. JAMA Network, November 4, 2021.

172 Ramirez, Quixem. *2 vehicles, 3 people plunged into water after Skagit River Bridge collapsed on this day in 2013*. KING-TV, May 23, 2023.

173 Intelligencer Staff. *Surfside Condo Collapse: What We Know The search has officially shifted from a rescue operation to the recovery of bodies*. New York Magazine, updated July 13, 2021.

174 *The Collapse of Ronan Point*. Hidden Histories, February 26, 2019.

175 Cook, Chris. *Ronan Point: A Fifty Year Building Safety Problem*. BBC News, June 15, 2018.

176 *Grenfell Tower: What Happened*. BBC News, October 29, 2019.

177 Van Steenwyk, Jason. *Deadly London apartment blaze highlights fire safety issues*. Buildium, July 11, 2017.

178 *Grenfell Tower Fire*. Wikipedia, https://en.wikipedia.org/wiki/Grenfell_Tower_fire

179 *Tacoma Narrows Bridge (1940)*. Wikipedia. https://en.wikipedia.org/wiki/Tacoma_Narrows_Bridge_(1940)

180 *Leon Moisseiff*. Wikipedia. https://en.wikipedia.org/wiki/Leon_Moisseiff

181 *Tacoma Narrows Bridge Collapses*. History, A&E Television Networks LLC, last visited December 22, 2023.

182 *16 cases mired in dog handler's fraud*. wrongful-convictions, August 30, 2009.

[183] Paget, Sharif. *Bassam Youssef: The wild story of Égypt's Jon Stewart'*. BBC News, January 10, 2018.

[184] Bowen, Jeremy. *Arab Spring: How the uprisings still echo, 10 years on*. BBC News, February 11, 2021.

[185] Graumann, Angelina. *7+ VC Firms Funding the Future of Healthcare in 2024*. Visible, March 16, 2024.

[186] *The AOA's Code of Ethics provides guidance on medical ethics and professional responsibilities*. American Osteopathic Association, last visited September 7, 2024.

[187] *Renal Dialysis Equipment Market Size & Share Analysis – Growth Trends and Forecasts (2023-2028)*. Mordor Intelligence, 2023.

[188] *Dialysis Equipment Market Size, Share and Industry Analysis etc*. Fortune Business Insights, August 2019.

[189] Ornstein, Charles. *We've Been Tracking Pharma Payments to Doctors for Nearly a Decade. We Just Made a Big Breakthrough*. ProPublica, December 20, 2019.

[190] Harrity, Patricia. *Leaked Documents Show American Doctors Were Financially Rewarded For Pushing The Covid Jab*. The Expose, August 21, 2023.

[191] *Truth*. Stanford Encyclopedia of Philosophy, last revised August 16, 2018.

[192] *Voir dire*. Wikipedia, https://en.wikipedia.org/wiki/Voir_dire

[193] *Innocence Project*. https://innocenceproject.org/exonerations-data/

[194] *William Blake: The fool who persists in his folly will become wise*. The Socratic Method, last visited December 26, 2023.

[195] *Moody's*. https://www.moodys.com

[196] *S&P Global Ratings*. https://www.spglobal.com/ratings/en/

[197] Wojtowicz, Marcin. *CDOs and the financial crisis: Credit ratings and fair premia*. Elseview, Journal of Banking & Finance, Vol. 39, pgs 1-13. February, 2014. Last visited on ScienceDirect, December 26, 2023.

[198] Oxley, Sonia. *Wimbledon 2023: The Ball Boys from Barnardo's*. BBC News, June 28, 2023.

[199] *Effectiveness of torture for interrogation*, Wikipedia.

[200] Tavris, Carol; Aronson, Eliot. *Mistakes Were Made (but not by me): Why we justify foolish beliefs, bad decisions and hurtful acts*. Mariner Books, April 28, 2020.

[201] *Misattribution of memory*, Wikipedia.

[202] *Grass Fed versus Corn Fed: You Are What Your Food Eats*, HighQuest Group, 2016.

[203] *E. Coli*. Mayo Clinic, last visited December 30, 2023.

[204] Spunt, Georges. *When Nature Speaks: The Life Of Forrest C. Shaklee, Sr.* Frederick Fell Publishers, January 1, 1977.

[205] Schmidt, LAC, Eric. *How Rockefeller Created the Business of Modern Medicine*. Meridian Health Clinic, last visited December 30, 2023.

[206] Jacqueline. *The Hidden Connection of Rockefeller, Homeopathy & Chiropractic.* Deep Roots at Home, June 8, 2024.

[207] Bunea Ph.D., Emilia. *The Truth About Corporate Psychopaths*. Psychology Today, May 12, 2023.

[208] Price, Catherine. *The Age of Scurvy*. Distillations Magazine, Health & Medicine. August 14, 2017.

[209] *The British 'Limeys' Were Right: A Short History of Scurvy*. Health.mil, Military Health System and Defense Health Agency, last visited December 7, 2023.

[210] *Estimated share of African slaves who did not survive the Middle Passage journey to the Americas each year from 1501 to 1866.* Statista, last visited December 7, 2023.

[211] Yanes, Javier. *Low-Cost Technology from Poor Countries that Saves Lives in Rich Countries*. BBVA Open Mind, October 27, 2021.

[212] *Space Shuttle*, Wikipedia. https://en.wikipedia.org/wiki/Space_Shuttle

[213] Malik, Tariq. *NASA's Space Shuttle By The Numbers: 30 Years of a Spaceflight Icon*. Space.com, July 21, 2011.

[214] Forrest, Jeff. *The Space Shuttle Challenger Disaster, A failure in decision support system and human factors management*. Metropolitan State College, November 26, 1996.

[215] Wall, Mike. *Documentary Probes Challenger Disaster on 30th Anniversary (Exclusive Video)*, National Geographic, 2016.

[216] Levine, Peter A. *Waking the Tiger: Healing Trauma*. North Atlantic Books, July 7, 1997.

[217] Clayton, Ph.D., Ingrid. *What is the Fawning Trauma Response?* Psychology Today, March 24, 2023.

[218] *The Great Pacific Garbage Patch*. The Ocean Cleanup, last visited December 26, 2023.

[219] *What is industrial and organizational psychology?* Psychology 2e, Openstax, last visited December 26, 2023.

[220] VonMinden, Nathan. *The Challenger Disaster*. Vertical Entertainment, 2019.

[221] *The meaning of "existential."* The Britannica Dictionary, last visited December 7, 2023.

[222] Ranga, Dana. *I Am In Space*. Journeyman Pictures, 2014.

[223] Mises Institute- https://mises.org/

[224] *100 Most Famous Aries in History*. On This Day, last visited December 26, 2023.

[225] *Leopold II*. Encyclopediae Brittanica, last visited December 27, 2023.

[226] *Kim Il-Sung*. Encyclopediae Brittannica, last visited December 27, 2023.

[227] *Philip IV*. Encyclopediae Brittanica, last visited December 27, 2023.

[228] *Stanley Kubrick*. Biography, August 14, 2019.

[229] Eby, Douglas. *Gifted and Shy: Kubrick; Kidman and Others*. High Ability, 2023.

[230] Miele, Ph.D., Laura. *How a Coach's Attitude Can Affect an Athlete's Mentality*. Psychology Today, February 22, 2022.

[231] Phillips, Tom. *The Cultural Revolution: all you need to know about China's political convulsion*. The Guardian, May 10, 2016.

[232] Szczepanski, Kallie. *The Great Leap Forward: Millions died of starvation*. ThoughtCo., September 3, 2019.

[233] *Stockholm Syndrome*. Cleveland Clinic, last visited December 27, 2023.

[234] Rouan, Rick. *Fact Check: Stat grossly misleading about slave ownership in 1860*. USA Today, July 16, 2021.

[235] *The Mill Girls of Lowell*. National Park Service, last visited December 27, 2023.

[236] *Is there any truth to the claim that freed slaves who moved to Liberia enslaved the local population?* History.stackexchange.com, 2013. https://history.stackexchange.com/questions/10267/is-there-any-truth-to-the-claim-that-freed-slaves-who-moved-to-liberia-enslaved

[237] *History of Liberia*. Wikipedia. https://en.wikipedia.org/wiki/History_of_Liberia

[238] Wilson, Richard. *William Tolbert Jr.'s Triple Legacy to Liberia*. Good Faith Media, May 27, 2014.

[239] *Nzinga of Ndongo and Matamba.* Wikipedia.

[240] *The Arab Muslim Slave Trade of Africans, The Untold Story.* Alliance of Progressive Young Africans, last visited December 27, 2023.

[241] Gillan, Joanna. *Remembering the Barbary Slaves: White Slaves and North African Pirates.* Ancient Origins, February 2, 201.

[242] Davis, Robert C. *Christian Slaves, Muslim Masters: white slavery in the Mediterranean, the Barbary Coast and Italy, 1500-1800.* Internet Archive, 2004.

[243] Gillan, Joanna. *Remembering the Barbary Slaves: White Slaves and North African Pirates.* Ancient Origins, February 2, 2021.

[244] *China's Belt and Road Initiative turns 10. Here's what to know.* World Economic Forum, November 20, 2023.

[245] Nyabiage, Jevans. *China finds manufacturing opportunities in low-wage Africa.* myNews, June 1, 2020.

[246] *Habitat for Humanity.*

[247] *Livable Wage by State 2024.* World Population Review, last visited August 25, 2024.

[248] Bhutada, Govind. *Purchasing Power of the U.S. Dollar Over Time.* Visual Capitalist, April 6, 2021.

[249] Daniel, Warren. *How Much Did a House Cost in 1960?* MSS, July 17, 2022.

[250] Yayan. *Unsung Heroes: The Thankless Struggle of Volunteering.* VolunteerPeninsula.org, October 7, 2023.

[251] Savage, Gail. *How cruelty became the point of our labor and welfare policies.* The Washington Post, May 26, 2021.

[252] Madhok, Diksha. *Daniel Kahneman, the Nobel Prize winner who wrote Thinking, Fast and Slow, dies aged 90.* CNN, March 28, 2024.

[253] Perera, Ayesh. *Framing Effect in Psychology.* SimplyPsychology, September 7, 2023.

[254] Chen, James. *Hindsight Bias: Causes, Examples and FAQ.* Investopedia, September 29, 2022.

[255] Holzman, Randall. *How The Representativeness Heuristic Affects Decisions and Bias.* Verywellmind, January 15, 2023.

[256] Weinschenk, Ph.D., Susan. *Great Stories Release Brain Chemicals.* Psychology Today, May 13, 2016.

[257] Melamede, Yeal. *(Dis)Honesty – The Truth About Lies*. Bond/360, 2015.

[258] *Police officers accused of issuing dozens of bogus tickets.* Associated Press, April 22, 2021.

[259] *Nuns among worst perpetrators of horrific violence and sex abuse in Jesuit-run schools and missions on Indian reservations*, The Missoulian. Montana, June 5, 2011.

[260] Beasley, Jessica; Bottle, Ana. *12 of the greatest civil engineers of all time.* Institution of Civil Engineers, February 18, 2022.

[261] *Theranos Scandal: Who is Elizabeth Homes and why was she on trial?* BBC, November 19, 2022.

[262] Burgemeester, Alexander. *11 Famous Narcissistic Leaders in History.* The Narcissistic Life, July 3, 2023.

[263] *Robert Mugabe.* Wikipedia. https://en.wikipedia.org/wiki/Robert_Mugabe

[264] *On the Origin of Species.* Encyclopaedia Britannica, last visited December 15, 2023.

[265] Wong, Kate. *How Scientists Discovered the Staggering Complexity of Human Evolution.* SCIAM, September 1, 2020.

[266] *Cuckoo tricks to beat the neighborhood watch.* University of Cambridge, via PhysOrg, August 2, 2012.

[267] Featherstone, Nicky. *How Do Beaver Dams Affect the Environment?* Forest Wildlife, September 13, 2021.

[268] Johnystamy. *Long Term Effects of Malaria on Labour Productivity.* Effective Altruism Forum, October 29, 2015.

[269] Justine Hausheer. *How Do Elephants "Talk" to Each Other?* National Audubon Society.

[270] Zahavi, Amotz A. *The Handicap Principle: A Missing Piece of Darwin's Puzzle.* Oxford University Press, August 7, 1997.

[271] Sumner, Thomas. *ScienceShot: Did Lead Poisoning Bring Down the Roman Empire?* Science, April 21, 2014.

[272] Eugene M. McCarthy, PhD. *What do lions eat? Almost any animal they* can, December 5, 2012.

[273] Matthew 7:7. *'Ask and You Shall Receive' Bible Meaning.* Christianity.com, last visited December 29, 2023.

[274] Goddard, Neville, *Feeling is the Secret.* Textbook Classics, 2012.

[275] *The Unexamined Life is Not Worth Living* – Socrates. Wikipedia.

[276] Goddard, Neville, *Feeling is the Secret.* Textbook Classics, 2012.

[277] Conatus, Wikipedia.

[278] Phillips, DDS, Ellie. *Ancient Wisdom: The History of Xylitol.* DrEllie.com, last visited August 20, 2024.

[279] *What is dental amalgam?* Consumers for Dental Choice, Inc.

[280] *Dentist Laser May Spell End for Fillings.* Dailyrecord.co.uk, February 18, 2008.

[281] Honkala, E. et al. *Chewing of xylitol gum – a well adopted practice among finnish adolescents.* PubMed, Caries Res. 1996;30(1):34-9. doi: 10.1159/000262134.

[282] *Does Asbestos, One of Nature's Most Useful Minerals, Deserve Its Bad Reputation?* The Natural Handyman, last visited August 20, 2024.

[283] Levine, Peter A. *Waking the Tiger: Healing Trauma.* North Atlantic Books, July 7, 1997.

[284] Dwoskin, Hale. *The Sedona Method.* Sedona Press, July 30, 2003.

[285] *The History of the Axe.* Gränsfors Bruk, last visited March 11, 2024.

[286] Lemke, Eric. *Finnish 'Leveraxe' Looks to Go Mainstream in U.S.* Gearjunkie, August 14, 2015.

[287] Tavris, Carol; Aronson, Eliot. *Mistakes Were Made (but not by me): Why we justify foolish beliefs, bad decisions and hurtful acts.* Mariner Books, April 28, 2020.

[288] *What is Family Constellations?* Hellinger Institute, last visited March 31, 2024.

[289] *John D. Rockefeller.* Wikipedia. https://en.wikipedia.org/wiki/John_D._Rockefeller

[290] *Steve Jobs.* Astrodienst Astro-databank, last visited December 28, 2023.

[291] McLeod, Saul, Ph.D., *Stanley Milgram Shock Experiment: Summary, Results, & Ethics.* SimplyPsychology, June 16, 2023.

[292] Burke, Hilda. *Pets in prison: the rescue dogs teaching Californian inmates trust and responsibility.* Guardian News & Media Limited, April 19, 2020.

[293] Maidenberg, Michelle. *14 Strategies for Building Confidence in Your Children.* Psychology Today, March 2, 2021.

[294] *H. H. Holmes.* Wikipedia. https://en.wikipedia.org/wiki/H._H._Holmes

[295] Cherry, MSEd., Kendra. *Sigmund Freud's Life, Theories and Influence.* Verywellmind, August 15, 2022.

[296] *A new perspective on you.* MBTI, last visited December 28, 2023.

[297] *DiSC Personality Assessment.* Truity, last visited December 28, 2023.

[298] *List of tests.* Wikipedia.

[299] Baumer, MD, MEd., Nicole ; Frueh, MD, Julia. *What is neurodiversity?* Harvard Health Publishing, November 23, 2021.

[300] Kolber, Jerry & Margol, Bill. *Brain Games.* Magical Elves Productions, National Geographic Television. October 9, 2011.

[301] *World Population.* Wikipedia.

[302] *Volkswagen Emissions Scandal.* Wikipedia.

[303] Vaknin, Sam. *Acquired Situational Narcissism.* HealthyPlace Inc., last visited December 28, 2023.

[304] *United States v. Microsoft Corporation* 253 F.3d 34 (D.C. Cir. 2001).

[305] Jenkins, Gregory T.; Robert W. Bing (January 2007). *Microsoft's Monopoly: Anti-Competitive Behavior, Predatory Tactics, And The Failure Of Governmental Will.* Journal of Business & Economic Research 5 (1): 11–16. Retrieved 23 February 2013 - Wikipedia.

[306] Kawamoto, Dawn, *Gates Deposition Called Evasive.* C|net August 28, 1998.

[307] Wasserman, Elizabeth, *Gates deposition makes judge laugh in court.* CNN.com, November 17, 1998.

[308] Richman, Sheldon. *Clinton's Legacy: The Financial and Housing Meltdown.* Reason, October 14, 2012.

[309] Henry, Ed et al., *Bush: Bailout plan necessary to deal with crisis.* CNN.com, 1998.

[310] Bader, Hans, *Obama Justice Department Forces Banks to Make Risky Loans, Planting the Seeds of a Future Financial Crisis.* Competitive Enterprise Institute, August 31, 2011.

[311] Armitage, Richard, *Bulling in children: impact on child health.* BMJ Paediatr Open. 2021; 5(1): e000939.

[312] Callaway, Ewen, *Starvation in pregnant mice marks offspring DNA.* Nature, 2014.

[313] Agostinis, Valentina. *Blow up of "Blow Up."* Minimum Fax Media, December 16, 2016.

[314] Brooks, Jon. *13 Crazy Facts About Iceman Wim Hof That Nobody Talks About.* HighExistence, June 26, 2023.

[315] Greene, Robert. *The Laws of Human Nature.* Viking, October 23, 2018.

[316] Stoffelen, Anneke; Griend, Robert van de. *The outside world knows Wim Hof as the eccentric Iceman. His family suffered domestic violence.* de Volkskrant, September 28, 2024.

[317] *Narcissistic personality disorder. Mayo Clinic, last visited January 8, 2024.*

[318] *5 Types of Narcissism and How to Spot Each. PsychCentral, last visited June 7, 2024.*

[319] Elving, Ron. *Latest Tell-All, By Former National Security Adviser McMaster, Is Not All About Trump.* NPR, September 21, 2020.

[320] *Schulze et al. Universitätsmedizin Berlin, 2013, quoted in: Davis, Shirley. The Neuroscience of Narcissism and Narcissistic Abuse. CPTSD Foundation.org, June 22, 2020.*

[321] *Corelli, Carla. Understanding Antagonistic Narcissism – Traits, Characteristics and Behaviours. October 15, 2023.*

[322] *American Masters: Inventing David Geffen. PBS, November 20, 2012.*

[323] Huff, Ethan. *Shocking incident on X proves that psychiatrists and psychologists are power-hungry, narcissistic psychopaths.* Deception.news, July 9, 2024.

[324] Sarkis, Ph.D., Stephanie. *Why Toxic People Are So Harmful.* Psychology Today, June 27, 2023.

[325] Voss, Christopher. *Never Split the Difference: Negotiating As If Your Life Depended On It.* Harper Business, 2016.

[326] Ingham, Harry. *Dana Twidale and The Big Swindle – victims of Hull wedding planner speak out on Quest Red show.* HullLive, May 27, 2023.

[327] Harrison, Jody. *Explained: What are Scotland's New Hate Crime Laws?* The Herald, March 14, 2024.

[328] Cowling, Patrick; Forsyth, Alex. *Huge rise in domestic abuse cases being dropped in England and Wales.* BBC News, October 15, 2021.

[329] Main, Nikki. *Electric cars release MORE toxic emissions than gas-powered vehicles and are worse for the environment, resurfaced study warns.* Daily Mail, March 4, 2024.

[330] Delbert, Caroline. *Supercapacitors Are About to Blow Past Batteries as the Kings of Power.* Popular Mechanics, June 10, 2024.

[331] *Philby, Kim.* Astro-Databank, last visited November 13, 2024. https://www.astro.com/astro-databank/Philby,_Kim

[332] Musser, George. *The Origin of Cubicles and the Open-Plan Office.* Scientific American, August 17, 2009.

[333] Bernstein, Ethan; Waber, Ben. *The Truth About Open Offices.* Harvard Business Review, Nov.-Dec. 2019.

[334] Carmelo, Sammi. *How to Stay Productive in a Loud Office.* Business News Daily, updated May 31, 2024.

[335] Lam, Vivian. *Open-plan office noise increases stress and worsens mood: we've measured the effects.* The Conversation, July 4, 2021.

[336] Lam, Vivian. A new study should be the final nail for open-plan offices. The Conversation, July 17, 2018.

[337] *Top +45 Complex PTSD Quotes.* Ineffable Living, last visited September 30, 2024.

[338] *CPTSD (Complex PTSD).* Cleveland Clinic, last visited November 29, 2023.

[339] *Complex PTSD.* U.S. Department of Veterans Affairs, last visited December 26, 2023.

[340] *Pete Walker,* http://www.pete-walker.com

[341] *The Fawn Response: How Trauma Can Lead to People-Pleasing.* PyschCentral, last visited December 26, 2023.

[342] Doyle, Dr. Glenn Patrick. X Post, June 26, 2024.

[343] Perkins, M.Ed., Cynthia. *The Long-Term Effects of Stress on Health.* Holistic Help, last visited July 28, 2024.

[344] *Amygdala Hijack: When Emotion Takes Over.* Healthline, last medically reviewed September 17, 2021.

[345] *Daniel Goleman.* https://www.danielgoleman.info

[346] Bernstein, Jules. *America's most widely consumed cooking oil causes genetic changes in the brain.* University of California, January 23, 2020.

[347] Mercola, Dr. Joseph. *Soybean Oil May Cause Irreversible Changes In Your Brain.* Principia Scientific International, March 10, 2022.

[348] Humphreys, Lisa. *FDA Authorizes Qualified Health Claim for Soy Oil.* United Soybean Board, US Soy – August 1, 2017.

[349] Sosland, Josh. *F.D.A. okays Bunge petition on soybean oil health claims.* Food Business News, July 31, 2017.

[350] Cryan, John. *Fermented foods and fibre may lower stress levels – new study.* University College Cork via World Economic Forum, November 7, 2022.

[351] Mensik, Hailey. *A third of manager harbor unconscious fear, leading to a $36 billion productivity loss.* Worklife, November 4, 2023.

[352] *Understanding the Consequences of Non-Compliance: Risks and Penalties.* Financial Crime Academy, August 2, 2023.

[353] Blakemore, Erin. *When Native Americans Briefly Won Back Their Land.* History.com, updated July 10, 2023.

[354] Benton, Lauren. *Maritime Humanities-1400-1800: Piracy in World History.* Amsterdam University Press, last visited July 26, 2024.

[355] Acemoglu, Daron; Johnson, Simon. *Machinery and Labor in the Early Industrial Revolution, and in the Age of AI.* National Bureau of Economic Research, 2024.

[356] Cirruzzo, Chelsea; Leonard, Ben. *Pharma Lobbying Up in 2024.* Politico, April 24, 2024.

[357] Grimalda, Gianluca, et al. *Egalitarian redistribution in the era of hyper-globalization.* ECONSTOR, Review Of Social Economy, 2020, Vol. 78, NO. 2, 151–184 https://doi.org/10.1080/00346764.2020.1714072

[358] The Global Warming Policy Forum. *Ancient society adapted & flourished in face of climate change, archaeologists discover.* Posted on Iowa Climate Science Education, October 31, 2020.

[359] Fix, Blair. *How the Labor Theory of Value Emerges from Egalitarianism.* Economics from the Top Down, September 11, 2021.

[360] Post, Ted. *Magnum Force.* Warner Bros., 1973.

[361] Circle of Mamas. *The Tennessee Sudden Infant Death Syndrome cluster: How Wyeth concealed the DPT vaccine SIDS link.* Signs of the Times, September 17, 2018.

[362] A Midwestern Doctor. *The Century of Evidence That Vaccines Cause Infant Deaths.* State of the Nation, August 26, 2022.

[363] *Equipoise.* Wikipedia.

[364] Sanchez-Perez, Jorge H., et al. *Peru's COVID-19 Vaccine Scandal shows the shady deals made with pharma companies.* The Conversation, March 17, 2021.

[365] *Dominick Dunne's Quarter Century.* Vanity Fair, October 6, 2008.

[366] *Dominick Dunne.* Wikipedia, last visited March 8, 2024.

[367] de Garis, Kirsty; Jolley, Timothy. *After the Party,* Road Trip Film Pty Ltd., 2009.

[368] Dormehl, Luke. *Today in Apple History: Steve Jobs Leaves and Rejoins Apple.* Cult of Mac, September 16, 2023.

[369] *Steve Jobs Discovers the Macintosh Project.* Mac-History.Net, last visited March 10, 2024.

[370] *Dean Kamen.* Wikipedia.

[371] *Isambard Kingdom Brunel.* Wikipedia, last visited March 10, 2024.

[372] *Alfred Nobel.* Wikipedia, last visited March 10, 2024.

[373] Jarecki, Andrew. *The Jinx.* HBO Documentary Films, 2015.

[374] *Robert Durst.* Wikipedia, last visited July 15, 2024.

[375] Earp, Brian D. *Do the Benefits of Male Circumcision Outweigh the Risks? A Critique of the Proposed CDC Guidelines.* PubMed Central. Front Pediatr. 2015; 3: 18. Online publication March 18, 2015.

[376] Calvès, Anne-Emmanuèle. *Empowerment: The History of a Key Concept in Contemporary Development Discourse.* Revue Tiers Monde Volume 200, Issue 4, 2009, pages 735 to 749. https://www.cairn-int.info/article-E_RTM_200_0735--empowerment-the-history-of-a-key-concept.htm

[377] *Revolutionary War Strategy.* American Battlefield Trust.

[378] Dost, Stephen; Fitzpatrick, Kevin. *Signs of a Psychopath*: *Chase Me* (S1E1). Red Marble Media, August 23, 2020.

[379] Gladwell, Malcolm. *The Tipping Point: How Little Things Can Make a Big Difference.* Little, Brown, February 29, 2000.

[380] *Suicide Legislation.* Wikipedia. https://en.wikipedia.org/wiki/Suicide_legislation

[381] Coyne, Ellen, et al. *'Shocking' levels of abuse allegations at over 300 religious-run schools laid bare in report.* Irish Independent, September 3, 2024.

[382] *Suicide Prevention.* Centers for Disease Control and Prevention, last visited SEptember 1, 2024.

[383] Ibraev, Gennady. *Heavy Metal Nano Contaminants In Vaccines Slowly Kill Us.* Principia Scientific International, March 3, 2021.

[384] *Suicide Rate by Country 2024.* World Population Review, last visited September 1, 2024.

[385] *Prozac Lawsuit.* DrugDangers, Seeger Weiss LLP, last visited September 2, 2024.

[386] Helena. *Stolen Lives*. Antidepressant Risks, last visited September 2, 2024.

[387] CMAJ. *Troubling Rise in Suicides Linked With Common Food Preservative*. Neuroscience News.com, July 18, 2022.

[388] *The Story Behind the United Kingdom's Unkillable Soldier*. Past Factory, last visited September 2, 2024.

[389] Page, M.S., Donna. *Astrology of Depression and Suicide*. Donna Page, Professional Astrologer. Last visited September 2, 2024.

[390] Pt. Punarvasu. *Astrological indicators for suicidal tendencies*. Indastro, September 10, 2019.

[391] Geller, Bruce. *Misson: Impossible* and, for example, *Mission: Impossible- Dead Reckoning*. Paramount Pictures, 2023.

[392] Quaglia, Sofia. *Scientists find way to remove polluting microplastics with bacteria*. The Guardian, April 28, 2021.

[393] Kendra MSEd, Cherry. *How False Memories are Formed in Your Brain*. Verywellmind, May 9, 2023.

[394] *Cognitive dissonance: What to know*. MedicalNewsToday, September 9, 2022.

[395] Pink, Daniel H. *When: The Scientific Secrets of Perfect Timing*. Riverhead Books, January 18, 2019.

[396] Nanay Ph.D., Bence. *"Know Thyself" Is Not Just Silly Advice*. Psychology Today, February 18, 2018.

[397] *Space Shuttle Columbia Disaster*. A&E Television Networks; History.com, updated January 24, 2023.

[398] *Thomas Bouch*. Wikipedia. https://en.wikipedia.org/wiki/Thomas_Bouch

[399] *Mianus Bridge*. Wikipedia. https://en.wikipedia.org/wiki/Mianus_River_Bridge

[400] Jacqueline. *The Hidden Connection of Rockefeller, Homeopathy & Chiropractic*. Deep Roots at Home, modified June 12, 2024.

[401] *Medical Error Statistics*. MyMedicalScore, last visited September 5, 2024.

[402] *The Rockefellers, The Flexner Report, The AMA, and their Effect on Alternative Nutritional (botanical) Medicine*. Truth in Plain Sight, April 25, 2021.

[403] *Flexner Report*. Wikipedia, https://en.wikipedia.org/wiki/Flexner_Report

[404] *American Stroke Association*, https://www.stroke.org/?form=stroke_df

[405] Fonarow, M.D., Gredd, et al. *Door-to-Needle Times for Tissue Plasminogen Activator Administration and Clinical Outcomes in Acute Ischemic Stroke*

Before and After a Quality Improvement Initiative. JAMA. 2014;311(16):1632-1640. doi:10.1001/jama.2014.3203.

[406] Haynes, M.D., Alex B. et al. *A Surgical Safety Checklist to Reduce Morbidity and Mortality in a Global Population.* The New England Journal of Medicine, January 29, 2009.

[407] Pearl, M.D., Robert. *Medicine Is An Art, Not A Science: Medical Myth Or Reality?* Forbes, June 12, 2014.

[408] Stelle, Laurelle. *Explosive report argues major industry 'created and perpetuated' a global crisis...* The Cool Down Company, August 2, 2024.

[409] *Center for International Environmental Law.* https://www.ciel.org

[410] *Napoleonic Wars Casualties.* Military History Fandom, last visited September 3, 2024.

[411] Jay, Martin Evan. *Sigmund Freud, Austrian Psychoanalyst.* Encyclopaedia Brittanica, updated August 18, 2024.

[412] Tannenbaum, Austin. *An Introduction to Carl Jung.* Medium, July 30, 2020.

[413] *Kerplunk Experiment.* Wikipedia, https://en.wikipedia.org/wiki/Kerplunk_experiment

[414] Alampur, Raj. *Legacy of John B. Watson: Pioneer of Behaviorism.* Medium, April 25, 2024.

[415] Sagan, Carl. *Cosmos: A Personal Voyage.* Internet Archive (KCET), September 28, 1980; also see *Cosmos*, Random House, May 7, 2002.

[416] Wickenburg, Joanne. *Your Hidden Powers: Intercepted Signs and Retrograde Planets.* American Federation of Astrologers, January 25, 2011.

[417] *Saturn Retrograde Meaning & More.* Astrology.com, last visited July 30, 2024.